THE AMERICAN EXPLORATION AND TRAVEL SERIES

ALEXANDER ROSS

THE FUR HUNTERS OF THE FAR WEST

ALEXANDER ROSS

THE FUR HUNTERS

OF THE FAR WEST

Edited by Kenneth A. Spaulding

UNIVERSITY OF OKLAHOMA PRESS : NORMAN

A Plains Reprint

The University of Oklahoma Press is committed to keeping its best works in print. By utilizing digital technology, we can reprint titles for which demand is steady but too small to justify printing by conventional methods. All textual content is identical to that of the most recent printing. Illustration quality may vary from the originals.

EDITED BY KENNETH A. SPAULDING

On the Oregon Trail: Robert Stuart's Journal of Discovery (Norman, 1953)

Alexander Ross, *The Fur Hunters of the Far West* (Norman, 1956, 2001)

Title page drawing: *Fort George,* by Henry James Warre. Courtesy Yale University Library.

ISBN: 0–8061–3392–9

Library of Congress Catalog Card Number: 56–5995

FOR THOMAS CLAUDE AND WILLIE CLANTON SPAULDING

ACKNOWLEDGMENTS

THIS BOOK could not have come into being without the generous assistance of many people. Those to whom thanks are particularly due are William Robertson Coe, who bequeathed to Yale University the magnificent collection of which the Ross manuscript is part; James E. Babb, librarian, and the Library Committee of the Yale University Library; Archibald Hanna, curator of the Western Americana Collection, Yale University Library; Dorothy W. Bridgwater, assistant reference librarian, Yale University Library; Mrs. T. C. Spaulding; and above all my wife Elizabeth, without whose very real assistance the work could not have been done.

Kenneth A. Spaulding

Storrs, Connecticut

February 12, 1956

CONTENTS

ILLUSTRATIONS

EDITOR'S INTRODUCTION

THIS BOOK holds between its covers the essential story of an era as adventurous as any that our continent has known. The years 1810 and 1825 bracket the Far Western fur trade from its active beginning to its initial decline. During those fifteen years a handful of men pushed their way by boat, by horseback, and on foot up the Columbia and Snake rivers, through the Cascade Mountains and the Rockies, and even into the catastrophic geography through which the Salmon River pours. They set their traps in all the tributary streams and even tried their luck in some of the tiniest creeks. They battled the ever-trying elements, contended either peacefully or savagely with the inhabitants, and toiled back and forth across some of the most difficult terrain that the American continent can offer. They traveled, hunted, and sometimes died, ostensibly in pursuit of the fortune that often proved a will-o'-the-wisp. But often they discovered, as Alexander Ross did, that when the time came for them to leave they had not yet had their fill of the Indian country. These were the mountain men of the Far West.

Ross was one of them. The account which follows is one of the most complete that has come down to us, and it has, in addition to the interest that might be expected, a virtue that makes it unique among journals of the period. This work spans the era of active fur hunting west of the Rockies. Ross was present when the Americans began the adventure at Fort Astoria and did not leave the area until the activities of the Hudson's Bay Company were waning perceptibly. During this time he saw the Americans establish the first post at the mouth of the Columbia, the North West Company engulf the American enterprise, and the Hudson's Bay Company incorporate and succeed the North West Company. When he left for Red River and retirement, beaver plews were hard to come by and worth very little even when they could be obtained. In reality the Far Western trade was finished.

Yet the knowledge acquired and transmitted by the fur traders was to have a worth far transcending the money value of furs. It was this little group of men who made the young nation and the world aware of a vast area previously unknown except on isolated coastal reaches and along the narrow trail followed by Lewis and Clark. Most of the information necessary for the ultimate occupation of this region was gathered by those who drove from the West Coast eastward, having come initially either from British Columbia or from the sea. Like the western arm of an encircling movement these parties swept toward the Rockies from the Pacific Coast, while the exploring bands to the east were working their courses up the main tributaries of the Mississippi. America was explored from the west as well as from the east, and it is the discovery from the west that the following account so richly describes.

Alexander Ross was born at Nairnshire, Scotland, in 1783. Attracted like so many of his young contemporaries to the bright prospects offered by the fur trade, he emigrated to Canada in 1805. There he taught school for several years, but in 1810 traveled to New York, where he enrolled as a member of John Jacob Astor's Pacific Fur Company. On the sixth of September of that year he set sail with the rest of the ocean-going contingent, bound for the mouth of the Columbia. After a voyage marked more by quarrels than by gales, the *Tonquin* put in at her destination on April 12 of the following year.

Here Ross began the activities which were to occupy him for the next fifteen years. That autumn he was sent to establish a subsidiary post at the mouth of the Okanogan River, where he stayed for several months and apparently collected a considerable quantity of furs. The following May he traveled northward, probably to explore the area around Shuswap Lake. He returned to Astoria in June and, the following November, was given official charge of the Okanogan post. On December 12, 1813, the British sloop of war

Raccoon took possession of Fort Astoria, and subsequently it passed to the North West Company.

Ross, as his journal recounts, was one of the former Astor employees who elected to join the British company. Thus, the years from the beginning through 1825 in the fur trade of the Northwest are before us in his own description. Upon retirement he became a settler in the Red River area, where he had been given a grant of one hundred acres by General George Simpson, the governor of Rupert's Land. Here he settled with his family, becoming a well-respected citizen and a holder of public offices. In 1856 he died at Colony Gardens (now Winnipeg), leaving behind him a son just graduated with honors from Toronto University.

Essential to an understanding of the Ross manuscript is a sense of the broad struggle in which the author was participating. The true antagonists were not the North West or the Hudson's Bay companies in opposition to a handful of American free traders but one aspect of British tradition arrayed against the new social concepts beginning to emanate from the small nation east of the Mississippi. This struggle had its foundation in ideas about men and their relations to one another, and, on this point, the opponents were deadlocked.

The British companies in America represented the conservative tradition as it had existed in eighteenth century England. Their outlook was at bottom essentially feudal, society being viewed as a network of interwoven but essentially personal loyalties. But though the relations extended from one person and one class to another, the classes themselves were rigidly fixed as the places of individuals in the hierarchy tended to be. The officials of the North West Company saw in the practices of serving three different grades of tea to the three grades of employees nothing but a minor exemplification of the strata which must necessarily exist in an orderly society. Conversely, when the imported Iroquois took unauthorized leave of the British companies to trade with the Americans they were taxed not with a breach of legal obligation but with personal disloyalty. The fact that they had been promised five times as much money by the Americans was not in point.

True to these concepts, the large British parties were always divided into three classes. The Britons provided leadership and kept the books, the French Canadians handled the boats and sometimes trapped, and the hired Indians both trapped and did the menial tasks. Goods were supplied to employees, apparently at retail prices, and the costs marked up as debts in the Company books. The allowance for each beaver pelt turned in by an employee was less than a dollar, though the same pelt was worth ten dollars or more in the big fur markets. It was this situation which moved the Iroquois to complain that they were forever in debt to the Company. They argued that, if allowed to go off by themselves in a small party, they could take a great many more pelts per person and so increase their chances of paying off their obligation.

For Ross the argument had a teasing plausibility. It was true that a small party could take as many beavers from a given stream as could a larger group; it was also true that the Iroquois were in debt, and that in his camp they constituted a group of perennially dissatisfied persons. But the first reason for opposing such an arrangement (Ross always states it in terms of character weakness) was also real. A small party was much more likely to be attacked than was a larger one. The second reason, perhaps as real as the first even though Ross leaves it unstated, existed just to the east of the Snake country, across the Continental Divide.

On the drainages of the Missouri and Yellowstone rivers were the posts of the Americans, and they were quite willing to trade with the Iroquois or other employees of the North West Company who might find money a stronger inducement than loyalty to their employer. These American posts followed in good part a principle of free trade and would buy furs at a relatively high rate from any trapper who came along. The "freemen" whom Ross berates could make a living by operating as their own masters and then selling the produce of their hunts to the Americans. Many of the trappers east of the mountains were already operating under this arrangement and, apart from the increase in danger incurred when men traveled in small groups of two, three, or four, it held every advantage for those who were actually setting the traps.

xviii

Events within the borders of the Louisiana Purchase constituted, from the British view, a revolution in the business of taking furs. In eastern Canada the arrangement had been to establish a post and then wait for the local tribes to bring in furs to trade. This plan, the traditional system of the North West Company, had never been successful in the Columbia area, and its failure was underscored by the rapidity with which independent trappers were trapping their own pelts in American territory. Naturally loath to copy the detested Yankees, the Company men nevertheless watched their own business fail for several successive years. In the end they were driven by the energetic Donald McKenzie and by orders from headquarters to make at least a partial adaptation to new conditions.

Though their reluctance may seem strange, it was based on at least a dim realization that the changes, necessary as they might be for business survival, were an attack on the traditional and feudal society that they revered. Under a plan by which the Company men went out independently for many months, the old system of interdependence was doomed. Nor did the new demands that employees leave the comfortable life at the posts in order to assume the discomforts and dangers of the trail make the proposals more popular. The Company had offered its employees something of a sinecure, but now they were being called upon to run about the countryside like Yankees.

These men were menaced not only by a condition particular to one section of the fur trade but also by an idea. Had there not been opposition from the citizens of another nation they could have arrived at a compromise with the geography, the weather, and the native inhabitants of the Columbia region. But apart from these inherent problems was the rapidly approaching menace from the east; for the British time was running out, while for the Americans every year meant an increase in the number of energetic trappers who pushed farther and farther west in their search for good beaver streams. By the time Ross left the fur country it was obvious that American trappers would soon appear in the Snake area, not as isolated groups like the Smith party but in numbers.

In the 1820's the Americans were making the fur trade pay. Accustomed to acting individually, they felt no need to wait upon a weak government for the aid it could not have given them in any event. The beaver were there and the price was right; the risks were to be assumed with the rewards. Besides, the cost of equipment was small, and fur was free for the taking. The country was open, beautiful, untrodden, and the hostile Indians would help keep it that way. A man could buy his necessities at the post and live on the bountiful game; what he needed was elbowroom, and as little interference as possible. Being limited only by his personal capacities, he could make a fortune or he could lose his life; in either event he was paid according to the abilities which he had manifested in action. The reward was just, and he was free to seek it according to his insights.

Oregon was the specific prize at the center of the conflict. Bounded by the Louisiana Purchase on the east, by Russian Alaska and the territory of the North West Company on the north, by the Pacific Ocean on the west, and by Spanish settlements on the south, it lay like a hollow center among contending interests and nations. Because of its location Oregon received relatively belated attention, but by 1809 David Thompson had failed in an attempt to carry the British flag to the mouth of the Columbia, and in 1810 the Astorians arrived. Some ten years after Ross left, the first settlers were looking for home sites in the Willamette Valley.

The twenty-five-year span intervening between the establishment of Astoria and the arrival of settlers saw an important test of the Jeffersonian ideal. In this neutral and distant arena, individualism met in conflict with a concept of social organization which required the subordination of the personal will to the written and unwritten laws of the organization. The economic motivation, which is so obvious, operated as an equally forceful stimulant for the representatives of both views and therefore did not determine the final outcome. It was not the failure to desire money but the concepts embodied in its pursuit that ended British influence in Oregon and, in so doing, helped open the way for the thousands of white-topped wagons that were to roll—from the United States—with an inexorable patience through canyons, over stream beds, and across prairies as wide as the sky towards the Northwest.

Ross has given us the climactic years of the struggle. When he resigned from the fur business in 1825 the Hudson's Bay Company, with which he was then affiliated, was in the process of discovering that a few successful forays into the difficult Snake country were not enough to counteract the less energetic efforts being made by the Company elsewhere in the area. With the presence of the Yankees east of the mountains already distracting Hudson's Bay employees and the knowledge that the source of distraction would soon cross the mountains in force, the officials must have been aware that the outcome would soon be obvious. The events described by Ross include the high beginning, not long after the British triumph over Astoria, and conclude with the British cause on the verge of defeat. Within this crucial decade two forces met, joined in a widespread though remarkably bloodless struggle, and contrived between them to determine the future of the American Northwest. This is the story which Ross has to tell.

The Ross manuscript was first published in London in 1855, under the title *The Fur Hunters of the Far West; a Narrative of Adventures in the Oregon and Rocky Mountains*. In 1924 the first of the two original volumes was reprinted by R. R. Donnelley and Sons Company, under the editorship of Milo Quaife. The style of the manuscript was extensively revised by the 1855 editor to make it conform to accepted rhetorical practices current in mid-nineteenth century England, and many manuscript passages were expunged, sometimes for prolixity, sometimes for earthiness of expression, and sometimes to avoid giving offense to persons or institutions.

The present work allows the account to stand in the words of the author wherever the meaning is not obscure. The manuscript was written over one hundred years ago, by a man more active than scholarly. The manuscript itself—and the version given here—reflects these matters. Though sometimes rough, the style of the original writing carries a sense of personality that is lacking in the smooth sentences of the 1855 edition. For example, Ross noted in one instance that he was "bent on making a spoon or spoiling a horn." This expression was carefully deleted in 1855, possibly on the ground that it was not sufficiently refined for the sensibilities of nineteenth century readers. Certainly the result of the change is to rob the passage of force, vigor, and the sense of personality with which the phrase infused it. Pungent descriptions of the habits and manners of North Westers were likewise eliminated, perhaps for the same reason.

The present edition was designed to capture precisely the qualities of immediacy, emotional attitude, and imagery that the 1855 work eliminated. The words of Ross have been carefully retained, and in their original order. Those passages omitted from the previous edition and not reinserted here are absent only because they are quite uselessly repetitious. Apart from the removal of what had already been stated, the words stand in their original order and choice.

But Ross was not a good or a consistent speller, and his sentences are pointed in a manner that sometimes borders on the irrational. In order to make the meaning of the text as clear as it ought to be the spelling of words now commonly known has been made to conform to modern usage, and the punctuation has been made to approximate that to which we are accustomed. Since the 1924 publication is a reprinting of Volume I of the 1855 edition, it compares to the present work in the same manner as its predecessor.

Unlike the publication of 1924, the present work includes four chapters of the second volume. The remaining chapters were omitted only because they contrast sharply both in subject matter and interest from the rest of the manuscript. At the middle of Chapter Thirteenth, Ross began a travelogue interlarded with philanthropic proposals concerning contemporary matters. Here the present edition has been ended, because at this point the narrative of the fur trade is over. The remaining chapters are the observations of a man vacationing through a pleasant and moderately well-known countryside. The description is conventional, as are the philanthropic proposals for the care of good Indians and bad half-breeds, until the reader is inclined to believe that Ross was caught up by an urge to be commonplace in a literary way and not by a desire to commit important matters to paper. Interest falls away sharply at this point, and for that reason the final three chapters were omitted.

ALEXANDER ROSS

THE FUR HUNTERS OF THE FAR WEST

1. REVENGE AT THE CASCADES

IN A WORK published by this writer a few years ago, he traced the history of the Pacific Fur Company, the first commercial association established on the waters of the Oregon or Columbia River, through all the windings of its short-lived existence: an association which promised so much and accomplished so little; like the May fly of an hour, it rose, flittered, and died. From the boldness of the undertaking, and the unyielding energy displayed in the execution, it must be allowed that it deserved a better fate. But the vicissitudes of fortune, and an unbroken chain of adverse circumstances, from its commencement in 1810, continued till its premature downfall paved the way for a more successful rival in 1813. The great Astor project which had for its object the monopolizing of all the fur trade on the continent, and by means of the China market, to have enriched the American, ceased to exist. Besides the history above alluded to, there has been a very interesting romance written on the Pacific Fur Company, by the able and accomplished pen of Washington Irving, entitled "Astoria."

In the present work we propose taking up the subject of Oregon and the Rocky Mountains, beginning with Astor's rival, the North West Company from the time that it occupied the entire trade of the Oregon, till its first and final defeat by another rival, the Hudson's Bay Company, in 1821. The country which they worked is bounded on the West by the Pacific and on the East by the Rocky Mountains, on the south by Mexico, and on the north by the Russian settlements near Kamtschatka, a country as large as the body of Europe, and, at the time we are writing, inhabited only by savages, for the investigation of the curious.

This wide field of commercial enterprise, like a windfall, fell into the hands of the North West Company, almost without an effort, for misfortunes over which they had no control sealed the doom of unfortunate Astoria. The first ship called the *Tonquin*, employed by the Astor Company, was cut off by the Indians on the North West coast, and every soul on board massacred. The second, named the *Beaver*, was lost in unknown seas, and the third, called the *Lark*, was upset in a gale 250 miles from the Sandwich Islands and became a total wreck, and, to complete the catalogue of disasters, in 1812 the war broke out between England and the United States.

Let us take a passing glance at the negotiations between the late Pacific Fur Company and the North West Company, which were as follows: the whole of the goods belonging to the former were delivered over to the latter at 10 per cent on cost and charges. The furs on hand were valued at so much per skin. Thus the whole amounted to 80,500 dollars, and bills of exchange negotiable in Canada were accepted in payment thereof: at the same time, the name of Astoria, the great depot of the Astor Company, situated at the mouth of Columbia, was changed to Fort George. Even this last relic of Astor's venture in the Far West must be effaced, although it has been said that when Washington Irving hit on the happy idea of adding the *i* and *a* by which Astor became Astoria, so pleased was the great man that he presented the poet with 1,000 dollars![1]

The above transactions, which changed the aspect of affairs on the Oregon, took place on the 16th of October 1813. A proviso was also introduced providing a free passage for all American subjects wishing to leave the country. But before entering more fully on this new field we would alight for a little to notice what had been done by travellers in other parts of this most imposing region of the West.

The earliest notice of any adventurer crossing the continent in these regions is that of Mr. Hearne in the service of the Hudson's

---

[1] Ross here repeats a version of the widely circulated rumor regarding Irving's motivations for writing *Astoria*. Irving probably did supply the name, but he apparently received only the customary remuneration for the book. See Stanley T. Williams, *The Life of Washington Irving* (New York, Oxford University Press, 1935, 2 vols.), II, 75–76 and 350.

Bay Company during the years 1769 and 1772. In his third and last expedition, he started from Fort Prince of Wales, in 1770, and reached the mouth of the Copper Mine River on the 17th of July the following year. The ice was then just beginning to break up round the shores of the frozen ocean. We need scarcely mention that Mr. Hearne was here far within the Arctic Circle, where the sun never sets at this season of the year. The next instance we have on record is that of Sir Alexander W. McKenzie, a partner of the North West Company, who in the year 1789 performed his first expedition of discovery across the continent from Montreal to the Hyperborean Sea, and again in 1793 to the Pacific Ocean. This enterprising adventurer did much to develop the inland resources of the country, and was personally known to the writer.

In the early part of the present century Fraser and Stuart, also two partners of the North West Company, crossed the continent from the Atlantic to the Pacific still farther south than their predecessors. One of the great streams of the Far West still bears the name of "Fraser's River" as a tribute to the memory of the first discoverer. A somewhat curious anecdote is told of this expedition. On reaching the Pacific the Indians put on a bold and threatening aspect. The party had a small field piece with them and to relieve the insecurity of the moment by frightening the savages, the piece was loaded and fired off in the middle of the crowd, but it is hard to say which party was most frightened by the discharge for the gun burst and was blown to atoms. Yet strange as it may appear, no person was either killed or wounded by the accident. The momentary surprise, however, gave time to the party to shift their quarters and make their retreat.

Indeed, to the spirit of enterprise diffused among the fur traders, from the earliest days of the French down to the present time, we owe almost all that we know in these savage places; yet with all their zeal and enterprise in the pursuit of gain, they were always tardy in giving what they knew to the world. Not so much from selfish motives, to conceal the truth, as from the difficulty, in many instances, of getting that truth made public.

So far then, the north has been more favoured than the Far West, for no white man had as yet visited the Columbia to any extent; for if we accept Vancouver's discovery of its entrance, in 1792, and the transitory visit of Lewis and Clarke in 1805, the writer himself and his associates were the first explorers of that distant quarter.

First then of the North West Company, and the causes which effected its overthrow. While treating of this part of our subject on the West, it will be necessary to glance occasionally at its transactions, on the east side of the mountains, and in doing this we propose to trace out and notice such incidents, adventures, and other occurrences connected therewith as may seem either novel or interesting to the general reader. The nature of the work before us will embrace the general features of the country, varieties of soil and climate, its geography, trade and commerce, all new discoveries, especially travels in the Snake country, the aboriginal inhabitants, character, customs, languages. Their feelings towards white men, and towards each other: together with the author's own adventures among the natives, from 1810 to the period of his leaving the Oregon in 1825. But although he has undertaken this task, he cannot venture, in the midst of business and bustle, to hold out that sanguine prospect of interest and amusement to the reader which might naturally be expected from one who has been the actor in so many novel scenes, the visitor of so many different tribes, or the observer of so many phases of character.

We shall first endeavour to point out the position which the North West Company, as a commercial body, occupied in relation to others engaged in the same pursuit. This company was incorporated in the year 1787, and it may with truth be said that no body of men associated together for the purpose of carrying on trade with the Indians in our day has been more persevering, enterprising or successful than they; and now to cap the climax of their rising glory, they had added, by the fall of their no less enterprising predecessors, the last link to the lengthy chain of their growing trade: which extended from the Atlantic to the Pacific.

What more would enterprise, merit or ambition desire: They had now got all they asked, all they seemed to wish for; and we might here pause for a moment and enquire in the spirit of moderation, does attainment invariably produce contentment: Did the North Westers in the language of gratitude say, "We have enough." No: there is no fathoming the fountain of thought nor the limits of ambition. On the unchanging principles of human nature every new acquisition served only, on their part, to create a fresh desire for more; and in their folly and extravagance they began to wrangle and to encroach on their chartered territories, as we shall have occasion to notice more particularly by and by.

During my own time in Canada, the vanity and extravagance of the North Westers were proverbial, particularly in and about Montreal, which was then the center of attraction, from its being the great rendezvous and headquarters of the fur trade. There nothing seemed worthy of being talked about unless it was associated with the words "North West." That body took the lead in all assemblies, clubs, and other circles of society: their name influenced the tone of public opinion, within as well as without the city. The French Canadians were almost all children of the North West school. They are generally voyageurs in the proper sense of the word, and every voyageur a North Wester. The Tartars never held the Grand Lama in higher estimation than the Canadians did the North Westers in those days.

During these days it was no uncommon thing for a dashing North Wester to parade the streets of the city with his horse shod with silver shoes, nor to be seen throwing handfulls of small coins among the children of the habitants on his visits through the country. Yet a man of this class has been known during his strolls to enter a gentleman's house in Montreal leading his horse by the bridle, and on reaching the parlour, to order the waiter to bring him a pint of samtschu and a slice of bread for his horse! The obedient waiter did as he was desired; the Chinese beverage was set on the table. But just as they were administering the refreshment, the drums began to beat, but whether a tattoo or reveille I know not, but the noise startled the restive animal, which in the fright shattered to pieces a splendid mirror valued at twenty-five guineas. At this incident the waiter turned pale, and was beginning to stammer out something when the great man cut him short by saying,

7

"Tut man, it is nothing, bring me here pen and ink." Pen and ink were accordingly brought, when he was presented with an order on the North West House for fifty guineas to purchase another mirror! More money has been thrown away in acts of folly and tinsel grandeur by North Westers in those days, than would have paved the streets of Montreal with the precious metal!

But it was not only in Montreal that the North West figured. Fort William,[2] the great rendezvous of their trade throughout the North, was in show and grandeur little behind their princely establishments in Montreal. Their buildings there were elegant, their style of living costly, and altogether the establishment presented a very imposing spectacle to the eye of a stranger. Whenever a foreigner of any distinction happened to visit Montreal, he, as a matter of course, was ushered into the North West circle; and from Montreal was usually conducted in a gay painted canoe, with paddle and song, to Fort William. On all such occasions, their munificence towards strangers knew no bounds, and was just as proverbial as their vanity and extravagance among their own people.

On the arrival once every year of the winterers at Fort William the voyageurs and common men of every grade were in the habit of receiving from their employer a regale gratis. This practice was often productive of strange scenes, immoral and degrading. These true men of the North reveled for days together in the vice of drunknesses and all the waggeries of licentious indulgences, and here would the bullies of fighting renown, rendered yet braver by the potent draught, hold their annual exhibitions. But although fighting and carousing constituted their chief delight while at headquarters, yet seldom did instances of insubordination occur; the only evil arising out of such excesses was exclusively the portion of the misguided wretches themselves, who very often, in the course of a few days, I might say hours, spent in gambling, drinking and foppery the fruits of many years' labour! We might here remark that, when passion is indulged without control, the difference between civilized man and the savage is scarcely perceptible.

Having got over these preliminary remarks, we shall now pro-

2 On Lake Superior, where the present city stands.

A portrait of Alexander Ross

which appeared in the 1855 edition of The Fur Hunters

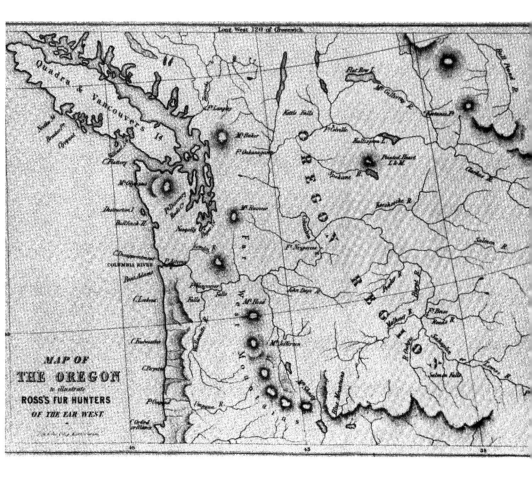

A map of the Oregon territory

which appeared in the 1855 edition of The Fur Hunters

ceed to those details more intimately connected with the subject of our narrative. And here we might notice that several individuals, partners as well as clerks and common men, belonging to the late Pacific Fur Company had entered into the service of the newcomers for such time, and on such conditions, as best suited their views. Nor was it difficult at this time to step from the one concern to the other, inasmuch as the newcomers were very anxious to secure the services of persons whose local experience might prove favourable in conducting the trade in their newly acquired territory; but as this anxiety arose chiefly from the necessity of the moment, on their part they would not, from partiality to their own people on the east side of the mountains, hold out the same prospect of promotion to those who joined them on the west and especially to those branded with the epithet "Yankee." Being, however, disappointed by the failure of the Astor concern, I refused to enter the service of the North West Company on any other condition than that which included promotion, and as I was the only one that acted on this principle, they met my views and we came to terms. So I became a North Wester.

Still bent on making a spoon or spoiling a horn, according to the vulgar expression, I engaged for a term of seven years, the time required according to North West rules to entitle one to promotion; and by so doing I had, as it were, to begin the world anew: in consideration, however, of the experience I had acquired in Columbia affairs, I had a better claim to promotion than what the most of the men of servitude gave them and my promotion was guaranteed to take place in 1822, by a written document signed at headquarters; while in the meantime I was appointed to the northern district, which being a titled charge was of itself a step towards preferment. But here we might as well explain what is meant by a "titled charge," according to North West nomenclature, clerks have charge of posts, Bourgeois of districts.[3] The hope of reward, it is said, sweetens labour and diminishes danger: looking therefore to what

[3] The post itself was one that would ordinarily be in charge of a clerk who was entitled to a share in the Company's profits. Ross hoped to become such a partner in 1822.

others as well as myself considered a certainty, the sting of past disappointment began gradually to be less felt, and I could now say, with the Shunammite of old, "I dwell among mine own people."[4]

While on the subject of promotion, it may not be amiss to notice how the chances generally run. There have always been two classes of expectants in the North West Company's service, who have invariably had the same promises held out to them. The one class has generally been fortunate; the other as generally unfortunate. The former, by way of distinction, we might call the aristocratic twigs of the day, or those connected with the men in power. These are easily known. An expectant of this class is generally seen basking himself in the sun, or loitering about his fort gate, amusing himself with his pipe or his gun; sometimes he may be observed listening to the long yarns of visitors. He talks loudly, laughs heartily, sings a good song, and keeps a pet dog; but he seldom troubles his head about trade, knows nothing of the country, the natives, their language or their habits. He seldom leaves his fort gate, or his pleasures, or soils his delicate hands with trading a skin; his apprentice keeps his accounts and his interpreter trades, his men go idle, and his post falls to ruin. But he can do what generally most men can do; he can write. His letters are in the hands of all the great of the trade; they are handed round the council hall with great eclât. His conduct is highly praised, he writes a captivating hand, his merit is very conspicuous; in short, he is altogether a remarkable clever fellow, merit must be rewarded, his name is at once put on the promotion list, gets his parchment, is dubbed a Bourgeois.[5]

The other class to which we have alluded consists of those who have taken energy and forethought on their side; but no patron, no friend. An expectant of this kind is always up early in the morning, all hands at work, and himself in the trading shop. His curiosity is never satisfied until he knows every hole and corner of the country, and every native in it by name. This activity of body and energy of

---

4 II Kings 4:13.

5 Promotion was neither swift nor sure in the North West Company. Ross may here have been troubled by the realization that he was by no means sure of being made a partner, even after his seven years as an apprentice clerk were served.

mind associate themselves to every hardship, privation and danger, in the pursuit of gain. His courage and perseverance accomplishes the most hazardous enterprises. He travels and learns from experience, calculates his returns, keeps correct accounts, and is never pleased unless his profits this year exceed those of last. The interest of his employers is always his first consideration. Spring comes, but in place of writing long letters, this zealous and faithful servant is journeying through ice and snow collecting his debts, or if not on the journey, he is either posting his books or pressing his packs. He has therefore no time to write letters to this one or that one; all his time is taken up in watching his master's interest, and who in return ought to think of his interest; but no: at headquarters his name is never mentioned, no promotion awaits him! But still he struggles on in the same zealous career, until at last his long service, grey hairs, and declining health admonish him that his zeal and faithfulness have all been in vain. At this stage he resolves either to leave the country pennyless, or to abandon himself with the savage. In either case he is lost to society, a burden to himself, and passes the remainder of his days not only in obscurity, but in all the bitterness of disappointed hope. Such is the fate of many who spend their lives in Indian countries, that boasted land of fortune hunting.

The first step the North Westers took, after inheriting their new acquisition, was to dispatch two of their partners and twenty of their men in two boats to convey the gratifying news to Fort William, the chief depot of their inland trade on Lake Superior. Everything was done to dissuade Messrs. Keith and Alexander Stuart from undertaking so perilous an adventure with so few men; but to no purpose: they made light of the matter, giving us to understand that they were North Westers! "We are strong enough," said they, "to go through any part of the country." Full of confidence in themselves they derided the danger as they did our counsel. While speaking on the subject of danger, one of those swelling fellows, such as may be ordinarily seen stuck up in the end of a North West canoe, with a bonnet of feathers surpassing in size the head of a buffalo bull turned round to us, and said—"Do you think we are

11

Yankees. We will teach the Indians to respect us." And with this, off they started.

The journey began and went on well enough till they arrived at the portage of the Cascades,[6] the first impediment was in ascending the river, distant 180 miles from Fort George, here the Indians collected in great numbers, as usual; but did not attempt anything until the people had got involved and dispersed in the portage; they then seized the opportunity, drew their bows, brandished their lances, and pounced upon the gun cases, powder, kegs, and bales of goods, at the place where Mr. Stuart was stationed. He tried to defend his post, but owing to the wet weather, his guns missed fire several times, and before any assistance could reach him, he had received three arrows, his gun had just fallen from his hand as a half-breed named Finlay came up and shot his assailant dead: By this time the people concentrated, and the Indians fled to their strongholds among the rocks and trees. To save the property in their moment of alarm and confusion was impossible; to save themselves, and carry off Mr. Stuart was the first consideration. They, therefore, made for their canoes with all speed and embarked. Here it was found that one man was missing, and Mr. Keith, who was still on shore, urged the party strongly to wait a little; but the people in the canoes called on Mr. Keith, in the tone of despair, to jump into the canoe or else they would push off and leave him also; being a resolute man and not easily intimidated, he immediately cocked his gun and threatened to shoot the first man that moved. Mr. Stuart, who was faint from loss of blood, seeing Mr. Keith determined and the men alarmed, beckoned to Mr. Keith to embark. The moment he jumped into the canoe they pushed off and shot down the current. During this time Mr. Stuart suffered severely and was very low, as his wounds could not be examined. And when this was done they discovered that the barbs of the arrows were of iron, and one of them had struck on a stone pipe which he carried in his waistcoat pocket, which fortunate circumstance he perhaps owed his life.

The chief object of this expedition has been noticed; but there

6 Near the site of Bonneville Dam.

was another which we shall just mention. A party of six men under a Mr. Reed had been filled out by the Astor Company for the Snake country the year before of which hitherto there had been no tidings: a part of the present expedition were to have gone in search of them. The unfortunate affair at the Cascades, however, put an end to the matter and taught the North Westers the lads of the Cascades did not respect their feathers. Thus terminated the first adventure of the North West on the Columbia. It was after that Mr. Reed and his party were all murdered by the Indians. This disaster set the whole North West machinery at Fort George in motion. Revenge for the insult, and a heavy retribution on the heads of the whole Cath-le-yach-e-yach nation, was decreed in a full council; and for a whole week nothing was to be heard about the place but the clang of arms and the din of war. Every man worth naming was armed and besides the ordinary arms and acoutrements, two great guns, six swivels, cutlasses, hand-grenades, and hand-cuffs, with ten days provisions, were embarked; in short, all the weapons and missiles that could be brought into action were collected and put in trim for destroying the Indians of the Cascades, root and branch.

Eighty-five picked men and two Chinook interpreters under six chosen leaders were enrolled in the expedition, and the command of it tendered to Mr. McKenzie, who, however, very prudently declined, merely observing that as he was on the eve of leaving the country, he did not wish to mix himself up with North-West affairs; but that he would cheerfully go as a volunteer. The command then disolved on Mr. McTavish; and on the 20th of January, with buoyant hearts and flags flying, a fleet of ten sail conveyed the men to the field of action. On the third day, they arrived safely and cast anchor at Strawberry Island,[7] near the foot of the rapids. On their way up, the name of this formidable armament struck such terror into the marauders along the river that they fled to the fastnesses and hiding places of the wilderness; even the two Chinook interpreters could neither sleep nor eat so grieved were they at the thoughts of the bloody scenes that were soon to be enacted.

[7] Hamilton Island.

On the next morning after the expedition came to anchor, the Indians were summoned to appear and give an account of their late conduct, and desired, if they wished for mercy, to deliver up at once all the property plundered from the expedition of Messrs. Keith & Stuart. The Cath-le-yach-e-yach chiefs, not the least intimidated by the hostile array before them, sent back an answer. "The whites have killed two of our people, let them deliver up the murderers to us, and we will deliver to them all the property in our possession." After returning this answer, the Indians sent off all their wives and children into the thick woods; then arming themselves, they took their stand behind the trees and rocks. Mr. McTavish then sent the interpreters to invite them to a parley, and to smoke the pipe of peace. The Indians returned for an answer that, "When the whites had paid according to Indian law for the two men they had killed, they would smoke the pipe of peace, but not till then. Their wives and children were safe, and as for themselves they were prepared for the worst." Thus little progress was made during the first day.

The next day the interpreters were sent to sound them again. Towards noon a few stragglers and slaves approached the camp and delivered up a small parcel of cloth and cotton, torn into pieces and scarcely worth picking up, with a message from the chiefs: "We have sent you some of the property; deliver us up the murderers, and we will send the rest." Some were for hanging up the Indians at once; others for detaining them. At length, it was resolved to let them go. In the evening two of the principal chiefs surrendered themselves to McTavish, bringing also a small parcel of odds-and-ends, little better than the last. Being interrogated as to the stolen property, they denied being present at the time, and had cunning enough to make their innocence appear and also to convince McTavish that they were using their utmost influence to bring the Indians to terms and deliver up the property. A council was then held to decide on the fate of the prisoners. Some were as in the former case for hanging them up; others for taking them down to Fort George in irons. The council was divided, and at last it was resolved to treat the prisoners liberally and let them go; they never

14

returned again; and thus ended the negotiations of the second day.

The third day the interpreters were at work again; but instead of making any favourable impressions on the Indians, they were told that if they returned again without delivering up the murderers, they would be fired upon. During this day the Indians came once or twice out to the edge of the woods. Some were for firing the great guns where they were seen in the largest numbers; others, more evident but less calculating, were for storming their haunts and bringing the matter to a speedy issue. Every movement of the whites was seen by the Indians, but not a movement of the Indians could be discovered by the whites; and the day passed away without any result. Next morning it was discovered that some of the Indians lurking about had entered the camp and carried off two guns, a kettle, and one of the men's bonnets, and the Indians were seen occasionally flying from place to place, now and then whooping and yelling, as if some plan of attack were in contemplation. This was a new symptom, and convinced the whites that they were getting more bold and daring in proportion as their opponents were passive and undecided. These circumstances made the whites reflect on their own situation. The savages, sheltered behind the trees and rocks, might cut them all off without being seen; and it was intimated by the interpreters that the Indians might all the time be increasing in numbers by foreign auxiliaries; whether true or false, the suggestion had its effect in determining the whites that they stood upon dangerous ground, & that the sooner they left it the better. They therefore, without recovering the property, firing a gun, or securing a single prisoner, sounded a retreat, and returned home on the ninth day—having made matters ten times worse than it was before.

This warlike expedition was turned into ridicule by the Cathle-yach-e-yachs, and had a very bad effect on the Indians generally, and on their way back, some were so ashamed that they turned off towards the Wallamitte[8] to hide their disgrace, others remained for some days at the Cowlitz, and McTavish himself reached Fort George in the night. And thus ended this inglorious expedition, which promised so much and did so little.

[8] The Willamette River.

It ought to be observed that the nature of the ground along the Cascades on both sides of the river is such as to afford no position secure from attack or surprise; and it showed a perfect want of judgment in an Indian trader to expose his people in such a dangerous situation, when the Indians might have way laid and cut them off to a man and that without quitting their fastnesses, whereas the whole difficulty might have been easily obviated by a very simple stratagem on the part of the whites who might have easily secured three or four of the principal men, who established as hostages, would have soon settled the whole affair, without noise or any warlike demonstration.

The North Westers were prone to find fault with the acts of their predecessors and yet, with all their fault finding, they had not laid down any suggestions or plans to guide their future operations, either with respect to the coast or inland trade, which appeared inexplicable to us and we waited in anxious expectations to see what time would bring forth.

One day as I was musing over affairs, Mr. McDonald called me into his room, and after some trivial observations, said, "Well, I suppose you have heard that I intend to leave the country this spring." "No," said I, "I have heard nothing of it." "But," resumed he, "you will have heard that the spring brigade is to leave in a few days for the interior." "Oh yes," said I, "I have heard of that." "Yes," continued he, "we intend to start in a few days, and I shall leave the country, and have wished to leave some settled plan for carrying on the Columbia trade; but there are so many conflicting opinions on that subject that we have not been able to come to any decisions: so that I fear the trade must go on the best way that it can for this year yet." "Then," said I, "you do not approve of the system we have been following," meaning the American; "it appeared to me to work very well." He shook his head and smiled, but said nothing. Then suddenly turning to the subject of the voyage, he said, "Will there be any danger in getting along, our party will be strong?" Mr. McDonald, having come out by sea, had never ascended or descended the waters of the Columbia. "A strong party, with the usual precautions," I said, "will carry on through with safety. Compared with former years," I said, "it is mere holiday work." At the words "usual precautions" he smiled. "Do you think," said he, "that North Westers do not know as well as the Americans how to travel among Indians?" "The North Westers," observed I, "know how to travel among the Indians of Athabasca and the north; but the Americans know better than North Westers how to travel among the Indians of Columbia." Continuing the subject, he remarked, "The Indians along the communication must be taught to respect the whites, the rascals have not been well broken in; you will soon see a specimen of our mode of travelling among Indians, and what effect it will produce." "Well, I shall be glad to see it," said I, "but I hope it will not be such a specimen as was exhibited at the Cascades, nor produce the same results." On my mentioning the word "Cascades" his cheeks reddened and he appeared somewhat nettled, but recollecting himself, he changed the subject and put the question, "Where are the worst Indians along the route?" To this I replied that, "The worse Indians are those at the Long Narrows[9] called Wy-ani-pame or Gamblers[10] some 60 miles beyond the Cascades; but with a strong party and good night watch, there will be nothing to fear." He next inquired how far the Americans had penetrated to the north. "To the island of Sitka," was my reply. "And how far to the south," enquired he again. "To the frontiers of California," I answered. He then asked if we had been as far east as the Rocky Mountains. To which I answered that we had, and crossed them too. "The Americans," he remarked, "have been very enterprising." "We are called Americans," said I, "but there were very few Americans among us—we were all Scotchmen like yourselves. I do not mean that we were the more enterprising for that."

On the subject of travelling, he next enquired "if we invariably used horses." I told him that no horses were used along the coast; that the natives kept none, nor would the thick forests admit of their being used; but that throughout the interior all journeys were performed on horseback. "You must," continued he, "have travel-

9 Five Mile Rapids.
10 The Cathlasco tribe.

led over a great part of the country." "Yes, we did," said I, "it has often been remarked that before we were a year on the Columbia, we had travelled in various directions more than 10,000 miles." "That is a reproach to us," said he, "for we have been here upwards of six months, and with but one exception, have scarcely been six miles from our fort gates." He then asked me what I thought of the manner in which the Americans carried on the trade with the Indians. "I always approved it," said I. "They treated them kindly, traded honestly, and never introduced spirits and liquors among them." "Ha," said he. "But was it not a losing business." I said it was. Astor's underhand policy, and the war breaking out at the time it did ruined all. "But," I remarked, "the country is rich in valuable furs," and that the North West would now inherit these riches. "Time will tell," was his only answer. After attending briefly to our trials, hardships, and experience on the Columbia: "Well," said he, "I suppose we shall have to do the best we can, as you did, for this year at least, and follow the system pursued by the Americans." He then requested me to make out an estimate of men and goods for the different posts of the interior. I could not help smiling to see the great man reduced to the necessity of walking in the footsteps of his predecessors! after all was said to the contrary. But we must be candid; the futile genius of the North Westers do not always follow the example of their predecessors, they sometimes follow their own and here we might give our readers an instance in point.

The style of living and table etiquette of North Westers on the Columbia differed considerably from the simple and unceremonious custom observed by their predecessors. With the latter, at breakfast, dinner or supper there was no restraint, no unnecessary punctilio about who sat here or who sat there; once the chair at the head of the table was filled, all the others took their seats sans ceremoni, sometimes in one place, sometimes in another, as they might find it most convenient, without the least attention being paid as to who sat above or below them. And all from one end of the table to the other partook of the same eatables and the same drinkables without distinction. When one rose all rose—and to use an American phrase, "liberty and equality" reigned around the festive board.

Not so, however, with the North Westers, with them a very different system was pursued. Grand and imposing, according to their ideas of the strict rules of subordination, particularly at headquarters. Here you take your seat, as a Chinese Mandarine would his dress, according to your rank. The titled Bashaws, like so many Teutonic Knights, sit as a matter of course near the seat of honour, the head of the table. The subalterns next, and lastly a squad of all grades consisting of guides, interpreters and hangers on down to the serfs fill up the rear. The state of the native society being yet in its infancy, no woman sits at table. On the ringing of the bell, all flock to the dining hall as fast as they can. The saying "quick at meat, quick at work" is never lost sight of. Nothing less than a house on fire must interrupt their speed. On entering, the different parties urge themselves along the feudal hall in a steady position like troops; with the word "attention," each grade forming as it were a group by itself and a decorum bordering on silence ensues among all the folks of small role till the great Satrap at the head of the table takes his place, then each falls in according to his station. But if a Grandee happens to be a minute or two behind time, the subalterns wait until he enters and is first seated, and then they sit down; or if a subaltern be a little out of time, the understrappers do him the same honour, stand till he is first seated. The etiquette of a North West table demands that these punctilios be strictly observed. Religious feelings, however, are seldom allowed to interrupt their temporal enjoyments. No time is lost in asking a blessing, either before or after meals, Sunday or Saturday—no blessing is ever asked. No wonder then that a blessing did not follow North Westers through life: and the repast is always gone through in double quick time: for North Westers do everything at a gallop. At breakfast or supper, when tea is generally used, it is not uncommon to see three tea pots in requisition at the same time, and on the same table, each holding a different quality of the China leaf, with as many different qualities of sugar: the refined loaf, the common crushed, and the inferior brown, each in its proper place.

19

If dinner, the cloth is no sooner removed and a motion made to substitute bottles in its place than the president, at the head of the table, gives a significant, I should say an arbitrary glance around, the meaning of which, like Colonel Pride's purge, is never mistaken, being a signal for all beneath the dignity of a Bourgeois to retire, and they retire accordingly: except now and then a favourite, who happens to get a tip on the shoulder, and is desired to sit down. But the poor fellow thus honoured has little to boast of, for what he gains among his superiors he generally loses among his equals. The moment therefore the waiters begin to remove the cloth, there is an instant and simultaneous rush to see who will first get out to breathe the sweet air of freedom. The first is so desired that in the twinkling of an eye the hall is emptied of all those not entitled to "strong drink." While the one party thus keeps emptying their glasses, the others in simple glee keep emptying their pipes and cracking their jokes at the expense of their superiors. Such things being quite novel and amusing to most of us, I have given them to the reader at some length, thinking they may prove so to him also. An hour past, the bell again, like the boatswain's whistle, calls all hands to work. Such is the ordinary routine of things throughout the year and this brings our narrative up to the first day of April 1814.

Before entering upon another year we might here call the attention of the reader to the fact that with all the ambition and enterprise the North West Company were so noted for, there were ten partners, twice that number of clerks and one hundred and fifty men lying idle about Fort George since last fall! Without taking a single step to advance or extend the trade in any quarter. How unlike this was to the energy displayed by their more enterprising predecessors: this assemblage of Americans and North Westers continued, however, to pass a very comfortable and merry winter of it: nor did the harmony and good feeling that existed during that time experience the slightest interruption, if we except now and then a bit of a turn out between the bullies of the one party and the braggadocios of the other, which only seemed to banish ennui and enliven the scene.

On the sixth day after my conversation with Mr. McDonald, the brigade took its departure for the interior. It was the first grand movement of the North West Company on the Columbia. On this occasion one hundred and twenty-four men, exclusive of the people of the late Astor Company who were on their way to Canada by land. The whole embarked in a squad on 14 boats: the papers, bills, and other documents belonging to the American adventurers were put in the possession of our respected friend Donald McKenzie Esq. in order to be delivered to Mr. Astor at New York, and along with the party was the Company's express for headquarters. The whole left Fort George under a salute with flags flying.

On passing the Cascades the friendly Cath-le-yach-e-yachs did not so much as come and shake hands with us nor welcome our arrival but kept at a distance, so we passed without the least interruption and all went on smoothly till we reached the Long Narrows, that noted haunt of Indian pillagers; there we had to put up and encamp for the night, but the usual camp regulations were neglected. No importance whatever was attached to the two little words "usual precautions," which I had so emphatically mentioned to Mr. Mc-Donald; such things were now looked upon as a useless relic of "Yankeeism," therefore no night watch was set; all hands went to sleep but it was not long before a voice called out, "To arms, to arms! the camp is surrounded." In the turmoil and confusion that ensued, every one firing off his gun at random as he got up, one of our own men, a Creole of the South, was shot dead and his life purchased a lesson again at another time. If any Indians were actually about our camp, they must have scampered off instantly and unperceived, which they could easily have done, for none were to be seen when the confusion was over; nor was it ever known who gave the fatal alarm. From Creole encampment, we reached the forks 160 miles beyond the Long Narrows. This is another great rendezvous for Indians but we passed it quietly without interruption: and from thence to Fort Oakinacken,[11] 200 miles above the forks, without accident or hindrance, always careful, however, to remember the "usual precautions" by setting a ring to watch. On arriving at

[11] At the mouth of the Okanogan River.

this place, the different parties separated for their respective wintering grounds—and here the Fort William express and our friends for Canada bade us adieu and continued their journey. And we shall have the affairs of the voyage, and take up the subject of horses and inland transportation.

On reaching Oakinacken, everything was at a dead stand for want of pack horses to transport the goods inland, and as no horses were to be got nearer than the Eyakema Valley,[12] some 200 miles south west, it was resolved to proceed thither in quest of a supply. At that place all the Indians were rich in horses; the Cayouses, Nez Perces, and other warlike tribes assemble every spring to lay in a stock of the favourite kamass and pelica,[13] or sweet potatoes, held in high estimation as articles of food among the natives. Here also the Indians hold their councils and settle the affairs of peace or war for the year; it is, therefore, the great national rendezvous, when thousands meet and on such occasions horses can be got in almost any numbers; but owing to the vast concourse of mixed tribes, there is always more or less risk attending the undertaking.

To this place I had been once before during the days of the Pacific Fur Company so it fell to my lot again, although it was well known that the fatal disasters which more than once took place between those tribes and the whites would not have diminished but rather increased the danger; yet there was no alternative, I must go, so I set off with a small bundle of trading articles and only three men, Mr. Thomas McKay, a young clerk, and two French Canadians, and as no more men could be spared, the two latter took their wives along with them to aid in driving the horses, for women in these parts are as expert as men on horseback.

On the fourth night after leaving Oakinacken, Lopa, a friendly neighbouring chief of the Pisscaws tribe,[14] on learning that we were on our way to the Eyakemas, dispatched two of his men to warn us of our danger, and bring us back. The zealous couriers reached our camp late in the night. My men were fast asleep; but there was no

12 The Yakima Valley.
13 Plants with bulbous, edible roots.
14 The Wenatchee tribe.

sleep for me, I was too anxious and heard their approach; I watched their motions for some time with my gun in my hand, till they called out in their own language, "Samah! Samah! Peelcousm, peelcousm." "White men, turn back, turn back, you are all dead men!" It was, however of no use, for we must go at all hazard. I had risked my life there for the Americans, I could not now do less for the North West Company: so with deep regret the friendly couriers left us and returned, and with no less reluctance we proceeded. The second day after our friends left us we entered the Eyakema Valley, "the beautiful Eyakema Valley," so called by the whites. But on the present occasion there was nothing either beautiful or interesting to us; for we had scarcely advanced three miles when a camp in the true Mameluke style presented itself. A camp of which we could see its beginning but not the end! This mammoth camp could not have contained less than 3,000 men, exclusive of women and children, and treble that number of horses. It was a grand and imposing sight in the wilderness, covering more than six miles in every direction. Councils, root-gathering, hunting, horse-racing, foot-racing, gambling, singing, dancing, drumming, yelling, and a thousand other things which I cannot mention were going on.

The din of men, the noise of women, the screaming of children, the tramping of horses, and howling of dogs was more than can well be described. Let the reader picture to himself a great city in an uproar. You see life in the struggles, the feelings, the passions, the propensities, as they ebb and flow in the savage breast. In this field of savage glory all was motion and commotion, we advanced through groups of men and bands of horses, till we reached the very centre of the camp, and there the sight of the chiefs' tents admonished us to dismount and pay them our respect, as we depended on them for our protection.

Our reception was cool, the chiefs were hostile and sullen, they saluted us in no very flattering accents. "These are the men," said they, "who kill our relations, the people who have caused us to mourn," and here for the first time, I regretted we had not taken advice in time and returned with the couriers: for the general aspect of things was against us. It was evident we stood on slippery

ground. We felt our weakness. In all sudden and unexpected rencontres with hostile Indians, the first impulse is generally a tremour
or sensation of fear, but that soon wears off. It was so with myself at
this moment, for after a short interval, I nerved myself to encounter the worst.

The moment we dismounted we were surrounded, and the savages giving two or three war whoops and yells drove the animals
we had ridden out of our sight; this of itself was a hostile movement. We had to judge from appearances, and be guided by circumstances. My first care was to try and direct their attention to
something new and to get rid of the temptation there was to dispose of my goods; so without a moment's delay, I commenced a
trade in horses; but every horse I bought during that and the following day as well as those we had brought with us were instantly
driven out of sight, in the midst of yelling and jeering: nevethe-
less, I continued to trade, while an article remained, putting the
best facet on things I could, and took no notice of their conduct,
as no insult or violence had as yet been offered to ourselves personally. Two days and nights had now elapsed since our arrival,
without food or sleep; the Indians refused us the former, our own
anxiety deprived us of the latter.

During the third day, I discovered that the two women were to
have been either killed or taken from us and made slaves, and so
surrounded were we for miles on every side that we could not stir
unobserved; yet we had to devise some means for their escape. To
get them clear of the camp was a task of no ordinary difficulty and
danger. In this critical conjuncture, however, something had to be
done and that without delay. One of them had a child on the breast,
which increased the difficulty. To attempt sending them back by
the road they came would have been sacrificing them. To attempt
an unknown path through the rugged mountains, however doubtful the end was, appeared the only prospect that held out a glimpse
of hope; therefore, to this mode of escape I directed their attention.
As soon as it was dark they set out on their journey without food,
guide, or protection, to make, under a kind providence, their way
hence!

INDIAN CANOE

A water color by Alfred Jacob Miller

CHINOOK INDIAN

A water color by Alfred Jacob Miller

"You are to proceed," said I to them, "due north, cross the mountains, and keep in that direction, till you fall on the Pisscaws River,[15] take the first canoe you find, and proceed with all diligence down to the mouth of it, and there await our arrival. But if we are not there on the fourth day, you may proceed to Oakinacken, and tell your story." With these instructions we parted, and with but little hopes of ever meeting again. I had no sooner set about getting the women off than the husbands expressed a wish to accompany them; the desire was natural, yet I had to oppose it. This state of things distracted my attention, my eyes had now to be on my own people as well as on the Indians, as I was apprehensive they would desert. "There is no hope for the women by going alone," said the husbands, "no hope for us by remaining here, we might as well be killed in the attempt to escape as remain to be killed here." "No," said I, "by remaining here we do our duty; by going, we should be deserting our duty." To this remonstrance, they made no reply. The Indians soon perceived that they had been outwitted. They turned over our baggage, and searched in every hold and corner. Disappointment creates ill humour; it was so with the Indians. They took the men's guns out of their hands, fired them off at their feet, and then with savage laughter laid them down again. Took their hats off their heads, and after strutting about with them for some time, jeeringly gave them back to their owners; all this time they never interfered with me; but I felt that every insult offered to my men was an indirect insult offered to myself.

The day after the women went off, I ordered one of the men to try to cook something for us for we had eaten nothing since our arrival, except a few raw roots we managed to get unobserved. But the kettle was no sooner on the fire than five or six spears bore off in savage triumph the contents, they even emptied out the water, and threw the kettle on one side, and this was no sooner done, than thirty or forty ill-favoured wretches fired a volley in the embers before us, which caused a cloud of smoke and ashes to ascend, darkening the air around us: a strong hint not to put the kettle on the fire any more and we took it.

15 The Wenatchee River.

At this time, the man who had put the kettle on the fire took the knife with which he had cut the venison to lay it by, when one of the Indians, called Eyacktana, a bold and turbulent chief, snatched it out of his hand; the man in an angry tone demanded his knife, saying to me, "I'll have my knife from the villain, life or death." "No," said I. The chief seeing the man angry, threw down his robe and grasping his knife in his fist with the point downwards raised his arm as if he intended using it. The crisis had now arrived! Instantly there was a dead silence, and the Indians were flocking in from all quarters. A dense crowd surrounded us. Not a moment was to be lost, delay was fatal and nothing now seemed to remain for us but to sell our lives as dearly as possible. With this impression, grasping a pistol I advanced a step towards the villain who held the knife with the full determination of putting an end to his career before any of us should fall; but while in the act of lifting my foot and moving my arm, a second idea flashed across my mind admonishing me to soothe and not provoke the Indian, that Providence might yet make a way for us to escape; that thought saved the Indian's life and ours too. In place of drawing the pistol as I intended, I took a knife from my belt, such as travellers generally use in this country, and presented it to him, saying, "Here, my friend, is a chief's knife, I give it to you, that is not a chief's knife, give it back to the man." Fortunately, he took mine in his hand; but still sullen and savage he said nothing. The moment was a critical one, our fate hung as by a straw; I shall never forget it! All the bystanders had their eyes now fixed on the chief, thoughtful and silent as he stood, we also stood motionless, not knowing what a moment might bring forth. At last the savage handed the man his knife, and turning mine around and around for some time in his hand, turned to his people, holding up the knife in his hand, exclaimed, "She-augh Me-yokal waltz." "Look my friend, at the chief's knife," these words he repeated over and over again. He was delighted. The Indians flocked round him. All admired the toy, and in the excess of his joy he harangued the multitude in our favour. Fickle, indeed, are savages. They were now no longer savages, but friends! Several others following Eyacktana's example harangued in turn, all in favour of the whites. This done, the great men squatted, threw ashes down, the pipe of peace was called for, and while it was going around and around the smoking circle I gave each of the six principal chiefs a small paper-cased looking glass and a little vermilion as a present; and in return they presented me with two horses and twelve beavers, and the women soon brought us a variety of eatables.

This sudden change regulated my movements. Indeed I might say the battle was won. I now made a speech to them in turn, and as many of them understood the language I spoke I asked them what should I say to the great white chief when I got home, when he asked me, "Where are the horses I bought from you? What shall I say to him?" At this question, it was easy to see that their pride was touched. "Tell him," said Eyacktana, "that we have but one mouth, and one word; all the horses you have bought from us are yours: they shall be delivered up." This was just what I wanted. After a little counselling among themselves Eyacktana was the first to speak, and he undertook to see them collected.

By this time it was sundown. The chief then mounted his horse and desired me to mount mine and accompany him: telling one of his sons to take my men and property under his charge till our return. Being acquainted with Indian habits I knew there would be repeated calls upon my purse, so I put some trinkets in my pocket and we started on our nocturnal adventure, which I considered hazardous but not hopeless. Such a night! The chief harangued, travelled and harangued the whole night; the people replied. We visited every street, alley, hole, corner, lengthways, crossways, east, west, south and north, from group to group, and the call was, "Deliver up the horses." There was gambling, there was dancing. Laughter in one place, mourning in another. Crowds passing to and from, whooping, yelling, dancing, drumming, singing. Men, women and children huddled together, flags flying, horses neighing, dogs howling: chained bears, tied wolves, grunting and growling; all pell-mell among the tents, and to complete the confusion, the night was dark. At the end of each harangue, the chief would approach me, and whisper in my ear, "She augh tamtay enim," "I have spoken well in your favour," a hint for me to reward his zeal,

27

by giving him something and this had to be repeated constantly. A string of beads or two buttons or two rings. I often thought he repeated his harangues more frequently than was necessary; but it answered his purpose and I had no choice but to obey and pay.

At daylight we got back, my people and property were safe and in two hours after, my 25 horses were delivered up and in our possession. I was now convinced of the chief's influence and had got so well in his good graces with my beads, buttons and rings, that I hoped we were out of all our troubles, and our business being done I ordered my men to tie up and prepare for home, which was glad tidings to them. With all this favourable change we were much embarrassed and annoyed in our preparations to start. The savages interrupted us every moment. They jeered the men, frightened the horses and kept handling, snapping and firing off our guns. Asking for this, that or the other thing. The men's hats, pipes, belts and knives were constantly in their hands. They wished to see everything, and everything they saw they wished to get, even to the buttons on their clothes. Their teasing curiosity had no bounds; every delay increased our difficulties. Our patience was put to the test a thousand times; but at last we got ready, and my men started. To amuse the Indians, however, till they could get fairly off I invited the chiefs to a parley which I put a stop to as soon as I thought the men and horses had got clear of the camp. I then prepared to follow them, when a new difficulty arose. In the hurry and bustle of starting my people had left a restive, awkward brute of a horse for me, wild as a deer, and as full of latent tricks as he was wild. I mounted and dismounted, at least a dozen times. In vain I tried to make him advance. He would rear, jump and plunge, but refused to walk, trot or gallop. Every trial to make him go was a failure. A young conceited fop of an Indian, thinking he could make more of him than I could, jumped on his back, the horse reared and plunged as before; "Kap-sheesh-she cam," "the bad horse," and gave me another; for the generous act, I gave him my belt, the only article I had to spare. But although the difficulty I had with the horse was galling enough to me, it proved a source of great amusement to the Indians, who enjoyed it with roars of laughter. Before taking my leave of the chief Eyacktana, it is but justice to say that with all his faults, he had many good qualities, and I was under great obligations to him.

I now made the best of my way out of the camp, and to make up for lost time took a short cut, but for many miles could see nothing of my people and began to be apprehensive that they had been waylaid and cut off. Getting to the top of a high ridge, I stopped a little to look about but could see nothing of them; but had not been many minutes there before I perceived three horsemen coming down an adjacent hill at full tilt. Taking them for enemies I descended the height, swam my horse across a river at the bottom of it, and taking shelter behind a rock, dismounted to wait my pursuers. Here I primed my rifle anew and said to myself, "I am sure of two shots, and my pistols will be more than a match for the other." The moment they got to the opposite bank I made signs for them to keep back or I would fire on them; but my anxiety was soon removed by their calling out, "As-nack-shee-lough, As-nack-shee-lough," "Your friends." These friendly fellows had been all the time looking about in anxious suspense to see what would become of us. Two of them were the very couriers who had, as already stated, strongly tried to turn us back. I was overjoyed at the meeting yet still anxious, as they had seen nothing of my men, to find whom we all set off and came up with them a little before sundown. When we first discovered them, they were driving furiously; but all at once, the horses stood still. I suspected something and told the Indians to remain behind while I alone went on to see what was the matter; when, as I had expected, seeing four riders following them at a gallop, they took us for enemies as I had done before and left the horses to take up a position of defence behind the trees where they might receive us, and we should have met with a warm reception, for McKay, although young, was as brave as a lion. But they were soon agreeably surprised and the matter was soon explained. I then made signs for the Indians to come forward. The moment we all joined together we alighted, changed horses, and drove on until midnight, when we took shelter in a small thicket of woods, and passed the night with our guns in our hands.

At dawn of day we again set off, and at 3 o'clock in the afternoon reached the banks of the Columbia, some six miles beyond the mouth of the Pisscaws River, where we considered ourselves out of danger. I then started on ahead in company with the friendly Indians to see if the two women had arrived, and as good luck would have it we found them there with a canoe ready to ferry us across. They had reached the place about an hour before us, and we could give our readers a brief outline of their adventures.

On leaving us, instead of taking directly to the mountains, they in the darkness of the night bridled two of the Indians' horses and rode them for several hours, till they were far beyond the camp; but as soon as it was daylight they turned the horses adrift and entered the mountains on foot. In the hurry of starting, they forgot to take a fire steel or anything to make fire with and had been there three days and nights without food or fire; a short time, however, before I had reached them they had met some friendly Indians who had ministered to their wants. During the four days of their pilgrimage, they rode 18 miles, travelled 54 and paddled 66, making in all 138 miles. We now hasten to resume our narrative.

In a short time the two men and all the horses arrived, but could give no account of McKay. I therefore immediately sent them back with an Indian in search of him while I and the other Indians were occupied in passing over the horses, for during high water the Pisscaws River is very broad at its mouth. Sometime after dark the men arrived with the news that they had found McKay lying some distance from the road in almost a lifeless state and unable to ride or be carried. In this state of things I had no alternative but to send back the two men with two Indians to have him brought in the canoe. About midnight they all arrived, but poor McKay was in a very low and dangerous state, having by some mishap which he could not explain dislocated his hip joint, which after much trouble I got placed again, and he gradually came around; but as he could neither ride nor walk, I was reduced to the necessity of hiring two of the Indians to paddle him home in the canoe, meanwhile the two men, women and myself continued our journey and reached Oakinacken in safety, after an absence of seventeen days; but the

Indians only got there with McKay four days after us, and from the hot weather and hardness of the canoe, he suffered very much. The limb had again got out of joint, and was so much swollen that it resisted all my efforts to get it reduced, so that he never got the better of it but remained lame till the day of his death. Thus terminated the most trying and hazardous of trips I ever experienced in the country.

As soon as Mr. McKay was out of danger I left him and set off with all haste to Fort Spokane,[16] distant 160 miles southeast from Oakinacken, with 55 of our horses: and on our way both going and coming, made a short stay at a place called the Grand Coulé, one of the most romantic picturesque marvellously formed chasms west of the Rocky Mountains. If you glance at the map of Columbia you will see some distance above the great forks a barren plain extending from the south to the north branch of that magnificent stream, there in the direction of mainly south and north is the Grand Coulé, some 80 or 100 miles in length. No one travelling in these parts ought to resist paying a visit to the wonder of the West. Without their being able to account for the cause of its formation. We shall now digress for a short space and return to Fort George. We shall proceed to give a brief description of this wonderful chasm or channel as it now is and perhaps has been since the creation.

The side or banks of the Grand Coulé was for the most part formed of basalt rocks and in some places as high as 150 feet, with shelving steps formed like stairs to ascend and descend and not infrequently vaults or excavated tombs, as if cut through the solid rocks like the dark and porous catacombs of Kiev. The bottom or bed, deep and broad, consists of a conglomerate of sand and clay paved and smooth when not interrupted by rocks; the whole form is in every respect the appearance of a deep bed of a great river or lake, and now dry and scooped out of the level and barren plain. The sight in many places is truly magnificent. But perils and pleasures succeed each other: for while in one place the solemn

---

16 Spokane House was the original headquarters of the North West Company, in the Columbia territory. It was located between the forks formed by the Spokane and Little Spokane rivers and, according to Ross, was founded in 1809.

gloom forbids the wanderer to advance, in another the prospect is lively and inviting and almost everywhere studded with ranges of columns, pillars, battlements, turrets, and steps above steps, in every variety of shade and colour. Here and there, endless vistas and subterraneous labyrinths add to the beauty of the scene, and what is still more singular in this arid and sandy region, cold springs are frequent; yet there is never any water in the chasm, unless after recent rains. Thunder and lightening is known to be more frequent here than in other parts, and a rumbling in the earth is sometimes heard. According to Indian tradition, it is the abode of evil spirits. In the neighbourhood there is neither hill nor dale, lake nor mountain, creek or rivulet to give variety to the surrounding aspect. Altogether it is a charming assemblage of picturesque objects to the admirer of nature.

In 1811 three men belonging to the Pacific Fur Company had been murdered by the natives; but as the matters could not be traced out, the deed was never avenged. We however had no sooner taken our departure for the interior than the murderers considered it unnecessary to conceal the deed any longer, as the Americans, as we were called, had left the country; they thought all was safe and consequently joined their relations at Fort George. Their return to the neighbourhood had been known to the whites, who, in order to make an example of them and strike terror into evil doers wished to apprehend them; for some time they contrived to elude their vigilance and it threatened for a time the security of the North West Company's possession on the Columbia.

The whites, however, were not to be foiled in their attempt to get hold of them. To attain the desired end they were obliged to have recourse to some of the friendly Indians, who found out their secret haunts, hunted them up, and delivered them into their hands. Three were implicated and found guilty of murder on Indian evidence and were condemned to be shot. Capital punishment was inflicted upon two of them; but the third was pardoned and set at liberty. The conduct of the murderers may serve to throw some light on their knowledge of right and wrong, and on the character of these Indians generally. The three villains fled toward the south as soon as they had committed the deed, nor did they ever return or make their appearance in that quarter until they heard that the Americans left the country.

The punishment of the offenders, however, gave great offence to many of the surrounding tribes, who thought the North Westers had no right to kill their relations; the deed not being committed in their day, nor on their own people, they said the act on their part was mere cruelty, a hatred of the Indians, and that in consequence, they must be their enemies. Jealousy had also its influence: seeing that those Indians friendly to the whites had been so liberally rewarded for their zeal in apprehending the criminals, others were displeased that they had not come in for a share of the booty. The Indians took up arms and threatened to expell the whites from the country. This manifestation of hostility on the part of the natives gathered strength daily and kept the whites in constant alarm, more especially as there were but few of them to resist so formidable a combination.

In the midst of this hostile flumen, as good fortune would have it, the long expected ship *Isaac Todd* from London arrived, and cast anchor in front of Fort George, with ample supplies both of men and means, and her seasonable appearance struck such awe into the rebellious savages that partly through fear and partly in anticipation of the state of things to come they sued for peace, which was granted, and all became quiet and tranquil once more. The *Isaac Todd*'s presence spread a momentary gleam of light over the North West affairs, in short gave a new impulse to all their measures in the Far West. After a short stay at the Columbia smoothing down all difficulties with the Indians and taking on board the furs and peltries belonging to the late American adventurers, the vessel sailed for Canton.[17] The transient joy which her timely arrival caused was but of short duration and had scarcely time to be announced in another express to Fort William, when again the report of affairs was clouded by a misfortune which bowed down the proudest spirit and drew a tear of sympathy from every eye.

17 Canton, China, one of the world's largest fur markets.

On the 22d of May some time after the arrival of the *Isaac Todd,* a boat containing Messrs. Donald McTavish and Alexander Henry, two partners of long standing and high reputation in the service, with six men was swamped, all hands perishing with the exception of one man, in crossing the river. Although the accident took place in broad daylight and in front of the fort, the circumstance was not perceived nor known for some hours after when John Little, the man that was saved, arrived at the fort and communicated the intelligence. We shall give his sad tale in his own words.

"We pushed from the wharf," said John Little, "at 5 o'clock in the afternoon, the wind blowing a gale at the time, and the tide setting in. The boat was ballasted with stones, we were eight on board and a heavy surf, about two miles out in the stream she filled and she sank like a stone. A terrible shriek closed the scene! The top of the mast was still above the surface of the water, I got hold of it, but the first or second swell swept me away. In a moment nothing was to be either heard or seen but the rolling waves and whistling winds. Jack, a young sailor lad, and I took to swimming and with great exertions reached a dry sand bank in the channel, about three-quarters of a mile ahead of us; but the tide flowing at the time and forced by the gale soon set us afloat again. Here we shook hands, bade each other farewell, and took to swimming again. At the distance of a mile we reached another flat sandbank, but the tide got there nearly as soon as ourselves and we were again soon afloat. Jack was much exhausted, I was little better, and the wet and cold had so benumbed us that we had scarcely any feeling or strength. We now shook hands again, anxiously looking for relief towards the fort. Here poor Jack began to cry like a child and refused for some time to let go my hand. I told him to take courage and pointing to a stump ahead of us said to him, 'If we get there we shall be safe.' Then bidding each other adieu we once more took to swimming in hopes of reaching the stump I had pointed to, being better than half a mile off. I reached and grasped it with almost my last breath; but poor Jack although within ten yards of it could not do so, it was too much for him and I could render him no assistance. Here he struggled and sank, and I saw him no more. I had been grasping the stump with the grasp of despair for more than half an hour when fortunately a little before dark an Indian canoe, passing along shore, discovered my situation and saved my life. The water had reached my middle, and I was insensible." One of the Indians who had brought Little to the fort remarked, "When we got to him he was speechless, and yet his fingers were sunk in the wood, so that we could hardly get his hands from the stump."

Peril by water was not Little's only danger, as we learned from one of the Indians who rescued him. He was within an ace of being shot as well as drowned. The moment the people in the canoe came in sight of the stump, one of the Indians, pointing to it, said to his comrades, "Look! what is that leaning on the stump?" Another called out, "A sea otter or a seal, come let us have a shot at it." Both at that instant taking up their guns made signs to the person steering to make for the stump slowly, while the canoe was thus making for the stump, the two men held their guns ready cocked, to have a shot. "Shoot now," said one of them to the other. The canoe all this time nearing the object, and the two anxious marksmen on their knees, with their guns pointed! when a woman who happened to be in the canoe, bawled out to the men, "Alke, Alke, Tilla-kome, Tilla-kome." "Stop, stop, a man! a man!" At this timely warning the men lowered their guns to look and in a few moments the canoe was at the stump: and seeing Little, the fellows put their hands to the mouths, exclaiming in the Chinook dialect, "Naw-wet-ka, naw-wet-ka," "It is true, it is true." To the keen eye of this woman poor Little owed his life at least.

Following the *Isaac Todd* there arrived from the same port a schooner called the *Columbia*. This vessel was intended for the China and coasting trade, and Angus Bethune Esq., a North West partner, was appointed super cargo. A voyage or two across the Pacific, however, convinced, the North Westers that the project would not succeed. The post duties at Canton connected with other unavoidable expenses absorbed all the profit, and this branch of their trade was relinquished as unprofitable. And even the coast trade itself was far from being as productive as might be expected, owing to the great number of coasting vessels which came from all parts of the states, especially Boston, all more or less connected with the Sandwich Islands and China trade. Competition had therefore almost ruined the coast trade and completely spoiled the Indians.

Having glanced at the affairs of Fort George and the coast trade, we now resume the business of the interior. It will be in the recollection of the reader that we left the spring brigade at Oakinacken, and our friends journeying on their way to Canada. From Oakinacken, I proceeded northward some 300 miles to my own post at the She-whaps;[18] there being now no rivalry there or elsewhere to contend with I put the business in train for the season, and immediately returned again with the view of being able to carry into effect a project of discovery which I and others had contemplated for some time before, that was of penetrating across land from Oakinacken due west to the Pacific on foot, a distance supposed not to exceed 200 miles, and for the performance of which I had allowed two months.

The undertaking had often been talked of but as often failed to be put into execution. This was, however, the first time the thing had been attempted by any white man; and as the part of the country held out a good prospect for extending the tract I was anxious to see it explored, and the question set at rest. Men, however, being scarce with us this year, I determined on trying with Indians alone, placing at that time more faith in their zeal, fortitude and perseverance than ever I felt disposed to afterwards. Having procured a guide and two other natives myself being the fourth person, we prepared with all the confidence that hope could inspire for the execution of my plan.

On the 25th of July we set out on our journey, our guns in our hands, each a blanket on his back, a kettle, fire steel, and three days provisions, depending upon our guns for our substance. Indeed, the only baggage we encumbered ourselves with consisted of ammunition for food and protection. Crossing the Oakinacken, we followed the west bank of the Columbia in a SW course distance 8 miles, till we reached the mouth of the Mea-who River,[19] a con-

18 Near Shuswap Lake, British Columbia. The post was located at the juncture of the Thompson and North Thompson rivers.

siderable stream issuing at the foot of the mountains, along the south bank of which we ascended, but from its rocky sides and serpentine courses, we were unable to follow it. We therefore struck off to the left, and after a short distance entered a pathless desert, in a course due west. The first mountain on the east side is high and abrupt. Here our guide kept telling us that we should follow the same road as the Red Fox chief and his men, and to go. Seeing no track nor the appearance of any now I asked him where the Red Fox road was; "This is it that we are on," said he, pointing before us. "Where?" said I. "I see no road here, not even so much as a rabbit could walk on." "Oh! there is no road," rejoined he, "But this is the place where they used to pass." When an Indian in his metaphorical mode of expression tells you anything, you are not to suppose that you understand him, or that he literally speaks the truth. The impression on my mind was that we should at least occasionally have fallen upon some sort of a road or path to conduct us along: but nothing of the kind was to be seen. The Red Fox here spoken of was the head chief of the Oakinacken nation[20] and had formerly been in the habit of going to the Pacific on trading excursions, carrying with him a species of wild hemp which the Indians along the Pacific make fishing nets of; and in exchange, the Oakinackens bring back any marine shells and other trinkets, articles of value among the Indians. After we entered the forest our course was 2 miles, NW 1, SW 1, W by S 1, W 3, distance 8 miles.

On the 26th we made an early start this morning. Course as nearly possible due west. But not half an hour had passed before we had to steer to every point of the compass, so many impediments crossed our path. On entering the dense and gloomy forest, I tried my pocket compass but to very little purpose, as we could not in many places travel fifty yards in any one direction; so rocky and uneven was the surface over which we had to pass that it made us lose too much time. And as I placed implicit confidence in my guide, I laid it by. On seeing me set the compass the guide, after staring with amazement for some time, asked me what it was. I told him it was

19 The Methow River.
20 The Okanogan tribe.

the white man's guide. "Can it speak?" said he. "No," replied I, "it cannot speak." "Then what is the good of it," said he. "It will show us the right road to any quarter," answered I. "Then what did you want with me, since you had a guide of your own." This retort came rather unexpected, but taking hold of my double-barrelled gun in one hand and a single one in the other, I asked him which of the two were best. "The two barrelled," said he, "because if one barrel miss fire you have another." "It is the same with guides," said I, "if one fail, we have another." Course today W. 4, N.W. 1, N.N.W. 1, S.W. 2, W. 5, N. by W. 6.

On the 27th. Weather cold and rainy, still we kept advancing through rugged and broken country, in a course almost due west. But camped early on account of the bad weather, having travelled about 10 miles. The next day we made a long journey general course W. by N. Saw several deer and killed one. The drumming partridges were very numerous so that we had always plenty to eat. We met with banks of snow in course of this day. Distance 18 miles.

On the 29th. This morning we started in a southerly direction but soon got to the west again. Country gloomy, forest almost impervious with fallen as well as standing timber. A more difficult route to travel never fell to man's lot. On the heights the chief timber is a kind of spruce but not very large, only two or three feet in diameter. The valleys are filled with poplar, alder, stunted birch and willows. This range of mountains[21] lying in the direction of nearly S. and N. are several hundred miles in length. The tracks of wild animals cross our path in every direction. The leaves and decayed vegetation were uncommonly thick on the surface of the ground, and the mice and squirrels swarmed, and have riddled the earth like a sieve. The fallen timber lay in heaps, nor did it appear that the fire ever passed in this place. The surface of the earth appeared in perfect condition. And the rocks and yawning chasms gave to the whole an air of solemn gloom and undisturbed silence. My companions began to flag during the day. Distance 15 miles.

On the 30th. The sixth day in the evening, we reached a height of land which on the east side is steep and abrupt. Here we found

21 The Cascade Range.

the water running in the opposite direction.[22] My guide unfortunately fell sick at this place and we very reluctantly had to wait for two days until he recovered when we resumed our journey; but his recovery was very slow, and on the second day he gave up altogether and could proceed no farther. We were still among the rugged cliffs and deep groves of the mountain, where we seldom experienced the cheerful sight of the sun: nor could we get to any elevated spot clear enough to have a view of the surrounding country. By getting to the top of a tall tree now and then we got some relief but little, for we could seldom see to any distance so covered was all around us with a thick and almost impenetrable forest. The weather was cold, and snow capped many of the higher peaks. In such a situation I found myself without a guide. To go forward without him was almost impossible. To turn back was labour lost and to remain where we were was anything but pleasant, to abandon the sick man to his fate was not to be thought of. The serious question then arose, what were we to do? At last we settled the matter so that one of the Indians should remain in touch with the guide and the other to accompany me, I still intending to proceed; so we separated. Observing every now and then as we went along to mark with a small axe some of the larger trees to assist us in our way back in case our compass got deranged, although, as I have already noticed, we but seldom used it while our guide was with us. But the case was different now; in fact, it was the only guide I had. Course today W. 5, N. 1, N.W. 2, N.E. 1, W. 9, distance 18 miles.

August 4th. We were early on the road this morning and were favoured occasionally with open ground. We had not gone far when we fell on a small creek[23] running by compass W.S.W. but so meandering that we had to cross and recross it upwards of forty times in the course of the day. The water was clear and cold and soon increased so much that we had to avoid it and steer our course from point to point on the north side. Its bottom was muddy in some places, in others stony, banks low and lined with poplars; but

22 The north fork of the Cascade River, near Cascade Pass.
23 One of the headwaters of the Cascade River.

so overhung with wood that we could oftener hear than see it. On this little encouraging stream flowing no doubt to the Pacific we saw beaver lodges and two of the animals themselves, one of which we shot. We shot a very fine otter also, and notwithstanding the season of the year the fur was black. Tired and hungry, we put up at a late hour. Courses W. 8, N.W. 5, W. 7, S.W. 2; distance travelled today 22 miles.

On the 5th. I slept but little during the night; my mind was too occupied to enjoy repose, so we got up and started at an early hour. Our journey today was through a delightful country of hill and dale, wood and plains. Late in the afternoon, however, we were disturbed and greatly agitated by a fearful and continuous noise in the air, loud as thunder, but with no intervals. Not a breath of wind ruffled the air; but towards the southwest, from whence the noise came, the whole atmosphere was darkened, black and heavy. Our progress was arrested; we stood and listened in anxious suspense for nearly half an hour, the noise still increasing and coming, as it were, nearer and nearer to us. And if I could compare it to anything, it resembled the crash of a heavy body of water falling from a height, till it came near to where we stood, when in a moment, we beheld the woods before it bending down like grass before the scythe! It was the wind accompanied with a torrent of rain; a perfect hurricane, such as I had never witnessed before. It reminded me at once of those terrible visitations of the wind peculiar to tropical climates. Sometimes a slight tornado or storm of the kind has been experienced on the Oregon, but not often. The crash of falling trees, the dark and heavy cloud, like a volume of condensed smoke, concealed from us at the time its destructive effects. We remained motionless all the time. An hour passed, and the storm was over. And although it was scarcely a quarter of a mile from us, all we felt of it was a few heavy drops of rain, as cold as ice, with scarcely any wind; but the rolling cloud passed on, carrying destruction before it as far as the eye could follow. In a short time we perceived the havock it had made by the avenue it left behind, having levelled everything in its way to the dust. The very grass was beaten down to the earth for nearly a quarter of a mile in breadth, leaving a hollow track behind it. But this was not the only difficulty that now presented itself; the Indian I had along with me was so amazed and thunderstruck with superstitions and fear at what he had seen that his whole frame became paralysed. He trembled and sighed to get back, and all I could either say or do could not turn him from his purpose. He refused to accompany me any further. At last he consented, and we advanced to the verge of the storm-fallen timber and encamped for the night. We saw a good many beaver lodges along the little river and some small lakes; and deer grazing in herds like domestic cattle, and so very tame that we might have shot as many of them as we chose. Their curiosity exceeded our own and often proved fatal to them. The little river at this place seemed to take a bend nearly due north and was 22 yards wide and so deep that we could scarcely wade across it. I gave it the name of "West River."[24] Here the timber was much larger than any we had yet seen; some of the trees measuring five and six feet in diameter. Course today W. 12, N.W. 2, S. 1, S.W. 2, W. 9. Distance was 26 miles. Making from Oakinacken to Point Turn About[25] 151 miles.

After we had put up for the night it was evident my companion was brooding and unsettled in his mind, for he scarcely spoke a word: and although he had consented to continue the journey I could easily see his reluctance. Being apprehensive that he might try and play me a trick, I endeavored to watch his motions as closely as possible during the night; yet in spite of all my watchfulness, he managed to give me the slip, deserted and in the morning I found myself alone! I looked about in all directions for him but to no purpose, the fellow had taken to his heels and returned. There was no alternative but to yield to circumstances and retrace my steps, and this was the more galling as I was convinced in my own mind that in a few days more I should have reached the ocean and accomplished my object.[26] I paused and reflected, but all to no purpose. Fate had decreed against me, and with reluctant steps I turned round and made the best of my way back to where I had

24 The Cascade River.
25 Just below the forks of the Cascade River.
26 He was about fifty miles from Skagit Bay.

left my guide and reached the place after intense anxiety at 4 o'clock in the afternoon of the third day, having scarcely taken a mouthful of food all the time. I reached the place as the men were in the act of tying up their bundles and preparing to start on their homeward journey.

The guide was still somewhat ailing, and the fellow who had left me was little better for, in his hurry back, he had overheated himself, which together with the fright had thrown him into a fever: nor was I in too good humour, hungry, angry, fatigued and disappointed. I sat down as grim and silent as the rest, nor did a word pass between us for a while. After some time, however, I tried to infuse some ambition and perseverance into the fellows to get them to resume the journey; but to no purpose; they were destitute of moral courage, a character peculiar to their race. I had been taught a good lesson which I remembered ever after, not to place too much faith in Indians. After remaining over night at the guide's encampment, we turned our faces towards home. Wild animals were very numerous, far more so than on our first passing. Whether it was the storm that had disturbed them in another quarter or some other cause, we could not determine, but they kept rustling through the woods, crossing our path in every direction as if bewildered. We shot several red deer, three black bears, a wolf and fisher and arrived at Oakinacken on the 22nd of August, after a perilous and disagreeable journey of thirty days. And here my guide told me that in four days from Point Turn About, had we continued, we should have reached the ocean.

After remaining for a few days at Oakinacken I visited the Shewhaps, but soon returned again to the former place to meet the fall express from the east of the mountains. After a few hours' delay at Oakinacken the express proceeded on its way to Fort George, but was stopped at the forks on its way down, the Cayouse and Nez Perces, Indians of the plains, being encamped there in great numbers. On perceiving the boat sweeping down and keeping the middle of the stream, as if anxious to pass the camp unnoticed, according to North West custom, the Indians made signs for the whites to put on shore. The first signal passing unheeded, a shot was next fired ahead to bring them to, and this also passing without notice a second shot was fired at the boat; the gentleman in charge ordered the sternsman to make for the land. On arriving at the camp, the Indians plunged into the water and taking hold of the boat hauled her up on the beach high and dry, with the crew still on board: nor would they allow the people to depart till they had smoked themselves drunk, then pushing the craft into the water again they made signs for them to depart, at the same time admonishing them never to attempt passing their camp again without first putting on shore and giving them a smoke.

On the departure of the express, I took a trip as far as Spokane House. This district with its several outposts was under the superintendence of John George McTavish Esq. to whom I related the result of my trip of discovery. Returning home, I passed the remainder of the winter at Oakinacken, being now part of the northern district. The spring being somewhat early this year and all hands mustered at the forks, the general rendezvous for mutual safety, we took the current for headquarters and arrived at Fort George on the 10th of June 1815.

2. THE WHITE WOLVES

A COUNCIL sits annually at headquarters which regulates all the important matters of the Company for the current year; but no person of less dignity than a Bourgeois or proprietor is admitted to a seat, except by special invitation. The council of this year was strengthened by the arrival of three new functionaries from the east side of the mountains, yet nothing new transpired. The members sat for four days, nearly double the usual time, but no new channel was opened for extending the trade: nor was there the least deviation from the old and continued system of their predecessors. The decision of the council was that there existed no new field that could be opened to an advantage, so that everyone was again appointed to his old post—and I of course to mine.

During the sittings there is always a strong manifestation of anxiety out-of-doors, each one being desirous to know his appointment for the year: for it not unfrequently happens that they are changed without much ceremony, particularly if there be any individual who is not easily managed. And for an obnoxious individual to be removed to the most remote corner of the country this year and to some other equally remote next by way of taking him is not at all uncommon.

But this part of their policy is not confined to the subordinates; it reaches even to the Bourgeois, and he is not infrequently admonished by the example of others that he stands on the brink of a precipice; for if too refractory in their councils, he is sure to get his appointment at such a distance and under such circumstances as to exclude most effectually his attending their meetings for some length of time. This is the course generally adopted to get rid of an importunate and troublesome man, whether of high or low rank in the service, or for such as the company cannot dispose or cannot conveniently provide for.

The council being over, the business of the year settled, and the annual ship arrived, the different parties destined for the interior and east side of the mountains took their departures from Fort George on the 25th of June. And we shall leave them to prosecute their journey for a short time, while we glance at another subject.

No sooner had the North Westers inherited the Oregon,[1] notwithstanding the unfavourable decision of our western council, than ship after ship doubled Cape Horn in regular succession with bulky cargoes to the fulfillment of every demand, and constant selections of their partners, clerks, and Canadians crossed over the dividing ridge, but all proved abortive in bringing about that rich harvest which they had expected.

We may now remark on the effect produced on affairs by the country falling into the hands of new masters; but day after day passed by, yet the ordinary dull routine of things continued. And a spectator might have read in the countenances of our great men something like disappointment. The more they wished to deviate, the more they imitated the policy of their predecessors; with this difference, however, that in every step they took, their awkwardness pointed them out as strangers. They found fault with everything, yet could mend nothing. Even the establishment of Fort George could not please them; therefore a fort built upon a large scale, and greater elevation, was more consonant to their ideas of grandeur; in consequence, the pinnacle of Tongue Point was soon to exhibit a Gibralter of the West. An engineer was hired, great guns were ordered, men and means set at work, racks were levelled, and yet this residence more fit for eagles than for men was at last relinquished, and the condemned old fort was again adopted.

The inland brigade, whose departure has already been noticed, ascended the Columbia without any interruption until it had reached a little above the Walla Walla, near to the spot where the Cayouse Indians had in the preceding fall stopped the express and hauled the boat up high and dry on land, and here they intended

1 The Columbia River.

to play the same game over again, for when the whites were in the act of poling up a small but strong rapid along shore with the intention of stopping as soon as they got to the head of it, the Indians who were still encamped there, insisted on their putting to shore at once. This invitation was, however, under existing circumstances disregarded by the whites as being almost impossible at the moment. When suddenly a party of the Indians mounted on horseback plunged into the stream, and so barred the narrow channel through which the boats had to pass that great confusion ensued. Still the whites in their anxiety to get up the rapids paid but little attention to them, which forbearance encouraged the Indians to resort to threats by drawing up their horses and menacing the whites. In this critical conjunction the whites seized their arms and made signs to the Indians to withdraw, but this only encouraged them the more to resist, and throwing themselves from their horses into the water they laid hold of the boats. The struggle and danger now increased every moment, as the Indians were becoming more and more numerous and daring. The whites had not a moment to lose; they fired. Two Indians fell dead on the spot, and a third was badly wounded. All three floated down the current. The instant the shots went off, the Indians made for land, and the firing ceased. The whites in the meantime drifting down to the foot of the rapid crossed the river to the opposite side, and soon after encamped for the night on a sandy island. Had the whites done what they ought to have done from the lesson of the previous year at this place, put ashore at the foot of the rapid, no difficulties would have ensued and no blood would have been shed.

On the next morning the Indians assembled in fearful numbers and kept up an occasional firing at the whites on the island, at too great a distance to do any harm, but as they escaped without injury, they did not return the fire. The greatest arrogance was that the whites could not proceed on their journey before the natives mustered in too great numbers for it blew almost a hurricane, and the cloud of dust which the wind raised about their encampment was some punishment for the deeds they had committed. The whites seeing it impossible to remain any longer on the island adopted a

46

bold and vigorous resolution. After appointing fifteen resolute fellows to guard the property, they embarked to the number of seventy-five men, well armed, made for the shore, and landing a little from the Indians' camp, hoisted a flag inviting the chiefs to a parley: but the Indians were distrustful. Treacherous themselves, they suspected the whites would be also; they therefore hesitated to approach. At last, however, after holding a consultation they advanced in solemn procession, to the number of eighty-four. After a three-hour negotiation the whites paid for the two dead bodies, according to Indian custom, and took their leave in peace and safety, and this ended the disagreeable affair.

From the hostile island our friends continued their voyage without any other casualty until they reached the Rocky Mountains; but there fatal disasters awaited them. The waters being unusually high much time was lost in ascending the current, so that by the time they arrived at Portage Point,[2] their provisions got short, and some of the hands falling sick and unable to undertake the difficult portage of eighty miles on foot, the gentlemen in charge had no alternative left but to fit out and send back a boat from that place with seven men, three of whom being unable to undertake the portage. After being provided with some provisions the returning party took the current, but on reaching the Dalles des Morts[3] they disembarked contrary to the usual practice to hand the craft down by a line, when unfortunately they quarrelled among themselves and letting go the line, in an instant the boat wheeled round, was dashed to pieces on the rocks and lost.

The sick and frail party had now no alternative but either to starve or walk a distance of 300 miles, over a country more fit for goats than for men. All their provisions were lost with the boat; neither were they provided with guns nor ammunition for such a journey, even had they been in health. In this forlorn state they quarrelled again and separated. One of the strongest and most expert tried and reached the establishments below after suffering every hardship that human beings could endure. The other five

2 The mouth of the Wood River.
3 Death Rapids.

remained, out of which one man alone survived, deriving his wretched subsistence from the bodies of his fallen comrades. This man reached Oakinacken more like a ghost than a living creature after a lapse of two months.

From these sad details we now turn to record the passing events of the northern quest. After a short stay at Oakinacken I set out for my post at the She-whaps and reached that place in the month of August. During my absence a man by the name of Charette, whom I had left in charge, had been murdered. Charette was an honest fellow, and deserved a better fate. The murderer was a young Indian lad who had been brought up at the establishment. They had gone on a trip to Fraser's River, six days journey due north and had quarrelled one evening about making the encampment. During the dispute the Indian said nothing. But rising a short time afterward and laying hold of Charette's own gun, suddenly turned round and shot him dead without saying a word, and then deliberately sat down again! This was proved by a third person then present. Several instances of this kind have happened within my own knowledge, and it was a general remark that all those Indians who had been harboured among the whites are far more malevolent and treacherous than those who had never the same indulgence shown to them.

These remarks lead me to another circumstance which gave rise to great uneasiness among the natives along the banks of the Columbia who never fail to magnify and represent in a distorted light everything, however trivial.

One day Ye-whell-come-tetsa, the principal Oakinacken chief, came to me about a similar circumstance, saying he had bad news to tell me: adding, "I fear you will not believe me, for the whites say that Indians have two mouths and often tell lies, but I never tell lies, the whites know I have but one word and that word is truth." I said, "I never doubt the words of a chief; but come let us hear, what is it?" "My son," said he, "has just arrived from below, and has reported and his report is always true. That there is a great band of strange wolves some hundreds in number and as big as buffaloes coming up along the river, and they kill every horse, none can escape them. They have already killed thousands; we shall all be ruined. They are so fierce that no man can approach them, and so strong and hairy that neither arrows nor balls can kill them. And you," said he to me, "will lose all yours also, for they travel so fast that they will be here in two nights." I tried to console the melancholy chief, gave him some tobacco, and told him not to be discouraged, that if the wolves came to attack our horses we should certainly kill them. That we had balls that would kill anything. With this opinion he seemed pleased and went off to circulate the opinion of the whites among his own people. I had heard of the report respecting the wolves some time before the chief had told me, for these things spread like wildfire; I was convinced some horses had been killed, it was a common assurance for not a year passes when the snows are deep, and often when there is no snow at all; but such things happen; but as to anything else, I looked upon it as mere fable.

On the third day after my parley with the chief, sure enough the wolves did come, and killed, the very first night, five of our horses. On discovering in the morning the havock the unwelcome visitors had made, I got a dozen steel traps set in the form of a circle round the carcass of one of the dead horses, then removing the others and keeping a strict guard on the livestock, we waited with anxiety for the morning, when taking a man with me and our rifles, we set out to visit the traps.

On reaching the spot we found four of them occupied. One of them held a large white wolf by the foreleg, a foot equally large was gnawed off and left by another, the third held a fox, and the fourth trap had disappeared altogether. The prisoner held by the leg was still alive, and certainly as the chief said, a more ferocious animal I never saw. From the moment we approached it, all efforts were directed towards us. It had marked and cut the trap in many places. It had gnawed and almost consumed a block of oak which held fast the chain, and in its fruitless efforts had twisted several links in the chain itself. For some time we stood witnessing its maneuvers, but it never once turned around to fly from us, on the contrary, now and then it sprang forward to get at us with its mouth wide open, teeth all broken, and its head covered with blood. The part which the trap held was gnawed, the bone broken, and nothing holding it but the sinews. Its appearance kept us at a respectable distance, and although we stood with our guns cocked, we did not consider ourselves too safe for something might have given way, and if so we should have regretted our curiosity. So we sent two shots and put an end to its suffering. Its weight was a hundred and twenty-seven pounds. And the skin which I gave to the chief was considered a valuable relic. "This," said he, holding up the skin in one hand, "is the most valuable thing I ever possessed." The white wolf skin in season is esteemed an article of royalty, it is one of the chief honours of the chieftainship and much used by these people in their religious ceremonies, and the kind of wolves are not numerous. "While I have this," exclaimed the chief, "we have nothing to fear, strange wolves will kill no more of our horses, and I shall always love the whites." Leaving the chief in a joyful humour, the man and myself followed the faint traces of the lost trap which occasionally appeared upon the crust of the snow. Having proceeded for some miles, we at length discovered the wolf with the trap at his heels, making the best of his way over rugged and broken surface of rocks, ravines, hills and dales, sometimes north, sometimes south, in zig zag courses to suit his escape and deceive us: he scampered along at a good trot, keeping generally about a quarter of a mile ahead of us. We had not been long in pursuit, however, before the man I had with me, in his anxiety to advance, fell and hurt himself and had to return home; I, however, continued the pursuit with eagerness for more than six hours until I got a shot; it proved effectual. Had any one else done it I would have praised him for the act, for at the distance of one hundred and twelve yards, when nothing but its head appeared, my faithful and trusty rifle arrested his career and put an end to the chase, after nearly a whole day's anxious pursuit.

Some idea of the animal's strength may be conveyed to our readers from the fact that it had dragged a trap and chain weighing eight and a half pounds by one of its feet or claws the distance of twenty-five miles, without appearing in the least fatigued. The prize lay at my feet, when another difficulty presented itself; I took no knife with me and the skin must have. Taking therefore, according to Indian habit, the flint out of my gun, I managed to do the business, and home with the skin and trap I hied my way, no less fatigued, but pleased with the successful result.

There we succeeded in destroying the three ringleaders of the destructive game which had caused so much anxiety and loss to the Indians, nor were there more it would appear than three of the large kind in the troop; for not another horse was killed during the season, in all that part of the country; whenever several of the large wolves associated together for mischief, there is always a numerous train of small ones who follow in the rear and act as auxiliaries in the work of destruction. Two large wolves such as I have mentioned are sufficient to destroy the most powerful horse, and seldom more than two ever begin the assault, although there may be a score in the gang. And it is no less curious than amusing to witness their ingenious mode of attack. If there is no snow or but little on the ground, those two approach in the most playful and caressing manner, lying, rolling, and frisking about until the too credulous and unsuspecting victim is completely off his guard by curiosity and familiarity. During this time the gang squatted on their hindquarters, looking on at a distance. After some time spent in this way, the two assailants separate; when one approaches the horse's head, the other his tail, with a slyness and cunning peculiar to themselves. At this stage of the attack their frolicksome approaches become very interesting, it is in right good earnest, the former is a mean decoy, the latter is the real assailant and keeps his eyes steadily fixed on the hind strings or flank of the horse. The critical moment is then watched, the attack is simultaneous; both wolves spring at their victim the same instant, one to the throat, the other as stated, and if successful, which they generally are, the hind one never lets go his hold till the horse is completely disabled, for instead of springing forward or kicking to disengage himself, he turns round and round without attempting to defend himself. The one before now springs behind, to assist the other. The sinews are cut, and in half the time I have been telling it, the horse is on

51

his side, his struggles are fruitless, the victory is won. At this signal the lookers on close in at a gallop, but the small fry of followers keep at a respectful distance until their superiors are gorged, then they take their turn unmolested. The wolves, however, do not always kill to eat; wasteful hunters, they often kill for the pleasure of killing, and leave the carcasses untouched. The helplessness of the horse when attacked by wolves is not more singular than its timidity and want of action when in danger by fire. When these animals are assailed by fire, in the plains or otherwise, their strength, swiftness and sagacity are of no avail. They never attempt to fly but get bewildered in the smoke, turn round and round, stand and tremble until they are burnt to death, which often happens in this country in a conflagration of the plains.

No wild animal in this country stands less in awe of man than the wolf, nor is any other animal that we know so fierce. The bear on most occasions tries to fly from man, and is only bold and ferocious when actually attacked, wounded, or in defence of her young. The wild buffaloes are the same; but the wolf to the contrary has often been known to attack man, and at certain seasons of the year, the spring for instance, it is man's wisdom to fly from them. Some time ago a gang of seventeen in a band forced two of our men to take shelter for several hours in a tree, and although they had shot two of the most forward of them before they got to the tree for protection, the others instead of dispersing kept close at their heels. Wolves are as ferocious among themselves as they are voracious. I have more than once seen a large one lay hold of a small one, kill it on the spot, and feast on the smoking carcass. When the Indians are apprehensive of an attack from them they always contrive to light a fire.

I passed this winter between the She-whaps and Oakinacken: sometimes at the one, sometimes at the other so as to be constantly employed in the pursuit of furs.

I had often puzzled myself as well as others to know what the North Westers had in view by grasping at the entire trade of the Oregon and running down the policy of their predecessors, since they had not taken a single step to improve the trade, or to change that policy which they condemned. The most indifferent could not but have remarked this apathy and want of energy among men whose renown for enterprise on the east side of the mountains put to shame all competition, and carried everything before it.

Three years had elapsed since they were in possession of the trade from sea to sea, and since they enjoyed the full and undivided commerce of the Columbia River. In this part, however, their trade fell greatly short of their expectations, or their known success elsewhere: and instead of the anticipated prize, they discovered after so long a trial nothing else but disappointment and a uniform series of losses and misfortunes. But the quantity of furs on an average did not diminish but rather increased from year to year; it was observed by the more discerning part that the country was not barren in peltries and that there existed some defect in the management of their concern.

Expresses were frequently sent to the company's headquarters at Fort William. Dwelling on the poverty of the company's headquarters at Fort William. Dwelling on the poverty of the country, the impractibility of trade, and the hostility of the natives. In this manner the company were kept in the dark as to the value of the country. The round of extravagance went on, every one in turn made the best of not deviating from the steps of his predecessor but adhering as much as possible to the old habits and convenience while jaunting up and down the river in the old beaten path.

In the meantime, the company who had placed implicit confidence in the assertions of their co-partners began to waver in their opinions of their recent acquisitions, and they found the coffers were drained for the support of an empty name. They became divided in their councils; a great majority were inclined to throw up this cumbersome portion of their trade, while a few more determined were for giving it a further trial. For the members of the Company were no less noted for their temerity of what they already possessed than for the eagerness to seize every possible opportunity of increasing their overgrown territory.

The maxims of trade followed by the company of the east of the mountains, their mode of voyaging and their way of dealing with

Indians has been mentioned by long experience as the best calculated for them. These maxims are, nevertheless, founded on false principles, and when they are reduced to practice in the Western districts, they are found to fail.

An Indian from the Hudson's Bay does well where he was brought up, in the woods and swamps of the north; but must perish from want on the barren plains of the Columbia while multitudes of inhabitants are never at a loss to find a livelihood, and the rule holds good if reversed. The temperature of the climate not being the same, the face of nature alters more or less in proportion. Then the height of land is very distant from the ocean, the rivers in their course face in with level countries which form them into immense lakes, but from the great duration of the winter, the means of subsistence is scanty and the natives are thereby scattered over the wide extent, familiarized with the trader, and have every dependence on him for the supply of their real and acquired wants.

On the waters of the Pacific, the case is different. A chain of mountains extends its lofty ridges in the vicinity of the ocean. The inclination of the land is precipitous, and the course of rivers direct. The heats are excessive, and they continue without a cloud or moistening shower for months together to replenish the source or feed their parched streams. Droughts check the salutary progress of vegetation. The winters are short, the waters abound with fish, the forests with animals, the plains with various nutritious herbs and roots, and the natives cover the earth in swarms, in their rude and unenlightened state. War is their chief occupation and the respective nations and tribes in their meandering life are no less independent of their trader than they are of one another.

The warlike nations of the Columbia stir about in such unexpected multitudes as surprise the unwary trader, and their barbarous and forward appearance usually corresponds with their unrelenting fury. A sudden rencontre with them may well appall the stoutest heart. They are too free and indolent to submit to the drudgery of collecting the means of traffic. But articles of merchandise or use will not the less tempt their cupidity, and when such things are feebly guarded, they will not hesitate to take them by force. They are well or ill disposed towards their traders in measure as they supply them with the implements of war, and withhold them from their enemies. It is therefore a nice point to pass from one tribe or nation to another and make the most of each in the way of barter. Many are the obstacles to be overcome, nor is it given to ordinary minds to open new rounds and secure a permanent trade.

It is not easy to overcome the force of habit and no set of men could be more wedded to its customs than the great Nabobs of the fur trade. And I might have by way of confirming the remark just point out one instance among many. The description of craft used on the waters of Columbia by Astor's concern consisted of split or sawed cedar boats, strong, light and durable, and in every possible way safer and better adapted for rough water than the birch rind canoes in general use on the east side of the mountains. They carried a cargo or burden of about 3000 lbs. weight, and yet nimbly handled were easily carried across the portages. A great partiality subsisted in favour of the good old bark canoes of Northern reputation, being of particular form and with all the kind of vessel of customary conveyance used by North Westers. And that itself was no small recommendation. Therefore, the country was ransacked for prime birch bark more frequently than for prime furs, and to guard against a failure in this fanciful article, a stock of it was shipped at Montreal for London, and from thence conveyed round Cape Horn for their establishment at Fort George, in case that none of equal quality could be found on the waters of the Pacific.

On the arrival of the annual express we heard that some strenuous measures respecting the affairs of Columbia had been adopted at Fort William, that the eyes of the Company had at last been open to their own interest, and that a change of system after a warm discussion was resolved upon. Such steps of course influenced in a more or less degree the decision of our council here, and gave rise to some equally warm debates, as will appear by-and-by, as to the practicability of carrying into effect the resolutions passed at headquarters. The new plan or system settled upon for carrying on the trade west of the dividing ridge, so far as it went, embraced in its

55

outline several important alternatives. By this arrangement the new Columbia quarter, the most northern district of the company's trade, instead of being supplied with goods as formerly from the east side was in future to derive its annual supplies through the channel of the Columbia. And the Columbia itself, in lieu of being confined to the northern branch and sea coast, as had been the case since the North West had the trade, would be extended on the south and east towards California and the mountains, embracing a new and unexplored tract of country. To obviate the necessity of establishing trading posts or permanent dwellings among so many warlike and refractory natives, formidable trapping parties were, under chosen leaders, to range the country for furs, and the resources thus to be collected were annually to be conveyed to the mouth of the Columbia, these to be shipped for the Canton market. To facilitate this part of the general plan and give a new impulse to the measure, the Oregon was to be divided into two separate departments designated by the coast and inland trade, with a chief man at the head of each.

Another object connected with this new arrangement was the introduction of Iroquois from Montreal. These people being expert hunters and trappers might by their example teach others. To the latter part of this plan, however, many objections might have been urged. It will be in the recollection of the reader that we left the inland party preparing for headquarters. At the accustomed time we all met at the forks, and from thence, following the current of the river with our annual return, we reached Fort George on the 7th of June 1816.

3. RENEGADE IN CHAINS

THE FORT WILLIAM express brought some new and important resolutions in addition to those we have noticed in the latter part of the preceding chapter. The first confirmed a division of the Columbia into two separate departments, and appointed the chief man or Bourgeois to preside at the head of each. The second altered and amended the mode of conveying expresses, and the third dwelt on the new system to be introduced for the improvement of the trade generally with some other points of minor importance.

As soon therefore as all parties had assembled at Fort George, the council was convened; but instead of two or three days' sitting as usual, a whole week was spent in discussions without result; they had not the power either to alter or amend, and therefore they acquiesced in the minutes of council at headquarters.

The warm debate and protracted discussions in our council here however were not alone occasioned by the introduction of the new system as opening a new and extensive field for energy and enterprise. But let me tell the reader that the little pronoun plural "we" is not intended to represent all hands but merely those of my own class, the subordinates. For the Bourgeois looked as sour as vinegar nor did it require any great penetration of mind to know the cause.

Mr. Keith, already noticed in our narrative, had been nominated to preside at the establishment of Fort George, and had the shipping interest, coast trade and general outfitting business under his sole management. The gentleman appointed to superintend the department of the interior was none other than the same Mr. McKenzie[1] who had been one of the first adventurers to this part of the country and who occupies so conspicuous a part in the first

1 Donald McKenzie.

division of our narrative. To his share fell the arduous task of putting the whole machinery of the new system into operation.

Mr. Keith being one of themselves, his appointment gave no offense; but that a stranger, a man to use their own words "that was only fit to eat horse flesh, and shoot at a mark" should have been put over their heads was a slur on their reputation. So strongly had the tide of prejudice set against him, McKenzie, that Mr. Keith, although a man of sound judgement and good sense, joined in the clamour of his associates.

In connection with the new arrangement, the costly mode of conveying express throughout the country hitherto in vogue was to be abolished, and henceforth they were to be entrusted to the natives with the exception of the annual general express. To give full speed to these messengers, it was strongly recommended at headquarters that the council here should enter into the new order of things with heart and hand. We now turn our attention to the annual brigade. The people bound for inland, consisting of one hundred and two persons, embarked on board of twelve boats and left Fort George, after a short stay of only fifteen days. The waters being but moderately high this year and the weather very fine, no stoppage or casualty happened to retard their progress till they had reached the little rocky narrows below the falls;[2] when there an accident unavoidably happened. While the men were engaged in hunting up one of the craft, the line broke, and the boat instantly reeling round filled with water close to the rocks. The foreman taking advantage of his position immediately jumped out and saved himself, and so might the sternsman, had he been so inclined; but under the infatuation of the moment he kept standing in the boat, up to the middle in water, laughing all the time, making a jest of the accident, when suddenly a whirlpool bursting under the bottom threw the craft on her side, it instantly filled and sank, and poor Amiolle sank along with it to rise no more.

From the rocky narrows the different parties got to their respective destinations in safety, and having done so we propose taking our leave of them for a little, and in the meantime return to Fort George, the place of my appointment as second to Mr. Keith.

The company's ship *Colonel Allan,* direct from London, reached the Columbia a few days after the arrival of the spring brigade from the interior, and soon after her a schooner followed from the same post, both heavily laden with ample cargoes for the trade of the country. It was pleasing to see the North West as compared with Astor's vessels. The former brought us a full supply of everything required; whereas the latter, according to Astor's crooked policy, brought but little, that little perfect trash, nor was half of what was brought left with us, he preferring to supply the Indians rather than his own people.[3] The *Colonel Allan* after a short stay at Fort George sailed for California and South America on a speculating trip, and returned again with a considerable quantity of specie and other valuable commodities consigned to some of the London merchants. This specie and cargo were stored at the establishment and subjected us for some months to the annoyance of guarding it day and night. We often wished it in the owner's pockets, or in the River Styx.

During this summer Capt. McClellan of the *Colonel Allan* was employed in making out a new survey of the bar and entrance of the river and I was appointed to accompany him, this business occupied upward of three weeks. On the bar several channels were marked out in course of the examination; but as the sandbanks frequently shift, even in the course of a day or two, according to the prevailing wind, no permanent reliance could be placed on any of them. The old channel was considered the best. In August the *Colonel Allan* started for China with the Columbia furs and specie.

Before taking our leave of this ship and formidable commander, we have to record a fatal incident which took place on board of her while lying at anchor in front of Fort George. It had often been a subject of remark among Columbians how unfortunate a certain class of professional men had been in that quarter. We are here speaking of physicians or surgeons. The first professional gentleman of this class in our time was a Doctor White, who soon after entering the river became suddenly deranged, jumped overboard

2 Celilo Falls.
3 It might here be noted that Astor was in business to "supply" the Indians.

and was drowned. The next was a Doctor Crowly from Edinburgh who came out to follow his profession on the Columbia for the North West Company but soon after his arrival he was charged with having shot a man in cold blood, and was in consequence sent home to attend his trial and this brings us to the circumstance we have just attended to.

While the *Colonel Allan* was lying in port, an American ship commanded by a Capt. Reynolds entered the river but had no sooner cast anchor than I was sent by Mr. Keith, according to usual custom, to ascertain her object and to hand Mr. Reynolds a copy of the company's regulations for his information and guidance respecting the natives and the trade. So that all things might work conveniently in support of justice and good feelings between all parties.

While I was on board the Boston ship Mr. Downie, surgeon of the *Colonel Allan,* in company with some other gentlemen came on board on a visit of pleasure. As soon as my little business with Captain Reynolds was over he invited us all down to his cabin to take what he called the "Liquor;" we went down and were treated to a glass of New England whisky. On taking the bottle in his hand Doctor Downie said, "Let us fill up our glasses; it will perhaps be the last." I and others took notice of the words but no remark was made at the time, except by the Captain who smiled and said, "I hope not." After passing but a short time in the cabin we all left the ship, I returning to the fort while Dr. Downie and the others went to the *Colonel Allan.* Twenty minutes had not elapsed from the time we parted at the water's edge when a message reached Fort George that Doctor Downie had committed suicide. As soon as the melancholy report reached us, Mr. Keith requested me to go on board the *Colonel Allan* and attend the inquest. Accordingly I went, and found Mr. Downie in a dying state. The moment he entered his cabin he had shot himself with a pistol. Being perfectly sensible at the time, I put a few questions to him; his only reply was, "Oh! my mother, my mother." He soon breathed his last. No cause could be assigned for the rash act. He was a very sober man, beloved and respected by all who knew him. Mr. Downie was a near relation of the unfortunate captain of that name who fell so gallantly on Lake Champlain.

Leaving the *Colonel Allan* to pursue her voyage, we take up the subject of the schooner which entered the Columbia as already noticed. This vessel after a cruise along the coast, sailed for the United States. On board of the schooner was a Russian renegade by the name of Jacob, a blacksmith by trade, whom the captain, on his arrival, handed over to us in irons charged with mutiny. This daring wretch had laid a plot for putting the captain to death and carrying the ship to a strange port; but his designs were detected in time to save both.

We have no great pleasure in dwelling on crime, but will briefly sketch Jacob's career. He was brought to Fort George in irons, and there in irons he lay until the schooner sailed. On the strength of fair promises however, and apparent deep contrition, he was released from his chains and confinement and introduced to the forge as a blacksmith; he did not long continue there before it was discovered that he had been trying old pranks again; but not succeeding in bringing about a meeting, he succeeded in bringing about disaffection and desertion.

It was always customary at Fort George to keep a watch by night as well as a guard by day. In this respect it resembled more a military than a trading establishment. Jacob from his address had got into favour with his Bourgeois, was one of the night watch, and for some time gave great satisfaction. His conduct was however more plausible than real, and from some suspicious circumstances I had noticed, I warned Mr. Keith that Jacob was not the reformed man he wished to make us believe. But Mr. Keith, a good man himself, could only see Jacob's favourable side. The master was duped, and the blacksmith was at his old trade of plotting mischief. He was bribing and misleading the silly and credulous to form a party and had so far succeeded that while on watch one dark night he and eighteen of his deluded followers, chiefly Owhyhees,[4] got over the palisades unperceived and set off for California in a body! He had made his dupes believe that if once there, their fortunes were made. But just as the last of the deserters were getting over the pickets I

4 Hawaiians.

happened to get wind of the matter and discovered their design. I immediately awoke Mr. Keith, but it was only after muster was called that we found out the extent of the plot, and the numbers missing. "I could never have believed the villain would have done so" was Mr. Keith's only remark.

On the next morning the interpreter with five Indians all in disguise were sent to track them out with instructions to join the fellows, and to act according to circumstances. If they found them determined to continue their journey they were not to make themselves known; but if on the contrary they found them warring and divided, they were to use their influence and endeavour to bring them back. The plan succeeded. Abandoning their treacherous leader the fugitive islanders wheeled about, and accompanying the interpreter, returned again to the establishment on the third day. Jacob finding himself caught in his own trap and deserted in turn by those whom he had led astray abandoned himself with the savages, nor was he long with them when he gave us a specimen of his capabilities as robber as well as mutineer and deserter, for he returned to the fort in the night time and continued to get over the palisades, twenty feet high, eluded the watch, broke into a store, carried off his booty and got clear!! Soon after this exploit, which in no small degree added to his audacity, he entered the fort in broad daylight, clothed in garb of a squaw, and was meditating in conjunction with some Indian desperadoes an attack upon the fort, we only learnt after his apprehension.

We had repeatedly sent him friendly messages to return to his duty, and promised him a free pardon for the past. In short, we had done everything to induce his return, but to no purpose. He thought the footing he had obtained among the Indians was sufficient to set all our invitations and threats at defiance.

During all this time our anxiety and uneasiness increased, and the more so as it was well known that Jacob had become a leading man among a disaffected tribe of Indians. Our interest, our safety, our all depended on dissolving this dangerous union before it gathered strength. At this critical moment I proposed to Mr. Keith that if he gave me thirty men I would deliver Jacob into his hands.

"You shall have fifty," said he, but continuing the subject, he remarked again, "No, it will be a hazardous undertaking and I have no wish to risk men's lives." "Better to run every risk," said I, "than to live in constant alarm." "Well then," said he, "take the men you want and go," so I immediately prepared to get hold of the villain at all risks.

For this purpose, forty armed men were got ready and having procured a guide we left the fort in two boats by night, but soon left our boats and proceeded through the backwoods to prevent the Indians from seeing or circulating any report of our departure. Next day we had got to the edge of the woods about sundown, encamped there and remained concealed until night encouraged us to advance to within a short distance of the Indians. From this place I dispatched the guide and two men to examine and report on the situation of the Indian camp. On their return, a little after midnight, we put everything in the best order we could, both for the attack and to guard against surprise. We had information as to the hut Jacob was in, and on it of course we kept our eyes; our Indian guide became uneasy and much intimidated. He said it was madness to attempt taking him as he was always armed, and besides that the Indians would fire upon us, "Look," said I to him, "do you see our guns, are we not armed as well as they? All the Indians in the land will not prevent us from executing our purpose. But if you are afraid you can return home." This declaration touched him keenly. "I am ready," said he, "to follow the whites, I am not afraid."

The night being dark, we should have waited the return of daylight, but the Indians were too numerous; our only chance of success was to take them by surprise. I therefore divided the men into two companies, one to surround the tent; the other to act as a guard in case the Indians interfered. All being ready, I took Wilson the gunner and St. Martin, the guide, two powerful men with us. Arming ourselves, we made a simultaneous rush on the tent; but at the moment we reached it, a shot was fired from within, another instantly followed; yet we fortunately escaped. On forcing our way into the tent, the villain was in the act of seizing another gun, for he had them by him, but it was wrested out of his hands and we laid hold of him; being a powerful man, he managed to draw a knife and making a dash at St. Martin, cut his arm severely; but he had not time to repeat the blow, we had him down, and tying his hands and feet dragged him out, by this time all our people had mustered together and in the darkness and bustle we appeared much more formidable than we really were.

In this confusion I perceived the chief of the rebellious tribe. Turning round to the fellow as he was sitting with his head on his knees, said to him, "You are a pretty chief, harbouring an enemy to the whites, a dog like yourself." Dog or woman are the most insulting epithets you can call an Indian by. "You dog," said I again to him, "who fired the shot? You have forfeited your life! But the whites who are generous forgive you, look therefore well to your ways in the future." A good impression might have been made had we been more formidable and able to prolong our stay among them; but as the Indians might have recovered from their surprise, and seeing our weak side been tempted to take advantage of it, we hastened from the camp carrying our prize along with us.

After getting clear of the camp we made a halt, handcuffed our prisoner, and then made the best of our way home. On arriving at the fort Jacob was locked up, ironed, and kept so until the autumn, when he was shipped on board of a vessel sailing for the Sandwich Islands. As in irons he arrived, so in irons he left us. From that day, I never heard any more about Jacob.

It was a fortunate circumstance for us the Indians did not interfere with our attempt to take him. The fact is, they had no time to reflect but were taken by surprise, which added to our success as well as safety.

On Jacob's embarking in the boat to be conveyed to the ship, he took off his old Russian cape, and waving it in the air round his head, gave three loud cheers, uttering in a bold voice, "Huzza! Huzza! for my friends, confusion to my enemies." While we were thus occupied on the west side of the mountains new and more deeply interesting scenes were exerting their influence on the east side. Which in the order of things, we next notice.

The North West Company were encroaching on the chartered territories of the Hudson's Bay Company. The North Westers, high in their own estimation, professed to despise all others, and threatened with lawless violence all persons who presumed in the ordinary course of trade to come within their line, a line without limit which fancy or caprice induced them to draw between themselves and all others. Many needy adventurers from time to time sought their way into the Indian countries from Canada; but few, very few indeed ever had the courage or good fortune, if good fortune we might call it, to pass Fort William and if in a dark night or misty morning they had passed the forbidden barrier, vengeance soon overtook them. Their canoes were destroyed. Themselves threatened and their progress impeded in every way, so that they had to return, ruined men!

It is a well known fact that the North West Company had no exclusive right to have any portion of the Indian country. Their right was in common with every other adventurer, and no more. And yet these were the men who presumed to burst through the legal and sacred rights of others. Many actions, however, which carried guilt and crime along with them were thrown upon the shoulders of the North West Company undeservedly. Many lawless acts and aggressions were committed by their servants which that highly respectable body never sanctioned. It was the unfortunate spirit of the times. One of the great evils resulting from competition in trade, in a country where human folly and individual tyranny among the subordinated often destroys the wisest measurers of their superiors. For at the head of the company of which we are now speaking were men of great sterling worth. Men who detested crime as much as they loved justice.

The North Westers had of late years penetrated through the very heart of the Hudson's Bay Company's territories as far as the Atlantic, which was of Hudson's Bay, and set at defiance every legal restriction or moral obligation. Their servants pillaged their opponents, destroyed their forts and trading establishments as suited their views, and not infrequently kept armed parties marauding from post to post, menacing with destruction and death every one that presumed to check their career, till at last party spirit and rivalry in trade had convulsed and changed the whole social order of things into a state of open hostility. And this was the complexion of affairs up to the fatal 19th of June of this year.

On that memorable day one of those armed parties to which we have just attested, consisting of forty-five men, had advanced on the Earl of Selkirk's infant colony at Red River when Governor Semple of the Hudson's Bay Company, with several other gentlemen and attendants, went out on behalf of the frightened colonists to meet them with the view, it has been stated, of ascertaining what they wanted. But the moment both parties met, angry words ensued, shots were fired, and in the unfortunate rencontre the Governor and his party, to the number of twenty-two, were all killed on the spot! The colonists were drove at the muzzle of the gun from their comfortable homes to a distance of three hundred miles from the settlement. Even to Norway House, at the north end of Lake Winnipeg. And if they had the good fortune to get off with their lives it was owing to the humane feelings of Mr. Cuthbert Grant, a native of the soil, who placing himself at the risk of his own life between the North West party and the settlers, kept the former at bay by his daring and determined conduct and saved the latter, for which meritorious and timely interference the settlement owes him a debt of gratitude which it can never repay.

On the words "shots were fired" hinged many of the decisions which took place in the courts of law. For the advocates of either party strenuously denied having fired the first shot. And perhaps the knowledge of that fact will ever remain secret; but the general opinion is against the North West party, and in that opinion we concur.

The triumph, however, was but of short duration, for the sacrifice of that day sealed the downfall of the North West Company. For no less than twenty-three individuals out of the forty-five which composed the North West party have fell victims, in the course of human events, to misfortune or to an untimely end!

We might here remark, in connection with this melancholy affair, that the going out of Governor Semple and so many men with him was an ill advised measure, and carried along with it the appearance of determination of their part to oppose force to force, and we cannot in the spirit of impartiality and fairness, close our eyes to the fact that they were all armed, and this was no doubt the light in which the North West party viewed their approach which led to the catastrophe that followed.

But we now hasten from this scene to notice the influence that it had on their opponents. No sooner had the news of the fatal disaster at Red River spread abroad, than the Earl of Selkirk with an armed force seized on Fort William, the grand depot and headquarters of the North West Company. We are not, however, either prepared to assert that Lord Selkirk was right in seizing on Fort William by way of retaliation. No one has a right to take the law into his own hands, nor to make himself judge in his own cause, but according to the prevailing customs of this lawless country power confers right. Soon after these aggressions the eyes of government were opened to the evils of the case, and two commissioners, Colonel Coltman and Major Fletcher, were sent up from Canada with authority to examine into the matter, seize and send down all guilty or suspected persons belonging to either side to stand their trials. And we cannot do better here than refer our readers to a perusal of the trials which took place in Canada in 1818 on the subject.

Before dismissing this part of our narrative, we might advert to what we have just mentioned, namely, "the Earl of Selkirk's infant colony," as it may afford some satisfaction to our readers to know something more about it, we shall for their information state a few facts. In the progress of his colonizing system, Lord Selkirk had purchased from the Hudson's Bay Company in 1811 a tract of land on the Red River, situated at the southern extremity of Lake Winnipeg in Hudson's Bay for the purpose of planting a colony there, and to which place several families had in 1812 and subsequent years been brought out from Scotland by his Lordship. These Scotch families were the first settlers in the Red River, and Red River was the first colony planted in Rupert's Land.[5]

5 Rupert's Land comprised what is now roughly the eastern half of Canada. The

The first settlers had to stand the brunt of troublesome times, and weather the sweeping storms of adversity during the early days of the colony. They were driven several times from their homes, and suffered every hardship, privation and danger by the lawless strife of the country. They even were forced to live and seek shelter among the savages, and like them had to resort to hunting and fishing to satisfy the pangs of hunger, and after order had in some measure been established, they were visited for several years by clouds of grasshoppers that ate up every green herb and left the fields black, desolate and fruitless.

What his Lordship's views were in planting a colony in such a frozen and out of the way corner of the earth as Red River is, few persons knew. For he must have foreseen that it must eventually fall into the hands of the Americans, however little they might benefit by it; for the march of improvement must, in the nature of things, be south, and not north. Its value therefore to Great Britain, excepting as the Hudson's Bay Company are concerned, will be nothing. But from its geographical position it may on some future occasion serve as a bone of contention between the two governments. The founder of Red River Colony could then have had no other real object in view than as a key to the fur trade of the Far West, and as a resting place for retiring fur traders clogged with Indian families. In this point of view the object was philanthropic, and to the fur trade, an item of real interest. For retiring traders in lieu of transporting either themselves or their means to the civilized world, as was the case formerly, would now find it to their interest to spend their days in perhaps a more congenial and profitable manner in Red River Colony, under the fostering care and paternal influence of the Honourable Hudson's Bay Company.

We have already adverted to McKenzie's appointment. In October that gentleman reached Fort George from Montreal to enter on his new sphere of labours. He was received by the Columbia managers with a chilling and studied politeness. It was no doubt morti-

territory under the aegis of the Hudson's Bay Company, it extended along the western shore of the Bay, southward to the present boundary of Minnesota, and on above the Great Lakes to the eastward. There were no precise boundaries.

fying to his feelings to witness the shyness in the conduct of his new associates, for if they could have driven him back from whence he came, it was evidently their object to do it. But McKenzie, as stubborn as themselves, knew the ground he stood upon and defied the discouraging reception he met with either to dampen his spirits or to cool his steady zeal. He, therefore, lost no time but intimated to Mr. Keith his wish to depart for the interior as soon as convenient, the season being far advanced, and the journey long.

Mr. Keith, however, raised many objections. He alleged the scarcity of men, the lateness of the season and want of craft. Nor were these objections altogether groundless. "Your departure," said he, "will derange all our plans for the year." In answer to which McKenzie handed him his instructions, a letter from the Agent at Montreal with a copy of the minutes of council at Fort William. After perusing these documents and throwing them on the table, he observed, "Your plans are wild, you will never succeed, nor do I think any gentleman here will second your views, or be so foolhardy as to attempt an establishment in the Nez Perce country as a key to your future operations and without which you cannot move a step." "These remarks are uncalled for. I have been there already," said McKenzie. "Give me the men and goods I require, according to the conditions of council. I alone am answerable for the rest." So saying they parted.

During all this time, the North Westers might be seen clubbed together in close consultation, avoiding as much as possible the object of their dislike; this shy and evasive conduct at length caused McKenzie to insist on his right. "Give me the men and goods," said he, "as settled at headquarters, I ask for no more, that I must have." "You had better," replied Mr. Keith, "postpone your operations till another year." "No," rejoined McKenzie, "my intentions are positive, I must proceed at once," and here the conference again ended.

Keith and his adherents had denounced every change as pregnant with evil and McKenzie's schemes as full of folly and madness. They therefore laboured hard to counteract both. The chief of the interior stood alone, I being the only person on the ground who seconded his views, and that was but feeble support. Yet although he thus stood alone, he never lost sight of the main object. The coolness between the parties increased; they seldom met. The wordy dispute ended, a paper war ensued. This new feature of the affair was not likely to mend the matter; but was just what McKenzie liked, he was now in his own element. This went on for two or three days, and all anxiously awaited the result. The characters of the men were well known. Both firm, both resolute.

At this stage of the contest, McKenzie called me into his room one day, and showed me the correspondence between them. "You see," said he to me, after I had perused the notes, "that in war as in love, the parties must meet to put an end to it." "I cannot see it in that light yet," said I, "but I can see that the wisest of men are not always wise. Delay is his object; you must curtail your demand, and yield to circumstances. You do not know Mr. Keith. He does everything by rule, and will hazard nothing; you on the contrary, must hazard everything. In working against you, they are working against themselves, and must soon see their error. It is the result of party spirit. Mr. Keith has been led astray by the zeal of his associates, left to himself he is a good man, and there is yet ample room for a friendly reconciliation."

Just as we were talking over these matters, a note from Mr. Keith was handed into the room. This note was written in a plain business-like manner and distinctly stated what assistance McKenzie could attain. After reading it over and throwing it down on the table among the other diplomatic scraps, McKenzie observed to me, "It is far short of what I require, far short of what I expected, and far short of what the company guaranteed; yet it is coming nearer to the point, and is perhaps, under all circumstances, as much as can be expected. It is a choice of two evils, and rather than prolong a fruitless discussion, I will attempt the task before me with such means as are available, and if a failure takes place, it will not be difficult to trace it to the proper source." Soon after this, the parties met and entered upon business in a friendly manner.

McKenzie now prepared for his inland voyage. But had the reader seen the medly of savages, Iroquois, Abanakees[6] and Owhyhees, that were meted out to him, he would at once have marked the brigade down as doomed; but that was not all, a question arose, according to the rules of the voyage, who was to be his second! and this gave rise to another serious difficulty. One said the undertaking was too hazardous ever to succeed. He would not go. Another, that it was madness to attempt it. And he would not go. And a third observed that as he had not been appointed by the council, he would not go. He was left to go alone!

Never during my day had a person for the interior left Fort George with such a motley crew, nor under such discouraging circumstances. And certainly, under all the difficulties of the case, he would have been justified in waiting until he had been fitted out better, or provided with means adequate to the undertaking; disregarding all dangers, his experience and zeal buoyed him up and ultimately carried him through in spite of all the obstacles that either prejudice or opposition could throw in his way.

Although McKenzie's personal absence was pleasing to his colleagues, yet in another point of view it was extremely unsatisfying, because they had failed in their effect either to discourage or stop him. Measuring, however, his capacity by their own, they still cherished a hope that the Indians would arrest his progress, his failure was therefore looked upon as certain.

Let us inquire how it happened that a man "only fit to eat horse flesh and shoot at a mark" should have been put over the heads of the Columbia manager, incomprehensible as it was to them, it was perfectly clear to us; because in the first place the trade of the Columbia rolled on, under their guidance, and had not advanced one single step beyond what it was when they first took possession of it. Nay, it was worse, which a very superficial glance at both ends might demonstrate beyond a doubt.

According to the articles of co-partnership, the shares of the stock in trade were divided into parts. The dividers, or as they were more generally called, "Agents," held a certain proportion in their own hand, as stock holders and general managers of the business. The Bourgeois, as they were called, or the native managers among the

6 Abenaki Indians, imported like the Iroquois from eastern Canada.

71

Indians, held the remaining shares. By the regulations of the concern, the Bourgeois were raised either through favour or merit
from the ranks, or step by step, to the more honourable and lucra-
tive station of proprietors, and their patronage in turn promoted
others. Their votes decided the election for or against all other
dictates. This was generally the manner in which the business of
promotion was carried on in the North West trade.

But the Agents were on a somewhat different footing for they
had not only a voice in common with the Bourgeois in all cases of
promotion; but they had what perhaps we might call an exclusive
right, as Agents, according to the interest they held, of sending into
the country any person or persons they thought proper, or who
possessed their confidence, whether connected with the company
or not. Such persons, however, entered the service at fixed salaries
without the prospect of promotion, because to have a claim to promotion in the regular way, an apprenticeship was indispensible.

To the Agents, therefore, our friend was known, his enterprize
and general experience gave them every hope; and to him in preference to any other they confided the difficult task of recovering the
Columbia trade and of carrying into effect the new system. Five
hundred pounds a year for five years secured him to their interest,
and on these conditions he returned again to the Columbia.

As soon as the brigade started for the interior, a party of ten men
were outfitted for the purpose of trapping beaver in the Wallamitte.
On their way up to the place, they were warned by the natives not
to continue for that they would not suffer them to hunt on their
lands, unless they promised an instant payment, by way of tribute;
this the hunters were neither prepared for, nor disposed to grant,
and they had the simplicity to imagine that the Indians would not
venture to put their threats into effect. Next day, however, as they
were advancing on their voyage, they were astonished at seeing the
banks of the river lined on both sides by the natives, who had stationed themselves in menacing postures behind the trees and
bushes. The North Westers were little acquainted with these people and thinking they only meant to frighten them out of some
articles of goods, they paddled up in the middle of the stream. A

AN INDIAN COUNCIL

A water color by Alfred Jacob Miller

AN INDIAN TOMB

A drawing by Henry James Warre

shower of arrows, however, very soon convinced them of their mistake. One of the number was wounded and in drifting down, for they immediately turned about, they fired a round upon the natives, and one of them was killed dead.

After this discomfiture the hunters made the best of their way back to the establishment, and the project of hunting in the Wallamitte was relinquished for some time. Soon afterwards, however, a party of twenty-five men under the management of a clerk was sent to pacify the natives and to endeavour to penetrate to the hunting ground. By reaching the spot where the first difficulty arose they found that the man who was killed had been a chief, and that, therefore, the tribe would not come to terms before a certain portion of merchandise was delivered as compensation for the injury done. This being accordingly agreed to the matter was compromised, and the party did advance but unfortunately soon got involved in a second quarrel with the natives, and having fired upon them killed three outright.

On their way back after putting up for the night, a band of Indians got in their camp and a scuffle ensued when one of the hunters got severely wounded, and the whole party owed its safety to the darkness of the night. By the disaster of this trip, every avenue was for the present shut up against our hunters in the Wallamitte direction.

One remark here suggests itself. When the first party of hunters were warned by the natives that they would not suffer them to hunt on their lands unless they produced an instant payment, by way of tribute. What was the amount of that tribute? Had they the moment the Indians threatened tribute, instead of paddling up in the middle of the stream stopped and made for shore, held out the hand of friendship, and smoked a pipe or two of tobacco with them there would have been an end to it, the affair would have been settled. This was the tribute the natives expected but the whites set the Indians at defiance by trying to pass them in the middle of the stream.

When any difficulty of this kind occurs, a friendly confidence on the part of the whites seldom fails in bringing about a reconciliation. The Indians at once come round to their views. This was the universal practice followed by us during our first years in travelling among the Indians, and we always got on smoothly. But in measuring the feelings of the rude and independent natives of Columbia by the same standard as they measured the feelings of their dependent slaves on the east side of the mountains the North Westers were not wise.

The result of this disaster shut us out entirely from the southern quarter. The loss was scarcely felt, and Mr. Keith with his usual sagacity and forethought lost no time in applying a remedy. But what remedy could well be applied? We considered ourselves aggrieved, the natives still more so, we had been wounded but they had been killed, and perhaps all by the conduct of one of our own people; yet under all the circumstances something required to be done, as the most prudent step to be adopted.

In order, therefore, to bring about a reconciliation, a party sufficiently strong to guard against miscarriage and give weight to our measures was filled out and put under my charge, and I was ably assisted by my experienced friend, Mr. Ogden.[7] This half diplomatic, half military embassy consisted of forty-five armed men, left Fort George in three boats and reached the Wallamitte Falls on the third day. It was there the Indians had assembled to resist any attempt of the hunters to ascend the Wallamitte. There we found them encamped on the left or west bank. We took up our position with two field pieces to guard our camp on the east or right hand side, which is low, rocky and somewhat uneven. Both parties were opposite to each other, with the river only between us. We early the next morning set the negotiations on foot and made several attempts, but in vain, to bring the Indians to a parley. I went to their camp, we offered them to smoke and held out the hand of friendship in every possible way we could; but to no purpose. They refused holding any communication with us; but continued to sing their war songs, and dance their war dances. We, however, were not to be discouraged by any demonstration on their part.

Patience and forbearance do much on these occasions. It is the

[7] Peter Skene Ogden.

best policy to be observed with Indians. Indeed, with all the natives of Columbia. Peace being our object, peace we were determined to obtain. We, therefore, quietly waited to see what time would bring about.

The first day past without our effecting anything, and so did the second likewise, with friendly offers constantly held out to them; but as constantly rejected. On the third day however, the chiefs and warriors crossed over to our side, and stood in a group at some distance from our camp. I knew what was meant by this, so I took a flag in my hand, and went along to meet them. Just as I had reached the party, the whole Indian camp burst into a loud and clamorous scene of mourning. That moment the chiefs and warriors formed a ring, squatted down, and concealing their faces with their garments, remained silent and motionless for about the space of half an hour, during all this time I had to stand patiently and await the result. Not a word was uttered on either side; but as soon as the lamentations ceased in the camp, the great men uncovering their faces stood upon their feet. I then offered the pipe of peace according to Indian custom, but a significant shake of the head from the principal chief was all I got in return.

After a momentary pause the chief turning to me exclaimed, in his own language, "What do the whites want?" Rather nettled at his refusing the pipe, I answered, "Peace. Peace is what we want," and in saying so I presented him with my flag. "Here," said I, "the great chief of the whites sends you this as a token of his love." A moment or two passed in silence; a whisper went around and the peace offering was accepted, and in return, the chief took a pipe painted and ornamented with feathers and laid it down before me. This was a favourable sign. On such occasions the calumet of peace is always an emblem of friendship. They were gratified with the toy; it pleased them. The chief asked to smoke. I then handed him the pipe he had but a little before refused and some tobacco, and they sat down and commenced smoking for that is the introductory step to all important affairs, and no business can be entered upon with these people before the ceremony of smoking is over.

The smoking ended, each great man got up in turn and made a

speech, and before they had all got through, nearly two hours elapsed, and all the time I had to stand and wait. These speeches set forth in strong language a statement of their grievances, a demand for redress, and a determination to resist in the future the whites from proceeding up the Wallamitte. As soon as the Indians had said all they had to say on the subject, they sat down.

After arriving at our camp and smoking there I stated the case on behalf the whites to oppose Indian determination to prevent us from ascending the Wallamitte, and bring about if possible a peace which was my object. I therefore endeavoured to meet every objection and proved to the chiefs that these people were the first aggressors by shooting their arrows at our people, but this being no part of Indian law, they either could not or would not comprehend it notwithstanding their people had been the aggressors in the first instance, our people had been guilty of great indiscretion, and to cut the matter short I agreed to pay for their dead, according to their own laws, if they would yield the other points which after a whole day's negotiation and two or three trips to their camp they at last agreed to. The chiefs reasoned the matter temperately and formally agreed to everything. But their acknowledged authority is but very limited, their power as chiefs but small, so that any rascal in the camp might at any time break through the most solemn treaty with impunity.

The conditions of this rude treaty were that the Wallamitte should remain open, and that the whites should have at all times free ingress and egress to that quarter unmolested; that in the event of any misunderstanding between the natives and the whites the Indians were not to resort to any act of violence; but their chiefs were to apply for redress to the white chief at Fort George. And if the whites found themselves aggrieved they were likewise not to take the law into their own hands nor to take any undue advantage of the Indians, the chiefs alone were to be accountable for the conduct of their people. And truth compells us to acknowledge that the Indians faithfully and zealously observed their part of it for many years afterwards.

The business being ended, the chief as a token of general consent scraped a little dust together and with his hand throwing it in the air, uttered at the same time the expressive word, "Hilow." "It is done." This was no sooner over than the chief man presented us with a slave as a token of his good will, signifying by the act that if the Indians did not keep their promise, we might treat them all as slaves. The slave being released again to the chief, we prepared to have the Indians. Paid our offering for the dead, shook hands with the living, satisfied the chiefs and pushed down the current.

On our way home, however, we were stopped about an hour at Oak Point[8] by the ice, a rather unusual circumstance, one that never occurred either before or after all the time I was in the country. On reaching Fort George the articles of the treaty were read over and I won from Mr. Keith a smile of approbation, and that was no small credit to me, for he was a very cautious man and not lavish of his praise. "Your success," said he to me, "removes my anxiety; and is calculated not only to restore peace in the Wallamitte, but throughout the whole neighbouring tribes."

We might here state that the Wallamitte takes its rise near the northern frontiers of California in about Lat. 42.30 North, not far from the Umpqua River. The former of these streams runs almost a northern course and empties its waters into the Columbia by two channels some ninety miles above Cape Disappointment, in North Lat. 46.40 being almost due east from the mouth of Columbia. The latter pursues a course almost due west, till it reaches the Ocean. The Call-law-poh-yea-as[9] is the name by which all the Wallamitte tribes, sixteen in number, are generally known. These people were always considered by the whites as a quiet and inoffensive nation, dull and unassuming in their behaviour; but when once roused, not deficient in courage.

We have more than once had occasion to notice the striking change in the natives during the reign of the North West Company on the Columbia. On his passage down McKenzie was greeted at the Long Narrows by an unexpected shower of stones, as he took the current at the lower end of the portage. The natives in this in-

[8] Near Quincy, Oregon.
[9] Kalapooia Indians.

stance were a few hundred strong, his party consisted of about forty, and judging it expedient to resent the first insult he briskly wheeled round to their astonishment, and ordered all arms to be presented. In this menacing attitude, he signified to his men to rest until he showed the example by firing the first shot. Then exhorting the natives to renew their insult with stones or resort to their arms, a fair challenge was offered. But whether the movement was too sudden, or that they were doubtful of the result, they declined and came forward with a satisfactory submission. The affair of the rifle on a former occasion was not perhaps forgotten. The attack was owing to the scarcity of tobacco. A very few pipes had been lighted, and they perceived he had a little of that article remaining and became enraged because they could not grasp the whole. A few days previous McMillan having gone down with an express with only twenty men, they robbed one of his people of his coat and others of various articles, at the moment of embarking; but this gentleman observed a very prudent forbearance, his party being in no way a match for them.

McKenzie's departure from Fort George has already been taken notice of, and without accident or loss of time he reached the dangerous pass of the Cascades. There, however, the rigours of the season checked his progress. For the Columbia was bridged over with ice.

We soon learnt, however, that McKenzie was at home. His party consisted of about forty men, such as they were, retaining therefore a certain number about himself and the property, he adopted the new measure of distributing the remainder in the houses of the different great men among the natives apparently as boarders but in reality as spies; so that every hour he had ample intelligence of all that passed in the respective villages or camp. The chiefs were flattered by this mark of his consideration. They were no less pleased with the trifles which from time to time they received in payment, and all the natives of the place became in a couple of months perfectly familiarized with the whites.

A great deal of information was collected from these people, considerable furs also, and altogether such a footing established among them as promised fair to be turned to advantage in time to come. The chiefs were no less pleased to see McKenzie than anxious to know the cause of his return to their country. And he was greeted with a hearty welcome from all classes.

"We are rejoiced," said an old chief to him one day, "to see one of our first and best friends come back again to live among us. We were always well treated by our first traders, and got plenty of tobacco to smoke. They never passed our camp without taking our children by the hand and giving us to smoke, and we have always been sorry since you left us. Our traders nowadays use us badly, they pass up and down the river without stopping. They never take our children by the hand, nor hold out the pipe to us. They do not like us. Their hearts are bad. We seldom go to see them. Are you," continued the chief, "going to remain long with us?" McKenzie consoled the friendly old man, and told him that he would be long with them to smoke and take their children by the hand, and would never pass nor repass without giving them a smoke as usual. At these words, the chief exclaimed, "Haugh owe yea ah! Haugh owe yea ah!" These exclamations of gratitude showed that McKenzie was perfectly at home among them. Every countenance he met smiled with contentment, and his authority was as much respected by the Indians as by his own people, so that he considered himself as safe and secure in the Indian camp as if he had been in his own house.

Nor had he sooner laid himself up in ordinary among the great Nabobs of the Cascades, than he was invited from wigwam to wigwam to partake of their cheer.

On the score of cheer, we might here qualify the curiosity of our reader with a brief description of one of their entertainments called an Indian feast. The first thing that attracts the attention of a stranger on being invited to a feast in these parts is to see seven or eight bustling squaws running to and fro with pieces of greasy bark, skins of animals, and mats to furnish the banqueting lodge as receptacles for the delicate viands. At the door of which is placed on such occasions a sturdy savage with a club in his hand to keep the dogs at bay while the preparations are going on.

The banqueting hall is always of a size suitable to the occasion, large and roomy. A fire occupies the centre round which, in circular order, are laid the eatables, and the guests form a close ring round the whole. Every one approaches with a grave and solemn step. The party being all assembled, the reader may picture to himself our friend seated like a epicure among the nobles of the place, with his bark platter between his legs, filled top heavy with the most delicious melange of bear's grease, dog's flesh, wappatoes, olellies, amutes,[10] and a profusion of other viands, roots and berries. Round the festive board, placed on terra firma, all the nabobs of the place are squatted down in a circle, each helping himself out of his platter with his fingers, observing every now and then to sleek down the hair by way of wiping the hands. Only one knife is used, and that is handed round from one to another in quick motion. Behind the banqueting circle sit in anxious expectation groups of the canine tribe, yawning, howling and growling; these can only be kept in the rear by a stout cudgel, which each of the guests keeps by him for the purpose of self defense; yet it not unfrequently happens that some of the more daring curs get out of patience, break through the front rank and carries off his booty; but when a mishap of this kind is committed, the unfortunate offender is generally well belaboured in his retreat, for the cudgels come down upon him with a well merited vengeance. The poor dog, however, has his revenge in turn, for the squabble and howl that ensued disturbs all the dormant fleas of the domicile in motion; his troop of black assailants jump about in all directions. So that a guest by helping himself to the good things before him, keeping the dogs at bay behind him, and defending himself from the black squadrons that surround him pays perhaps dearer for his entertainment at the Columbia Cascades than a foreign ambassador does in a London hotel!

In the breaking up of the ice our friends were again on their voyage; but had again the misfortune to break one of their boats while towing it up the Cascades. The lading consisted of sixty packages of ninety pounds each and the other craft were too much

10 An edible root, berries, and the wild strawberry.

laden to embark so great a surplus, and strange as it may appear, McKenzie lost not an hour in hastening his voyage but delivered over the whole of this valuable and bulky cargo into the hands of a chief named Shy-law-ifs until the period of his return.

And when the brigade returned from the ocean, the faithful and trusty chief delivered the whole over safe and untouched to McKenzie again, after being six months in his possession! Nor did we ever learn that the Indians or even his own relations molested him in the least during this seasonable act of friendship.

During his voyage, the chief of the interior visited several of the inland posts and set plans on foot for the ensuing year, and then joined the people of the spring brigade, who were assembling from all quarters. This party we had left, as will be remembered, on reaching their winter quarters and we now take up that subject in order to conduct them to their friends at headquarters.˙

In the Indian countries no sooner has the rigorous season begun to break up than the people of each wintering ground leave their respective stations and repair with all possible speed to the general rendezvous at headquarters. The mode of voyaging at that particular period varies according to the transportation of the climate, the face of the country, or the peculiar habits of the tribes. The station has been fixed in the vicinity of lofty mountains or level plains and whether the inhabitants live at peace or war with each other or endanger their trade is by their early sallies in the spring.

From some parts, therefore, the people carry their returns in canoes. The use of horses or sledges drawn by dogs is resorted to, as the most practicable for transporting property during the early stages of the season.

The time had now come when with lightsome hearts the winterers as they are generally called perform the annual trip to the ocean and an augmentation of returns this year brightened the features of our friends as they came down the Columbia to Fort George, where they arrived safely on the 16th of June 1817. Happy we were likewise that a twelvemonth had elapsed for the first time throughout the interior without casualty or bloodshed to thin their numbers.

4. PERILOUS RIVER

A FEW DAYS after the arrival of the spring brigade from the interior the company's annual ship reached at Fort George, and we shall commence the transactions of another year.

On the arrival of all hands at headquarters, the stay is generally short. Consequently at the head depot all is bustle and hurry; yet business of every description is transacted there with a degree of order and regularity not to be surpassed in countries more civilized. As soon, therefore, as the arrangements at the depot terminate and the annual appointment is made, for it is there unalterably fixed for the year, without any appeal each man returns to his post. But although the authority which determines the lot of each for the season is absolute; yet few instances of either oppression or injustice ever occur.

During the sitting of council this year an inclination was manifested to promote by every possible means the change of system and by so doing to give the chief of the interior the benefit resulting from general support, and after the council broke up the disposition was evinced to carry such a measure into practical operation; another operated in an opposite direction, tending to defeat any change for the better, and this disposition was strengthened by new and unforeseen difficulties over which the Columbia had no control.

In the various arrangements from year to year there is generally contentment and satisfaction among all classes, and this arises as much from that variety of scenes, that love of freedom which man is so universally fond of and which he here enjoys so fully, as from anything else, and pleasures there are at times in wild and savage country as well as in gay cities and polished circles, and on the whole few ever leave the scenes of the wilderness without deep regret.

In consequence of the East Indian Company's debarring the bulk of British subjects from sailing in the Indian Ocean, the North West Company's commerce in that quarter of the world became extremely circumscribed. Therefore they resolved to divest themselves of all their shipping and through the connexions they possessed in New England the inconvenience would be compensated by their investing their furs in China produce and their trade would not sustain any material injury.[1] We shall therefore not trouble ourselves nor our readers any more about the shipping interest; but confine our remarks to those measures which affected us nearer home.

The spirit of rivalry and opposition in trade east of the mountains had for some time past checked the progress of the North West Company and intercepted the reinforcements of men which had been dispatched to the Columbia quarter. On this account we found ourselves short of our usual complement and therefore had, at a great expense and loss of time, to send for a supply of Sandwich Islanders as substitutes.

But even this difficulty and delay might have been avoided had there been anything like willingness among ourselves to assist in bringing about the new order of things. Old habits and a love of ease predominated. The chief of the interior had therefore to depart with a motly and disaffected handful of men, chiefly Iroquois, to prosecute the introductory part of his reform plan.

Matters having been arranged the inland brigade, after a short stay of only eight days, left the head depot for the interior. I also accompanied the party for my own post the She-whaps, and the change was the more agreeable to me, as any place was to be preferred to the wet and disagreeable climate of Fort George.

It was not my intention originally to have conducted step by step

---

1 That is, rather than send their own ships into the territories forbidden them by governmental decree, the directors of the North West Company ordered furs to be sent to China in American ships, receiving in return either money or products to be sold in Europe.

every voyaging party ascending or descending the Columbia. Yet as I pledged myself to notice every incident that might occur, and moreover to narrate the subject of my own trials and hairbreadth escapes among the Indians that duty has again devolved on me, and as it will be found that we had more than ordinary difficulties to contend with during the present voyage, the reader may perhaps take some interest in the details.

On the brigade's starting counting only to forty-five men, being little more than half the usual complement we felt our own weakness and the more so at that season when the communication is resorted to by strange Indians being the great rendezvous of salmon fishing; but we had no alternative, few as our numbers were we had to face the difficulties that lay before us, so we hoisted sail and turned our backs on Fort George.

At Oak Point one of our men deserted and soon afterwards two others fell sick, diminishing our numbers and embarrassing us still more. At the mouth of the Wallamitte we were nearly getting into a serious quarrel. We had made a halt to trade some provisions from the Indians on Multnomah Island; but while in the act of doing so, some arrows were pointed our way without any apparent cause when two of the Iroquois immediately cocked their guns to fire upon the Indians; but were fortunately stopped in time, or we might have had a sad tale to tell. For one shot fired from any of our party would have been the signal of our ruin, and notwithstanding the Iroquois were checked in time yet the measure was noticed by the Indians and it raised a spirit of discontent which ran like wild fire among them, and our diminished numbers compared to former years encouraged the Indians to a boldness scarcely ever witnessed before. At this stage of the affair the natives were observed to collect in groups and to become shy towards us, a very bad sign, we however put the best face on things, tried to restore confidence and content them, after which we set sail and left them.

Arriving at the Cascades we found the natives in great numbers, and all completely armed. The utmost care and circumspection were needful in carrying our bulky ladings over that rocky and dangerous portage. And although strong guards were stationed at the frequent resting places, yet we could not manage to get through without repeated alarms. However, the good understanding we kept up with the principal men quieted all our apprehensions, and in spite of appearances it was found that we were in reality safe during the whole of our arduous day's labour.

Having encamped on a convenient spot at the upper end, the chief and great men were invited to come and smoke with us, they accepted the invitation and their suite of followers might have been five hundred. As soon as the order of the camp was finished and the proper precautions taken for the night, the chiefs were admitted within the lines and made to sit down at a convenient place set apart for that purpose by the doors of the tents, while the crowd received the same indulgence at some distance on the opposite side.

When the ceremony of smoking was over, a few words were addressed to the chiefs expressing the favourable sense we entertained for their character and their deportment during the day. We also bestowed on each a head of tobacco, and to every one of the motly group we gave a single leaf; which took a considerable quantity and some time to distribute. This kind treatment was so different to anything they had met with for years past that all with one voice called out in the Chinook language, "Haugh owe yea ah, Haugh owe yea ah," meaning "our friends, our friends." Turning then to the chiefs we pointed out the duties of the sentinels, signifying that they should explain the purpose to all the natives of the place in order that our slumbers might not be disturbed and the present happy intercourse not be interrupted. This done, the whole party instantly moved off in the most orderly manner: neither did any of them approach us during the night. We kept a strict watch till morning.

From the good understanding that existed between ourselves and the natives on a former occasion and particularly last winter, we anticipated the continuance of a friendly intercourse; but in this we were deceived. That friendship was but of short duration. It was in a moment dissolved by the most frivolous trifle.

I had with me an old favourite dog, a dwarfish little terrier of Spanish breed, which we had missed during the morning; but had not in the bustle and hurry made any enquiry about. One of the Indians as it afterwards appeared had got hold of it and carried it to his tent. The little captive in its struggles and anxiety for liberty happened to scratch one of his children in the face, got off, and made for us with all haste just as we were sitting down to breakfast. When happening to turn round, I perceived my little pet running towards us in great fright and two fellows following her at full speed with their guns in their hands. The poor little thing on reaching us lay down, and by its looks seemed to implore protection. No sooner had the rascals however got to us than one of them, with an air of bold affronting, cocked his gun to shoot the dog. I immediately jumped up, took the gun out of his hands, and tried to pacify him; but the fellow was furious and would give no explanation but again demanded his gun. I told him he might have his gun if he made no bad use of it. To this he made no reply, but with an air of insolent boldness, still demanded his gun. Laying hold of my own gun with one hand I handed him his with the other, accompanying the delivery with this admonition—"If you attempt to kill my dog you are a dead man."

The fellow stood motionless as a statue but made no attempt to kill the dog. His companion turned back to the camp the moment I laid hold of the gun, and in a few minutes we were surrounded by a hundred clamorous voices uttering the words, "Ma sats u-pa she shy hooks, Ma sats u-pa she shy hooks," "bad white people, bad white people." We, however, kept a watchful eye on their maneuvers, armed ourselves and waited the result. In a little time their excitement began to abate, and we had an opportunity of speaking in our turn; but our voice was scarcely heard in the crowd.

Had we measured the strength of both parties by our comparative numbers, we might at once have yielded to our opponents. But we drew no such comparison, we were compelled through sheer necessity to assert our rights and defend our property, which we did in defiance of all their threats; yet it is hard to say how the affair might have ended, had not our friend Shy-law-ifs run into the mêlé and stood up boldly for the whites, so after a great deal of loud clamour and threats the Indians had to return to their camp just as they came, and I saved my little dog.

I mention this trivial circumstance to show how fickle and unsteady Indians are, and how little is required to change their friendship into enmity. In this simple incident you have the true character of our Indian. He will purloin and conceal articles belonging to the whites, and then make a merit of finding them in order to get paid for his honesty! The hiding of a dog, the concealing of a horse, or anything else is a common practice of them, and the fellow who took the little dog had no other object in view but to make a claim on delivering it up.

After this affair we did not consider it good policy to depart from the place without coming to some understanding with the Indians. Putting our camp in a posture of defence to guard against surprise, McKenzie and myself went to the Indians and settled the matter in dispute, we gave the scratched bantling a small present, invited the chiefs to our camp to smoke, gave them a little tobacco, and parted once more the best friends in the world and all this did not take up two hours time nor cost five shillings. From this incident it would appear that the Indian is in some respect a mere child, irritated and pleased with a trifle.

Our cautious plans did not admit of our proceeding notwithstanding the apparent good feeling without having one of the considerable men to act the part of an interpreter and to proclaim our friendly footing to others as we advanced, particularly to the troublesome tenants of the falls: for we were not ignorant that false rumours might get the start of us and poison the minds of the natives against us.

Such conduct on the part of the Indians of the Cascades may seem rather strange, after the friendly manner in which our people had been treated by them during the last winter; but this can be easily accounted for were they less fickle than they are. In the winter season the natives of the place only were on the spot; but in summer the Cascades as well as the falls is a place of general resort for all the neighbouring tribes, as well as those of the place and this was the case on the present occasion. Thence their numbers and boldness.

The farther we advanced the more numerous were the natives, either dwelling in villages or congregated about the banks and rock ledge in tumultous crowds. We thought it necessary to make a short halt at each band, according to the rules of former days, and although the gestures were most suspicious at times yet we never failed to jump ashore and step into the midst of them with assumed confidence, at the same time accosting their great men and going over the same degree of ceremony as already noticed. We always passed as if we were old acquaintances on the most friendly terms. No steps without our power were neglected that could be any way conducive to our safety, an object which now imperiously claimed attention for rumours were in circulation that the natives had collected on the river in an unusual manner.

Whenever an occasion called us on shore, a couple of men from each craft appointed for the purpose instantly took their stand with fixed bayonets, and a line of privilege was always drawn which only the chiefs even allowed to pass for the purpose of acception.

Every step we then made was full of anxiety and apprehension increased in a twofold degree during the nights; every one of the party was at length so worn out by incessant watchings and fatigue that hope itself began to waver, and we even despaired of getting through, and not to our own puny arm nor to any further effort we could make but to a kind and superintending providence we owed our good fortune and safety.

Whenever the sun reached the summits of the hills the most commanding spot was situated for our encampment. In a few minutes the boats were carried out of the water and placed with the tents and baggage in form of a square, or such other figure as might correspond with the peculiar nature of the ground. This novel fortress had but one opening, which was wide enough to admit only a single person at a time. Of this the tents took up one angle, having the doors outward and before which a space was left vacant and appropriated for the chiefs. Beyond this was a station occupied by the guards and night watch, whose duty it was to keep at bay the

FORT VANCOUVER

A drawing by Henry James Warre

LES DALLES OF THE COLUMBIA RIVER

A drawing by Henry James Warre

tumultuous rabble, and here our solitary swivel was regularly pointed.

The chiefs, however, neither passed nor repassed without leave, and under the specious veil of respect for their exalted rank their influence was then made subservient to our views. Their persons were pledged to our safety. In this manner likewise they were in doubtful cases detained over night. Each of our party had a special occupation assigned, and the watch at night being divided into three we had each of us the direction of each man alternately. But in many instances we were all on foot and on these occasions had to pass a sleepless night.

When on shore the duties rested entirely on the gentlemen and sentinels, the farther we advanced the more we became sensible of the necessity of our newly adopted though simple system of strengthening our encampment nor could the natives have ever the enticing opportunity of seizing or pilfering any article to engineer a quarrel. Besides, as far as a breastwork could go the people were always sheltered from danger.

Fifteen minutes was the time generally taken to put the camp into a proper state of defence, about the same time only which it would have required to have jumbled everything pell-mell and the natives, the property and ourselves would have indiscriminately occupied but one and the same ground as had been done by the North West hitherto on the Columbia, and this mode of proceeding was one chief cause among others of that disorder and bold footing the natives had assumed, and by which the North Westers had so frequently got themselves involved in serious trouble on the Columbia. To reduce the natives to some order, however desirable, was no easy task and rendered more difficult by the fewness of our numbers. All we could therefore attempt on the present occasion was gradually to introduce the system of reform, leaving it to be followed up in the future.

During our passages through portages we were unavoidably more or less exposed. On this occasion the pauses or resting places were only the distances of a gun shot apart, and guards at each. First the craft were carried and placed in a double row with an area between sufficiently roomy for the baggage, which was properly ranged as it was brought forward, leaving a vacancy still large enough for the purpose of defense. The motions of the natives were closely scrutinised before we ventured to start again. Half the chiefs were stationed at one end of the pause, and half likewise at the other, it was on such occasions that the influence of these men came most into play; by these means therefore we advanced with considerable dispatch, and with all the degree of safety which the case would admit of.

On arriving at the Long Narrows, the most suspicious part of the communication, we found the natives mustered to the number of about one thousand warriors. The war song and yell warned us of hostile intentions, and the fears of our friendly Indian only served to confirm conjectures. We encamped at the commencement of the portage. The object of the natives we were told was to establish a perpetual tribute, which if granted would be the means of obtaining for us an undisturbed passage.

The subject of tribute had been the result of a general plan settled among the natives. The first appearance of it was manifested at the Wallamitte and had been gathering strength for years past, ever since the North West had possession of the country; and had the present expedition been conducted in the ordinary way of their travelling in these parts, no doubt it would have been enforced; but McKenzie's sudden and unexpected return, and the Indians' remembrance of him in former days, were favourable to us on the present occasion. His open, free, and easy manner often disarmed the most daring savage, and when one expedient failed another was always at hand. When the men stood aloof he caressed their children, which seldom failed to draw a smile of approbation from the rudest. His knowledge of their character armed him with confidence. In the most suspicious places, he would stroll among them, unarmed and alone, when he would allow no other man to step over the lines. He saw at a glance what was working within, and never failed to upset all their designs. Such a sagacious and prudent leader seldom fails to impart confidence to his followers.

We tried to put on as bold a front as possible. The guards were doubled all the night, not one of us slept. The chiefs were prevailed upon to remain in our camp, the hands were drawn out, and the arms inspected and the plan of proceeding for the ensuing day fixed and explained to the party. We were as desirous of reducing the turbulent natives as they were of reducing us; but the motly complement of voyageurs, composed of a mixture of Iroquois, Abanakees, Owhyhees, and some even of a worse description with the exception of a few staunch Canadians the whole were little better, in some instances worse, than Indians which made us unwilling to hazard a battle, our intention therefore was to stand on the defensive; should however the necessity of things bring on a combat we were each of us to lead a division, keeping those of each class unmixed and apart.

On the next morning the Indians were assembled by our camp at break of day. Our men were at their post close to the baggage, our swivel had likewise its station. The Indians eyed it with suspicion. The chiefs after a parley received a smoke, and by the medium of our interpreter they were given to understand the intent of our maneuvers; if they were advocated for peace and conducted themselves in an orderly manner, they should be presented with some tobacco at the farther end of the portage, as a mark of our friendship.

While thus engaged and the crowd thronging around us, a fellow more like a baboon than a man, with a head full of feathers and countenance of brass, having a fine gun in his hand, called out, "How long are the whites to pass here, troubling our waters and scaring our fish without paying us! look at all that bales of goods going to our enemies," said he, "and look at our wives and children naked." The fellow then made a pause, as if waiting an answer; but as good fortune would have it, the rest of the Indians paid but little attention to him. No answer was made, nor was it a time to discuss the merits or demerits of such a question. Happening however to be near the fellow when he spoke, I turned briskly round, "So long," said I, "as the Indians smoke our tobacco: just so long and no longer will the whites pass here." Then I put a question to him in turn. "Who gave you that fine gun you have?" said I. "The whites," said he, "And who gives you tobacco to smoke?" said I again, "The whites," he replied. Continuing the subject, "Are you fond of your gun?" said I. "Yes," said he, "And are you fond of your tobacco to smoke?" To this question the reply was "Yes." "Then," said I, "you ought to be fond of the whites, who supply all your wants." "Oh, yes," rejoined he. The nature of the questions and answers set the bystanders laughing, and taking no further notice of the rascal he sneaked off among the crowd, and we saw him no more. The question put by the feathered baboon amounted to nothing in itself; but it proved that the subject of tribute had been discussed among the Indians.

By the time the chiefs whom we were anxious to gain over to our side had promised to use their influence in our favour, we therefore lost no time in transporting our goods across the portage. All was suspense during this eventful day. A constant intercourse by pencil and paper was carried on from end to end of the pauses. The chiefs interested themselves for us, they spoke often and vehement-ly; but from the well known disposition of the Indian it was evident that the slightest mistake on our part would destroy the harmony that subsisted between us.

On reaching the further end of the carrying place, our craft were put into the water and laden without delay. The natives were in-creasing in numbers, and our party awaited the conclusion of the scene with anxiety. While I was distributing the promised reward to the chiefs, sixteen men under the direction of McMillan were placed as a guard to keep back the crowd; but they pressed us so hard that before we had done the guard as well as myself were forced into the water between the craft and the crowd, never was I harder pressed, or nearer being crushed than on that day. Two men were nearly losing their lives in the water, and more than once, we despaired of getting ourselves extricated.

The bows were strung, the arrows already out of their quivers. Signs were repeatedly made to the multitude to fall back, and just as the guard and all were hurrying to embark the word was issued for the men to raise their arms, and thrice was the order repeated before they obeyed. The interval was critical. I cannot describe it.

Let the reader picture in his own mind our situation. In this our perilous position a final notice was signified to the natives to depart, in this emergency the swivel was pointed from one of the boats. In a moment all was silent. The chiefs who had been overwhelmed by the crowd, now getting themselves extricated set the example, and the whole fell back a few paces. Our people taking advantage of the favourable moment embarked, while a third of our party were employed in getting the craft pushed off, the remainder with their arms facing the natives kept their posture until all was clear and ready for a fair start, then embarking we hoisted sail, our guns still pointed to the crowd, we were soon beyond their reach. Not an arrow flew, not a trigger was drawn, and that was all.

Had the Indians been aware of the movement made for defence at our departure, it is a question if they would have overlooked the opportunities that offered while we were more or less separated in making the portage. It never had been usual to take such precautions; but by this determined conduct their views were completely frustrated. No tribute was exacted: whereas had a different line been pursued and had things once gained the point of establishing it, in a few voyages the whole lading would no doubt have to pass for that purpose; and to the loss of property, that of lives must have inevitably followed. In dangerous or hostile rencontres the Indians generally single out the leaders as the first victims, considering the remainder of the party easily managed from their probable confusion. This appears to have been the case on the present occasion. For it was remarked that three daring persons of this description were seen hovering about us, when the adjusting of their weapons occupied very much their attention, and the surmise was confirmed by report.

The gentleman at the head of affairs,[2] after signifying the necessity of a sharp look-out, walked up and presented these three desperadoes with a stone to sharpen their arrows, then sternly eying them all three alternately, stamped with his foot, slapped the butt end of his gun, and opening the pans of his rifle and pistols, he primed anew to show them that his arms were likewise ready. He

2 Donald McKenzie.

then insisted on their sitting down and composing themselves. They did so with apparently great reluctance and at the same time laid down their arrows as a token of submission. This taking place in the full view of the crowd made the individuals look sheepish. The effect as far as we could judge did not operate amiss, and the demagogue who goes by the name of Red Jacket became useful and interested himself, no doubt to reclaim our favour and get a piece of tobacco.

During the first day after our leaving the Long Narrows we saw on almost every point crowds on their way to the great rendezvous, from which we inferred that the whole body of Indians had not yet been assembled at the appointed place and perhaps to that circumstance more than to any other we owed our safety. From the falls our friend from the Cascades, after being rewarded with a new suit, returned back to his people. During the remainder of the voyage the banks of the river, for a great way were covered with the natives. We made a short halt at each considerable camp, and the same attentions were paid to the chiefs in a greater or less degree, according as their respective merits and the aspect of things demanded. In passing by scattered bands, a few leaves of the envied plant were thrown upon the beach, sometimes this offering of friendship fell into the water, but this was productive of an equal effect as the natives in a twinkling plunged into the river to secure it. Some of the villages we passed had upwards of a thousand inhabitants, particularly those about the great forks.[3]

My craft happening to fall behind a little, one of the natives took offense at my handing to his companion a leaf or two of tobacco, which was intended for both; the villain lost no time in bending his bow and had he not been terrified in the act by my levelling my gun at him he would most likely have made sure of his mark.

At length arriving at the succession of bad steps called the Priest's Rapid[4] we were happily relieved from the importunities and annoyance of our numerous and designing neighbours on the south. Henceforth we travelled among those more friendly as we ad-

[3] The juncture of the Columbia and Snake rivers.
[4] About twenty miles down the Columbia River from Vantage, Washington.

vanced towards the north. The innumerable bands of Indians assembled along the communication this year rendered an uncommon degree of watchfulness necessary, and more particularly as our sole dependence lay on them for our daily subsistence. I have passed and repassed many times but never saw so many Indians in one season along the communication; we had reason to be thankful at our singular good luck throughout.

On arriving at Oakinacken six hundred miles from the ocean, I set out immediately for my winter quarters at the She-whaps, leaving my friends McKenzie and McMillan to do the same.

It may now occur to the reader that on arriving at Oakinacken our voyage was ended, and that henceforth we had nothing else to do. The case was however very different. I had still to put three hundred miles behind me before I reached my own destination, the others nearly as many; but the most singular circumstance was that some of the party after travelling so far north had at this stage of the voyage to wheel round and proceed again south, a most defective management.

Under existing regulations the first half of each brigade was at Oakinacken. This was the point of general separation, although the depot for the interior was still one hundred and forty miles farther east, at a place called Spokane House. Now whatever Oakinacken might have been, Spokane House, of all the posts in the interior, was the most unsuitable place for concentrating the different branches of the trade. But a post had been established at that place in the early days of the trade and after the country had become thoroughly known, people were adverse to change what long habit had made familiar to them. So Spokane House still remained. Thence both men and goods were year after year carried two hundred miles north by water, merely to have the pleasure of sending them two hundred miles south again by land, in order to reach their destination.

To obviate this serious difficulty it had been contemplated to have the depot of the interior removed from Spokane House to the Grand Forks or Walla Walla, making either of these places as being more central the general rendezvous. But many objections to this change were urged. The country was too dangerous, the natives too hostile. The measure was decreed impracticable. These were the ostensible reasons; but the real cause lay deeper under the surface.

Spokane House was a retired spot, no hostile natives were there to disquiet a great man. There the Bourgeois who presided over the Company's affairs resided, and that made Spokane House the centre of attraction. There all the wintering parties with the exception of the northern district met. There they were all filled out. It was the great starting point, although six weeks' travel out of the direct line of some, and more or less inconvenient to all! But that was nothing. These trifles never troubled the great man.

At Spokane House, too, there were handsome buildings. There was a ball room, and no females in the land so fair to look upon as the nymphs of Spokane. No damsels could dance so gracefully as they; none were so attractive. But Spokane House was not celebrated for fine women only, there were fine horses also. The race ground was admired, and the pleasures of the race. Altogether, Spokane House was a delightful place and time had confirmed its celebrity.

Yet with all these attractions in favour of the far-famed Spokane House, the unsparing McKenzie contemplated its removal. It was marked out by him as a useless and expensive drawback upon the trade of the interior, and Walla Walla pitched upon as the future, general rendezvous of the inland trade; this step deeply wounded the feelings of his colleagues and roused in the breast of all lovers of pleasure a prodigious outcry against him!

As to the reasons assigned against Walla Walla by those opposed to a change, we might here remark that the plan of non-intercourse which we had generally observed towards the natives was calculated rather to keep up a state of hostility than otherwise: for if we wished to reduce the turbulent spirit of the natives, it was not by avoiding them that we could do so; but by mixing with them. We must live with them and they with us, we must carry on a free intercourse with them and familiarize them by that intercourse. If this plan had been followed up at first the result, as in other similar cases, would have no doubt been favourable to both parties. At all events, a step so necessary and so essential to our interest and theirs ought to have had a fair trial.[5]

Some time before our arrival at the She-whaps one of the men I had with me named Brusseau, alias Aland, fell very sick, and was so feeble that he was unable to continue the journey. It being impossible for us to remain with him, I got a small place near wood and water fixed up and leaving a man to take care of him, and a spade in case of his death to bury him, we left him with but little hopes of recovery.

On the tenth day after we had left him, the man whom I had put to take care of Brusseau arrived at the fort with the news of his death, and on my asking him where the spade was, he said the Indians had stolen it. All this as a matter of course passed for truth until some time afterwards, when who should turn up but poor dead Brusseau, escorted by some friendly Indians.

It would appear that the cowardly and faithless fellow I had left to take care of him got frightened at the approach of some Indians, fled and abandoned Brusseau to his fate, who being left alone must have perished but for the timely appearance of some natives, who administered to his wants, thereby enabling him not only to leave the spot already doomed as his grave but also to bring home in his own hands the very instrument that was to have buried him.

In our original plan it was proposed to have the transactions of every year in a chapter by themselves; but finding as in the present instance that it would be of inconvenient length, I have resolved to deviate and keep it by dividing the operations of this year into two chapters.

5 Those who wished to stay at Spokane House argued that it was wiser to avoid contact with the Indians by remaining at a distance. Those who favored the mouth of the Walla Walla River as a location believed that in order to pursue the trade vigorously it was necessary to be situated in the Indian country.

5. A WOUNDED BEAR

HAVING in the preceding chapter closed our remarks on the voyage and reached our winter quarters, we shall now turn our attention to the transactions of the northern district.

In this extensive field but little had yet been done in the way of discovering the resources of the country; the greater part of which was unknown to its traders. I therefore received orders from headquarters to examine the eastern section lying between the Shewhaps and the Rocky Mountains, a large tract of wild country never before trod on by the foot of any white man. To ascertain the resources of this hitherto unknown waste as regards its furs and general appearance and to find out the shortest route between our starting point and Canoe River, lying at the foot of the mountains, this task I had to perform without guide or a single additional man beyond usual complements of the post.

Our readers will naturally suppose that an exploring party destined for the discovery of any new part of the country ought to be dignified with the name expedition, but there is no such appellation customary here. Whatever be the extent of the undertaking, there is no great preparation made before hand, because the ordinary routine of every day's duty is as full of adventure, and hardship, as it could be on a voyage of discovery even were it to the north pole. No salute is fired at starting, no feu de joie[1] on returning. The party set off with such means as are available at the time. Sometimes these means are more, sometimes less, according to circumstances, the rank of the leader, or the extent of the undertaking; but they are always simple. The traders, from the very nature of their employment, are daily familiarised with difficulties and

[1] A welcoming salute.

dangers, and not infrequently exposed to the severest privations; so that their ingenuity, sharpened by experience, seldom fails to overcome the greatest obstacles that can be presented by mountains or plains, by woods or by waters or by the still more dreaded arm of the lawless savage.

An experienced person in the Indian countries, with only one or two men, their guns, and a few loads of ammunition would think no more of crossing the desert from the Atlantic to the Pacific, in the most wild and unfrequented parts, than any other man in ordinary life would do to cross a country parish from one side to the other, and they seldom fail with means the most standard and we can take the present undertaking as an example, although a petty one. Yet those upon a large scale in this country differ in no material point, either as to man or means. After remaining at the She-whaps for a few days, settling the affairs of the place, I prepared for my journey; but had recorded experience to teach me this time not to depend altogether on the faith of Indians to leave me in the lurch as they had done before in my attempt to reach the Pacific.

Taking therefore two of my own best and most experienced hands together with two Indians, myself making the fifth person, we left Fort She-whap on the 14th day of August, intending to perform the journey on foot. Each man was provided with half a dozen pairs of Indian shoes, a blanket to sleep in, ammunition, a small axe, a knife, a fire steel and an awl; together with some needles, thread, and tobacco to smoke, all of which he had to carry on his back, and his gun on his shoulder. Each person had the same weight to carry; and this constituted the whole of our travelling baggage with the exception of a cooking kettle and a pint pot. It is the same equipment in all such cases, be the journey for a week, for a month, or for a year. Depending all the time on our guns for our subsistence and for a further supply of shoes, and clothes on the skins of the animals we might chance to kill on our way.

At the outset we proceeded up the North or Sun-tea-coot-acoot River[2] for three days, then turning to the right we took to the woods, steering our course in the eye of the rising sun nearly mid-

2 The North Thompson River.

99

way between Thompson's River on the south and Fraser's River on the north. The first day after turning our backs on North River we made but little progress; but what we made was in an easterly direction. The second day our courses per compass were E.S.E. 6 miles, E 4 miles, S.E. 2 miles, E. by N. 5 miles, E. 1 mile, N.E. 2 miles, N.N.E. 4 miles. And encamped. The country through which we passed this day was covered with heavy timber but clear bottom and good travelling, with here and there small open plains. During the third day the face of the country became timberless and frequently open clear ground, so that we made a long day's journey. In the evening we fell upon a small lake on the northern margin of which we encamped for the night.[3] Here we found two Indian families living on fish, roots and berries; which they were all employed in procuring and seemed in their wretched condition to live very comfortably and happy. They belonged to the Sun-tea-coot-a-coot tribe. One of the men belonging to these families who pretended to have a perfect knowledge of the country through which we had to pass volunteered to accompany us as a guide. For which services, I promised to reward him with a blanket and some ammunition when we returned. In consequence of this new acquisition to our party, we proceeded without having much recourse to our compass and without any doubt as to the difficulties of the road being overcome. Leaving this place, which we called Friendly Lake, we proceeded on our journey with feelings of great confidence as to our ultimate success.

We had now resolved to follow our guide, having every confidence in his knowledge of the country; but instead of taking us by an easterly direction, he bent his course almost due north for about sixty miles when we reached a small river called Ke-low-na-skar-am-ish, or Grizzly Bear River,[4] which we ascended in nearly an easterly direction for six days until it became so narrow that we could have jumped over it. While following this little stream, we passed several beaver lodges and other ravages of that animal. In many places trees were cut down, and the course of the water stopped and

[3] East Barriere Lake.
[4] The Adams River.

formed into small lakes and ponds by the sagacious and provident habits of the beaver. In one place forty-two trees were cut down, at the height of about eighteen inches from the root within the compass of half an acre. We now began to think we had found the goose that lays the golden eggs; this was but of short duration. Some low points were covered with poplars and other soft wood, and wherever that timber and water were plenty there were beaver, but not in great numbers. Few fur animals were seen after passing this place. From thence forward, the face of the country changed materially. It is in general too rocky, hard, and flinty for beaver. Huge rocks at every step barred our way. It is a country for goats. Elks and deer were very numerous. Great numbers of these animals were frequently seen and all of which appeared very tame for wild animals, a sure indication of their being but seldom disturbed. Never having been disturbed before by civilized man!

Along Grizzly Bear River we shot four elk, twenty-two deer, two otters, two beavers and three black bears without stepping out of our way; but the bears were poor, and the only cause we could assign for it was the scarcity of berries and fish. These animals generally frequent fruit and fish countries. Nor did we notice any fish in the river. But tracks of wild animals wherever the ground was soft were abundant, crossing the road in every direction.

In one of the thickets as we passed along, our guide took us a little out of our way to show us what he called a bear's haunt or wintering den, where that animal according to Indian theory remains in a dark and secluded retreat without food or nourishment for months together, sucking its paws! But there was nothing remarkable in the place. The entrance to the lair or den was through a long and winding thicket of dense brush wood; but its hiding place was not in a hole under ground but on the surface, deeply imbedded among the fallen leaves. The snow is often many feet deep, and their hiding place is discovered only by an air hole over the den resembling a small funnel, sometimes not two inches in diameter, through which the breath issues; but so concealed from view that none but the keen eye of the savage can find it out.

In this den the bear is said to lie in a torpid state from December till March. They do not lie together in families but singly, and when they make their exit in the spring, they are very sleek and fat. To their appearance at this season I can bear ample testimony, having frequently seen them. But no sooner do they leave their winter quarters and begin to roam about than they get poor and haggard. The bear is said never to winter twice in the same place. In their retreats they are often found out and killed by the Indians without making the least resistance.

A short distance from bear thicket is a towering height resembling a round tower, which we ascended. Here we had a pretty good view of the country around. But such a dreary prospect. The rugged rocks with their treeless and shrubless tops almost forbade us to advance.

On this hill or tower we shot a large white-headed eagle, which gave a name to the place, and here we inscribed on the south side of a dwarfy pine, "September 2nd, 1817." And had I had at the time a dram to have given my men, they would no doubt have identified the barren spot by a may pole or lop stick[5] on its top to commemorate our visit, according to North West custom. Here our guide told us that in five or six days more, we should reach our journey's end, adding that the She-whap Indians formerly passed that way on their travels to the east side of the mountains where they often, when numerous and strong, went to trade or make war; but that of late, they seldom ventured to meet the Assiniboins of the woods or Crees of the plains in that quarter. Not far from Eagle Hill we came to some water where we saw signs of beaver; but by no means so plentiful as to entitle it to the name of a beaver country. Our guide told us that these parts were in no respect what might be called a place for beaver. From Friendly Lake to Eagle Hill by the road we came on a rough calculation is 155 miles.

After passing several hours on this rocky pinnacle, we set out again on our journey; but in descending the rugged cliffs one of my men cut his foot very badly, which detained us for nearly a

5 A lop stick was made by peeling the bark or wood of a pole back and then allowing it to "lop" down in fuzzy circumference. It was designed to be unnatural in appearance, and hence to catch the eye.

whole day and so disabled the unfortunate man that we had almost made up our mind to leave him behind until our return; but as this would have deprived us of another man to take care of him we decided to keep together, so we dragged him along with us and he soon recovered.

Our course, after leaving Eagle Hill, was generally S.E. but in order to avoid clambering over rocks and mountains we had to wind in zig zag course the best way we could among the intricate defiles that every now and then crossed our path and often made but little headway. So that after an arduous day's travel we sometimes scarcely put ten miles behind us in a direct line. As we advanced the wild animals did not seem to increase in number, although our guns always procured us a sufficient supply of food; but the circuitous and in many places dangerous passes we had to wind our way through discouraged us. The precipitous rocks required the foot of a dog and the eye of a hawk to guard against accident at all times.

As we journeyed along our guide took us up to another height and pointing out to us the country generally, said he had passed and repassed through various parts of it seven different times, and in as many different places; he seemed to know it well, and observed that the road we had travelled, with all its difficulties, was the very best to be found. There was, he said, some other parts better furnished with water, and likewise several small lakes; but that beaver was scarce over all. And as to a water communication there was none. So that we at once condemned it as far as we had yet seen as both impracticable and dangerous: destitute of beaver and everything else so far as the purposes of commerce were concerned.

On the 10th of September being the ninth day after leaving Eagle Hill we reached what the guide called the foot of the mountains, but the ascent all along had been apparently as gradual and the country so very rugged with a broken and uneven surface that we could perceive no very perceptible difference in the height of the land until we came close under the brow of the dividing ridge; but there the difference was certainly striking. The guide had led us to a considerable eminence some distance out of our way, from which in looking back we beheld the country we had passed over, and certainly a more wild and rugged land the mind of man could not imagine; but in looking before us, that is, toward the mountains the view was completely barren, the almost perpendicular front met the eye like a wall, and we stood and gazed at what might be called one of the wonders of the world. One circumstance struck us very forcibly, and that was the increased size of the timber. Along the base of the mountains the timber which had been stunted and puny now became gigantic in size, the pines and cedars in particular. One of the latter measured forty-five feet four inches in girth, four feet from the ground.

After passing some time looking around us, we descended and encamped at the edge of the small and insignificant stream called Canoe River, celebrated among North Westers for the quality of the birch bark. So completely were its banks overhung and concealed with heavy timber, that it was scarcely visible at the short distance of fifty yards. It is a mere rill among rivers, in some places not more than fifteen paces broad. Its course is almost due south, and flows over a stony bottom, with low banks, clear cold water, and strong current. Here our guide told us that in two days' moderate travel we could reach its mouth, where it enters the Columbia near Portage Point. Everything here wore the appearance and stillness of the midnight hour. The aspect was gloomy, scarcely the chirping of a solitary silence. In all this extent of desert through which we had passed not a human being was to be seen, nor the traces of any.

At Canoe River we spent the greater part of two days strolling about its banks and having accomplished the object of our journey, rested ourselves, mended our shoes, we prepared to retrace our steps; but just as we were tying up our bundles to start, a fine moose deer plunged into the river before us; it had scarcely time to reach the opposite shore before it was shot down, and this detained us a few hours longer. We dined on this over-supply and bagging the tongue and nose we turned our backs on Canoe River and bidding a farewell to the mountains we took to the wilderness again, following as much as possible the road we had come; but at intervals deviating from it. The second day after starting we had very heavy thunder with a torrent of rain which impeded our progress, for the thick brushwood and long grass rendered travelling dry weather not overly pleasant; but in wet weather intolerable.

As the thunder and wind increased, I expressed a wish to take shelter under the cliff of a projecting rock until the storm abated; but our guide smiled at my ignorance. "Do not the whites know," said he, "that there is a bad spirit there," and he would not go near it, nor hear of our approaching the rock that offered us shelter. I said he might stop but I should go. "No, no!" said he, "the thunder may not kill you, but it will kill the Indians, do you wish us to die?" So I yielded the point, and we remained exposed to the fury of the storm all the time. "That rocky height,"[6] said he, pointing to one near us, "has fire in it, and the thunder keeps always about it." On my enquiring into the nature of the fire he observed, "Snow never remains there, it is hot, and smokes all winter, there is a bad spirit in it, three years ago two of our people who took shelter there were killed, the Kaslet-sam-muh dwell there." I then asked him if that was the only rock that smoked during winter in these parts! He answered, "No, there are several others a little further on that smoke; but the Indians never go near them, and wild animals in going past them are often killed. There are plenty bones there, the thunder is always loudest there. The bad spirit of Kaslet-sam-muh lives there." We, however, saw no indications of a volcanic nature, no lava near it. It was in my opinion pure superstition. The weather clearing up soon after we continued our journey.

On the seventh day from Canoe River we reached Eagle Hill, but made no stop there. From that place our guide took us a new road, I ought to say in a different direction, with the view of shortening our distance, but gained little by the change. Not far from Eagle Hill, we shot two grizzly bears and a bird of the vulture tribe; deer and elk were very numerous. In this direction we likewise passed a considerable lake[7] in which were several muskrat lodges. We shot some and saw two wolves prowling about, and for the first

6 One of the peaks in the Selkirk Range.
7 Adams Lake.

time saw tracks of the martin. Six days from Eagle Hill brought us back again to Friendly Lake, where the relations of our guide were left; but they had removed from the place where we left them, the guide went to the spot and after looking about for some time, noticed a small stick stuck up in the ground, rather leaning to one side, with a small notch in it. After examining the position of the stick and the notch, he observed to me, "My relatives are at such a place, the inclination of the stick pointed out." He said the direction they had gone and the notch meant one day's journey off and being in our line of march, we came to them at the very place the guide had stated.

With the guide's relations we passed a night and part of the next day, as two of my men had the soles of their feet blistered by walking. Starting from the Indians our guide still accompanied us. Here again we took another new road and crossed the woods in a southwest direction, thinking to shorten our distance considerably. By this course we avoided going to North River altogether until within a short distance of the fort. Here the woods assumed a more healthy appearance and became much stouter, and the rocks gave place to a rich and fertile soil.

On reaching a small open plain we perceived at some little distance off two large birds in the act of fighting, much in the same way as our domestic fowl. We made a halt, and I approached them till within gun shot unperceived and kept watching their motions for some time, at last I showed myself, when one of the birds tried to fly off; but was scarcely able to keep itself up and soon lighted again. I still approached when the bird tried to get up again; but when in the act of rising I fired and brought it to the ground; the other never stirred from its place. In taking up the bird I had shot, it proved to be a white-headed eagle. I then went to the other and taking hold of it, found it was a wild turkey cock, or what we call the Columbia grouse. A bold and noble bird. The grouse was almost blind. During the combat the eagle had almost torn out its eyes, yet it disdained to yield and might have ultimately come off the conquerer for the eagle was very much exhausted and nearly blind of an eye. The fight had been long and well contested, for the grass all round the spot for some twenty yards was beaten to the ground and their feathers strewed about by their fierce and bloody struggles. The grouse weighed 11¼ lbs., the eagle only 8¾ lbs. We carried both birds along with us.

By the road we last took we shortened our distance nearly a day's travel; but what we saved in shoes we lost in clothes, for almost all we had was torn to pieces before we got to the fort, which we reached after a làborous journey of forty-seven days on the 29th of September.

According to the most correct estimate the distance between the She-whaps and Canoe River does not by the route we travelled exceed 420 miles, and in a direct line, not much more than half that distance. From all I saw or could learn, however, in reference to the country generally little can be said in its favour. No road for the purpose of land transportation appeared to me practicable. Nor do I conceive it possible to make one without an expense that the prospects of the country would by no means warrant. And as to a water communication there is none except by Thompson's River, and that is practicable but a very small part of the way. Elsewhere there is none but Fraser's on the north. As a barren waste well stocked in wild animals of the chace and some few furs the trade on a small scale, apart from the She-whaps, might be extended to some advantage in this quarter, and the returns conveyed either to the latter post or to the mouth of Canoe River.

Leaving the affairs of my own district, we shall bestow a cursory glance at what was going on in another quarter. The season was now at hand when the company's dispatches were wont to arrive, and a brigade as usual escorted them from the interior to Fort George. As soon therefore as they arrived McKenzie made no hesitation to deliver over the important documents into the hands of the natives, to carry them to their destination. This appeared a strange mark of confidence in this almost hostile race. It seemed strange even to us that a novelty of this kind should succeed in this quarter, while it was remarked the same could never be brought to succeed by means of Indians in other than settled countries. At the falls a council of the chiefs and wise men was solemnly held over the dispatches, but after a very short delay, they sent them forward. At the Cascades more serious meetings disputed their fate; but after being determined by a variety of altercation for three days it seemed their good fortune again prevailed, and they went on from hand to hand with wonderful expedition, and the answer was conveyed back to the interior by the same hands with unheard-of rapidity.

In the contemplation of this plan, the council at headquarters had suggested the propriety of one set of couriers performing the whole journey; but McKenzie with his usual sagacity saw this would cause jealousy and eventually fail, he therefore managed so as to have the dispatches conveyed from one tribe to another, placing confidence in all to discharge the trust reposed in them.

By this means of conveyance a voyage which employed forty or fifty men was abolished, consequently saving the risk of lives, the loss of time, and heavy expenses, and the charges incurred were a mere trifle. Not only these advantages were obtained but that which strength and weapons could scarcely bring about, a slender sheet of paper conveying our ideas to one another, imprinted on the superstitious minds of the savages a religious degree of veneration for the superior endowments of the whites. They admitted the confidence placed in them, and this custom always afterwards continued. For a Columbia Indian was always ready to start in the quality of a courier for the boon of a few strings of beads or a few shots of ammunition.

When the different establishments were outfitted and put in train for the season, McKenzie with all the residue of the people set out on a voyage of hunting and discovery to the south of Lewis River, bordering on the Snake frontiers. This party consisted chiefly of such men as were otherwise found of little service in the wintering ground, being almost all composed of Iroquois and other refuse. They were five and thirty strong, and out of this motly number five Canadians was the only support he could trust to with confidence.

No sooner were they arrived in the midst of the Nez Perces on their way to their winter quarters than the Iroquois perceived their superiority in strength over the few whites, and instead of acting up to their respective duties they studied nothing but plotted the most against their leader and the slender band of Canadians that were about him, when a trifle which we mention blew the whole into flame.

The Iroquois contrary to the established rules of the trade and the general practice among the natives kept trafficking privately with the Indians, which conduct had once or twice before nearly caused serious quarrels between the natives and the party. The Iroquois had been repeatedly warned against such practices but without effect, they still continued to act as before. Grand Pierre, one of the Iroquois, bargained with an Indian for a horse. A misunderstanding arose between them and a quarrel was likely to ensue, when the Iroquois applied to his Bourgeois at the same time asking him for a variety of things to satisfy the Indian from whom he had got the horse. McKenzie was annoyed at the conduct of Pierre and the Iroquois generally, and wishing to put a final stop to such dangerous interference in future paid the Indian, and then drawing a pistol from his belt shot the horse dead upon the spot. The act ought to have warned Pierre and his companions of their misconduct. This caused a considerable talk at the moment, but the Iroquois grumbled and retired. From that moment, however, they meditated the destruction of their leader.

Being as cowardly as perfidious, in order to make sure of their blow they set to work to gain the natives to their side that they might keep the deed on their shoulders. But this only served to draw down upon them the contempt of the people, and eventually divulged their schemes before they were ripe for execution.

Sometime previous the Indians had mentioned something of the kind to our people, but they discredited the whole as a piece of deception got up to answer some purpose of their own; and it passed unheeded. The Iroquois learning however that the Indians had made their design known to the whites, were determined not to be foiled in their purpose. So one of the villains immediately arming himself and calling upon his comrades to follow him sallied forth for his master's tent, just at the break of day; but Ioachin, the

Iroquois interpreter, a faithful and zealous servant, having over-heard what was going on rushed into his Bourgeois' tent not half a minute before the assassin and one of his associates got there, and called out, "Murder! murder!" In the confusion McKenzie who had been asleep could not put his hands on his pistols, but grasping one of the tent poles he brought his assailant to the ground at the first blow. Another who followed close after shared the same fate. By this time, some of the Canadians and faithful Owhyhees arrived to their master's assistance and the Iroquois fled.

In this case McKenzie's strength and activity of body were of much service to him; but not more than his coolness and decision in the moment of danger.

Their plan was to murder their leader while asleep, and to escape with the property out of the country in a body; but the safety of McKenzie and the success of his affairs resting entirely on the promptness of action, he resolutely chastised the ringleader and others on the spot, nor had the tomahawks of the villains power to stop the timely punishment though brandished over his head! In the face of the natives, therefore, it was his good fortune to reduce his treacherous servants to a sense of their duty. But he did not think it prudent to trust them further in the prosecution of his plans, which by this unforeseen event experienced a partial failure for the year.

He dispersed the Iroquois. One was sent to me at Oakinacken, two to Spokane House, and the rest placed on a separate hunting ground in the neighbourhood under the eye of an influential chief, where they could do no harm. While with the remainder of his people he wheeled about in another direction, intending to carry on the project of hunting and of discovery for the season, although upon a more contracted scale. His primary object was to conclude an arrangement with the Nez Perces and in the Snake country to conciliate the Indians generally with reference to opening the way for extending the trade as soon as existing prejudices gave way; for he was surprised at the unfavourable change which the Indians had undergone during the short period the country had been under the domination of the North West Company, and frequently observed to me that a change of system was as necessary to reduce the Indians to order as to reclaim the trade; both being on the brink of ruin.

To this end he undertook at a late season of the year a voyage of three months long in deep snows, to traverse a rugged and mountainous country in order to keep up a good understanding with the strong and turbulent tribes inhabiting the south branch, where some of the scenes of his former years had taken place.

These roving and destitute bands inhabiting the borders of the Snake country still infested the communication, and held a valuable key of trade; but invariably continued hostile to the whites. At that hard season they are generally scattered about in small bands, and as it is much easier to gain on a few than on a multitude he visited them all and succeeded beyond expectation. In McMillan's wintering ground[8] everything went on in its usual successful train. But nothing happened in that old beaten path to elicit our notice; we now turn back to the north again.

Soon after my arrival from Canoe River, I was invited by the chiefs of my post to accompany a party of the natives on a bear hunting expedition for a few days. On these occasions they felt flattered by their trader accompanying them. The party were all mounted on horseback to the number of seventy-three, and exhibited a fine display of horsemanship. After some two miles' travel we commenced operations. Having reached the hunting ground the party separated into several divisions. We then perambulated the woods, crossed rivers, surrounding thickets, and scampered over hill and dale with yell and song for the greater part of two days, during which time we killed seven bears, nine wolves and eleven small deer; one of the former I had the good luck to shoot myself. In the evening of the third day however, our sport was checked by an accident. One of the great men, the chief Pasha of the hunting party named Ta-tack-it, Is-tso-augh-an, or Short Legs, got severely wounded by a female bear.

The only danger to be apprehended on these savage excursions is by following the wounded animal into a thicket, or hiding place; but with the Indians the more danger the more honour, and some

8 Probably Spokane House.

of them are foolhardy enough to run every hazard in order to strike the last fatal blow, in which the honour lies, sometimes with a lance, tomahawk or knife, at the risk of their lives. No sooner does a bear get wounded than it immediately flies for refuge to some hiding place unless too closely pursued, in which case it turns round with savage fury on its pursuers, and woe awaits whatever is in the way.

The bear in question had been wounded, and taking shelter in a small coppice the bush was instantly surrounded by the horsemen, when the more bold and daring entered it on foot armed with gun, knife and tomahawk. Among the bush rangers on the present occasion was the chief Short Legs, who, while scrambling over some fallen timber, happened to stumble near to where the wounded and enraged bear was concealed; but too close to be able to defend himself before the vicious animal got hold of him. At that moment I was not more than five or six paces from the chief; but could not get a chance of shooting so I immediately called out for help, when several mustered round the spot. Availing ourselves of the doubtful alternative of killing her, even at the risk of killing the chief, we fired and as good luck would have it shot the bear and saved the man, then carrying the bear and wounded chief out of the bush we laid both on open ground. The sight of the chief was appalling. The scalp was torn from the crown of the head down over the eyebrows! The chief was insensible, and for some time we all thought him dead; but after a short interval his pulse began to beat and he gradually showed signs of returning animation.

But it was a curious and somewhat interesting scene to see the party approach the spot when the accident happened. Not being able to get a chance of shooting they threw their guns from them and could scarcely be restrained from rushing on the fierce animal with their knives only. The bear all the time kept looking first at one then at another, and casting her fierce and flaming eyes around the whole of us, as if ready to make a spring at each; yet she never let go her hold of the chief but stood over him. Seeing herself surrounded by so many enemies, she moved her head from one position to another and these movements gave us ultimately an opportunity of dispatching her.

The misfortune produced a long and clamorous scene of mourning among the chief relations and we hastened home carrying our dead bears along with us, and arrived at the camp early in the morning of the fourth day. The chief remained for three days speechless. In cutting off the scalp and dressing the wound we found the skull, according to our imperfect knowledge of anatomy, fractured in two or three places, and at the end of eight days I extracted a bone measuring two inches long, of an oblong form, and another of about an inch square, with several small pieces, all from the crown of the head! The wound, however, gradually closed up and healed excepting a small spot about the size of an English shilling. In fifteen days, by the aid of Indian medicine he was able to walk about, and at the end of six weeks from the time he got wounded, he was on horseback again at the chace.

The tide of sympathy for the great man's misfortune did not run high for at best he was but an unprincipled fellow, an enemy to the whites and hated by his own people. Many were of opinion that the friendly bear had at last rid us of an unfriendly chief; but to the disappointment of all he set the bear and wounds both at defiance, and was soon, to our great annoyance, at his old trade of plotting mischief!

Wolf hunting as well as bear hunting occasionally occupies the attention of the natives. In these parts both species are numerous. The former is an inhabitant of the plains, the latter of the woods. Wolves and foxes are often run down on horseback, hunted with the gun or caught in traps. With all the cunning of the fox, however, the wolf is far more difficult to decoy or entrap, being shy, guarded and suspicious.

During the winter we are speaking of, a good many wolves and foxes were caught by the whites with hook and line as we catch fish, with this difference however that the one is taken in water, the other on dry land. For this purpose, three cod hooks are generally tied together back to back, baited, and then fixed with a line to the branch of a tree so that the hooks are suspended in the air at the distance of four or five feet from the ground. To get hold of the bait the animal has to leap up, and the moment the hooks catch their hold it finds itself either in a standing or suspended position, which deprives the animal of its strength, neither can it in that posture cut the line; it is generally caught, sometimes dead, sometimes alive.

The catching of wolves, foxes or other wild animals by the whites was however the work rather of leisure hours. In these parts as well as in many others the wolves kept prowling about night and day, having their favourite haunts on hillocks or other eminences on which they would stand to rest or look about them for some time. We therefore used to scatter bones or bits of meat as decoys to attract them and in the interval kept practising ourselves in shooting at these frequented spots, taking different elevations with the gun until habit and experience had brought us to hit a small object at a very great distance, and with as much precision as if the object had been near to us.

A band of Indians happening to come to the fort one day and observing a wolf on one of the favourite places of resort, several of them prepared to take a circuitous turn to have a shot at the animal. Seeing them prepare, I said: "And kill it from where you are." The Indians smiled at my ignorance. "Can the whites," said the chief, "kill it at that distance?" "The whites," said I, "do not live by hunting or shooting as do the Indians or they might." "There is no gun," continued the chief, "that could kill at that distance." By this time the wolf had laid hold of a bone or piece of flesh and was scampering off with it at full speed to the opposite woods. Taking hold of my gun, "If we cannot kill it," said I, "we shall make it let go its prey." "My horse against your shot," called out the chief, "that you do not hit the wolf." "Done," said I; but I certainly thought within myself that the chief ran no great risk of losing his horse, nor the wolf of losing its life; taking an elevation of some fifteen or sixteen feet over it, by chance I shot the rascal in his flight! To the astonishment of the chief as well as all present, who clapping their hands to their mouths in excitement, measured the distance by five arrow shots! and nothing but their wonder could exceed their admiration of this effect of fire arms.

When the ball struck the wolf it was in the act of leaping, and we may judge of its speed at the time from the fact that the distance from whence it took the last leap to where it was lying stretched measured twenty-four feet! The ball struck the wolf in the left thigh, and after passing through the body, the neck and head, I cut it out of the lower jaw with my pen knife. The chief on delivering up his horse, which he did cheerfully, asked me for the ball, and that ball was the favourite adornment of his neck for years afterwards. The horse I returned to its owner. The Indians then asked me for the skin of the dead wolf and to each of the guns belonging to the party was appended a piece, the Indians fancying that the skin would make them in future to kill animals at a great distance.

The incidents, adventures, and narrow escapes which in the course of this year we have had to notice may throw some transparent light over a fur trader's life in this country, his duties, his trouble, his amusements and his pleasures: and one of the greatest pleasures here alluded to consists in doing homage to the great. A chief arrives, the honour of waiting upon him in a servile capacity falls to your share, if you are not above the business. You go forth to meet him, invite him in, see him seated: and if need require it, you untie his shoes and dry his socks. You next hand him to eat, to drink, and to smoke. And you must smoke along with him. After which you must listen with grave attention to all he has yet to say on Indian topics, and you must always give him something new of your own in return. But the grand point of all this ceremony is to know how far you should go in these matters, and when you should stop. Nor must you forget that Indians are acute observers of men and things and generally possess retentive memories. By overdoing the thing you may entail on yourself endless troubles.

When not employed in exploring new and unfrequented parts, involved in difficulties with the natives, nor opposition in trade; the general routine of dealing with most Indians goes on smoothly. Each trading post has its leader, its interpreter, and its own complement of hands, and when things are put in a proper train according to the customs of the country, the business of the year proceeds without much trouble and leaves you sufficient time for recreation. You can take your gun or your book, you can instruct your family or improve yourself in reading and reflection and enjoy the pleasures of religion to better advantage, serve your God to more perfection, and be a far better Christian than were your lot cast in the midst of the temptations of a busy world.

Confining our remarks to the simple and uniform duties of a trading post. Activities of body, prudence and forethought are qualifications more in request than talent. In trade as in war there are gains and losses, advantages and disadvantages to be kept in view to guide one's conduct, and generally speaking the master of a department, district or post lives a busy and active life, and although in a manner secluded from the eye of the world yet he is just as interested and ambitious to distinguish himself in his sphere of life as if continually under the eye of a scrutinizing superior, for if he once loses his character through negligence or impropriety of conduct it is here tenfold harder for him to regain confidence than in any employment elsewhere. The apprehension of this alone is a great check against misconduct.

The usual time for mustering all hands at headquarters being now arrived, the different parties wintering throughout the interior, after assembling at the forks, made the best of their way to the emporium of the Far West and met at Fort George on the 5th day of June 1818.

6. PEACE PIPES

AT THE SITTING of the Fort George board of management in the preceding year an inclination was manifested to encourage the change of system agreeably to the minutes of council at headquarters. From the feeling at the time much was expected; but nothing was realized, for practically that disposition was rendered abortive by subsequent arrangements.

At headquarters however the council of Fort William this year took a decisive step that set all the vacillating measures of the managers at Fort George on one side by ordering one hundred men to be at McKenzie's disposal for the more effectively carrying out his measures. And that the Fort Nez Perces station, being more central for the general business of the interior than that of Spokane House, it should be forthwith established there. And I was appointed to take charge of that important depot. To these resolutions was appended a sharp reproof for the delays during the two preceding years.

The Fort George board of management had now no choice but to acquiesce in the decision come to at headquarters. The managers bit their lips and were silent. Men were provided and means also, and a new feature imparted to the order of things generally.

The council having sat, the brigade for the interior left Fort George and reached without accident or hindrance, after a short and prosperous voyage the Walla Walla, near the confluence of the two great branches of the Columbia, on the 11th of July. On that day McKenzie, myself, and ninety-five effective men encamped on the site pitched upon for new establishment of Fort Nez Perces, about half a mile from the mouth of the little river Walla Walla.

There our friends left us as a forlorn hope and proceeded on their journey to their several destinations. And as we have hitherto fully explained the customary mode of voyaging we shall now direct the attention of our readers to the operations in this new quarter: occasionally glancing at other parts as circumstances may require.

But before doing so we must in the first place give a brief description of the place itself, with such other remarks as may occasionally suggest themselves. And secondly present the reader with an account of our reception by the natives of the place and the almost insurmountable difficulties we had to encounter before we could bring about a full reconciliation with the turbulent and high minded Indians by whom we were surrounded.

On reaching the place instead of advancing to meet us at the water's edge as friends, on making for the shore the Indians, as if with one accord, withdrew to their camp! Not a friendly hand was stretched out; not the least joy, usual among Indians on such occasions, was testified to invite or welcome our arrival. These ceremonies, though trifling in themselves, are a very good indication of the reception likely to be met with and in the present case their total absence could only be considered as very unfavourable.

Shy and silent they sat on the mounds at some distance from us wrapped in their robes of dignity, observing a studied indifference. Even the little copper-coloured bantlings were heard to say, "What does the white people want here? Are they going to kill more of our relations?" alluding to some former occurrences there. Others again would remark, "We must not go near them because they will kill us." While all this was going on we kept a sharp lookout. The principal chief of the camp, instead of coming to us, kept walking round and round the assembled crowd urging the Indians to the observance of a non-intercourse until the whites had made them presents. Hints were given us that property would purchase a footing!

In the whole land this spot was among the most difficult, the most barren of materials for building, and as it was no common scheme, the same appeared to ordinary minds as a thing more wild than practicable. But plans had been formed, the country must be secured, the natives awed and reconciled, buildings made, furs collected, new territories added. No objections received a hearing, no obstacles were to be seen. After this manner therefore passed the order of the day, and in the dreaded spot we took up our stand to run every hazard and brave every danger.

The site was remarkable among the natives as being the ground on which some years before Lewis and Clarke of the American exploring expedition ratified, according to Indian report, a general peace between themselves and the tribes of the adjacent inland by the celebration of feasting and dancing for several days. It was rendered remarkable as a spot on which difficulties already noticed had taken place between the whites and the natives. And it was rendered still more remarkable as being considered the most hostile spot on the whole line of communication. A spot which the whites, it was said, could never hold with safety. The spot for Nez Perces fort was however marked out on a level point upon the east bank of the Columbia, forming something like an island in the flood, and by means of a tributary stream, a peninsula at low water.

The place selected was commanding. On the west is a spacious view of our noble stream in all its grandeur, resembling a lake rather than a river, and confined on the opposite shore by verdant hills of moderate height. On the north and east, the sight is fatigued by the uniformity and wide expanse of boundless plain. On the south the prospect is romantic, and abruptly checked by a striking contrast of wild hills and rugged bluffs on either side of the water, and rendered particularly so by two singular towering rocks similar in colour, shape and height called by the natives "Twins" situated on the east side, and they are skirted in the distance by a chain of the Blue Mountains, lying in the direction of east and west. To effect the intended footing on this straight and precarious spot was, however, certainly a task replete with excess of labour and anxiety.

In the charming security of a temperate atmosphere nature here displays in her manifold beauties, and at this season the crowds of moving bodies diversify and enliven the same. Groups of Indian huts with their spiral little columns of smoke, herds of animals give animation and beauty to the landscape. The natives in social crowds outdid each other in coursing their gallant steeds, in racing, and swimming, with other feats of activity. Wild horses in droves sported and grazed along the boundless plains. The wild fowls in flocks filled the air, and the salmon and sturgeon incessantly leaping ruffled the smoothness of the waters. The appearance of the country in a summer's evening was delightful beyond description.

Yet with all these alterations around us we were far from being free from anxiety. The natives flocked about us in very suspicious numbers, often through curiosity to see our work yet not at all times too well disposed; our situation was the more irksome as we depended for food on the success of trade and the degree of standing well or ill with the Indians.

By far the greater part of the timber had to be collected in the bush and conducted by water the distance of a hundred miles, for not a tree or shrub was on the spot itself! Divisions of our party consequently took place more often than was desirable, and our situation was ever exposed.

We had also to devise means to divert their attention and arouse the curiosity of the people; by being composed of different tribes the seeds of dissension were artfully sown among them to hold the balance equal and prevent their uniting against us. Each tribe imagining it possessed the pre-eminence in our consideration. And though they were as independent of us as we were the reverse of them, still they were taught to fancy that they could not do without us.

Soon after our landing the tribes began to muster fast, and the multitudes which surrounded us became immense and their movement alarming. They insisted on our paying for the timber we were collecting. They prohibited our hunting or fishing. They affixed an exorbitant price of their own to every article of trade, and they insulted any of the hands whom they met alone. Then they resolved to keep us in their power and withhold supplies until their conditions were granted.

Not knowing therefore how affairs might terminate, all work was suspended. We stood on our guard, and an enforced plan of non-intercourse between us of necessity took place for five long summer days, although we were at the time on very short allowance; one night all hands went to rest supperless! All this time the natives were mustering fast, plotting and planning. Our numbers however being collected they consisted of twenty-five Canadians, thirty-two Owhyhees, and thirty-eight Iroquois; and as a temporary enclosure had been put together we assumed a posture of independence and defiance.

The natives were offered such terms as were given in other parts of the country. That they should have the choice of cultivating a peaceable understanding with us and might profit by a friendly intercourse, or lay their account to undergo the vengeance of all the whites and ever after be deprived of the benefit resulting from a trade established among them. In the meantime while they were deliberating among themselves we were making every preparation for action.

Agreements enforced at the muzzle of our guns they could not it seemed withstand, and fortunately the chiefs advanced to bring the matters to an accommodation; they insisted as a preliminary step that we should bestow a liberal present on all the multitude around us to reconcile them to the measures. All the property we had would scarcely have been a mite to each! We therefore peremptorily refused. Their demands grew less and less as they saw us determined. They were therefore compelled at last to crouch to every condition, even the most minute, and we were left to use our own discretion. After these troubles which occupied many anxious days and sleepless nights all again became calm.

A trade with the natives now went on very briskly. Our people went to their work as usual and we enjoyed for a short time the comforts of peace and tranquility. But these enjoyments were however of short duration. True, we had obtained a footing on the ground and things in general wore the aspect of peace; but something else remained to be done before we could effect the object we had in view.

The principal cause which led to the establishing of this post was the establishing of the trade, consequently the great step was to pave the way for discoveries. To this end it was indispensable to the safety of the undertaking to have an understanding with the chief tribes who at all seasons infested the most practicable passes in the contemplated direction, which was overspread with the horrors of war, and seeing the natives extremely formidable we apprehended that they might be unanimous to prevent our advancing with their enemies.

With a view to effect this important point the chiefs and wise men of the different tribes were called together. They met. An endless round of ceremony took place among them during their discussion; yet nothing could be finally settled on account of the absence of one of the principal chiefs at the war in the very quarter we had our eye upon. And we considered his absence a great drawback on our proceedings. As he professed himself a sincere friend to the whites, we therefore placed our chief reliance on his influence and good offices.

For ten days our patience was put to the stretch by the intrigues of the many who busied themselves in thwarting our object; but while we were thus entangled in endless efforts to secure a peace, who should arrive but Tum-a-tap-um, the regretted chief. We now hoped that the business would be speedily and amicably settled. But new difficulties presented themselves. Instead of Tum-a-tap-um coming to join the assembled conclave to forward our business, all the great men deserted us to join him with his trophies of war and left us mere spectators to wait their convenience.

The arrival of the war party left us without either chief or slave to consult, and for three days we had to wait until they had exhausted their songs of triumph, without one single interview with the chief on whom we had placed so much confidence. This war party was reported to us to consist of four hundred and eighty men. Their hideous yells, mangled prisoners, and bloody scalps, together with their barbarous gestures, presented a sight truly savage. I only saw nine slaves. On the third day Tum-a-tap-um mounted on horseback, rode backward and forward round our little camp several times, without expressing either approbation or disapprobation of our measures. Then dismounting and drawing near to us with his men around him, they smoked some hundreds of pipes of our tobacco. The ceremony of smoking being over we had a long conversation with him on the subject of a general peace; but he was so elated with his own exploits and success on his late war expedition that we fancied him not so warmly interested in our cause as formerly.

Notwithstanding reiterated profession of friendship it was observed that his disposition was uncommonly selfish. He never opened his mouth but to insist on our goods being lavished on his numerous train of followers, without the hope of compensation. The more he received the more his assurance increased, and his demands had no bounds.

The natives were now to be seen clubbed together in groups; they were counselling day and night, and as all savage tribes delight in war it was no easy matter to turn their attention to peace. However, it was so managed that they were all got to meet again on the subject. "If," said Tum-a-tap-um, "we make peace, how shall I employ my young men? They delight in nothing but war, and besides, our enemies, the Snakes never observe a peace." Turning round, "Look," said he again, pointing to his slaves, scalps and arms, "am I to throw all these trophies away? Shall Tum-a-tap-um forget the glory of his forefathers, and become a woman?" Quahat, the Cayouse great war chief, next got up and observed, "Will the whites in opening a trade with our enemies promise not to give them guns or balls?" and others spoke to the same effect; but we tried to combat these remarks by expatiating on the blessings of peace and comforts of trade. Several meetings took place before we could accomplish the desired object.

At length a messenger came with notice that the chiefs were all of one mind and would present themselves in a short time. All our people were placed under arms assumedly to honour their reception; but really to guard ourselves. By-and-by the solemn train of chiefs, warriors and other great personages were seen to move from the camp in procession painted, dressed in their state and war garments, and armed. They entered our enclosure to the number of fifty-six where a place had been appropriately fitted up for the occasion. The most profound silence pervaded the whole, until the pipe of peace had six times performed the circle of the assembly.

The scene was in the highest degree interesting. The matter was canvased anew. Nothing appeared to be overlooked. The opinion of each was delivered briefly with judgement and with candour, and to the same end. Satisfied with the answers and the statements we had given, at sunset peace between themselves and the Snakes was decreed on the spot and a unanimous consent given for us to pass and repass unmolested. Then they threw down their war garments into the midst of the circle as if to say, "We have no further need of these garments." This manoeuvre had a double meaning. It was a broad hint for a new suit as well as a peace offering! The pipe of peace finally satisfied the treaty. Then all shaking hands, according to the manners of the whites, parted friends. Both parties apparently were pleased with the result. One condition of the treaty was that we should use our influence to bring the Snakes to agree to the peace, for without that it would be useless to ourselves. The only real object we had in view, or the only result that could in reality be expected by the peace business was, we might be enabled to go in and come out of the Snake country in safety, sheltered under the influence of its name. Nothing beyond this was ever contemplated on our part. All our manoeuvres were governed by the policy of gain. Peace in reality was beyond our power: it was but an empty name.

Does the reader ask, "Could the puny arm of a few whites, were they sincere, have brought about a peace between these two great and warlike nations, situated as they are?" I answer, "No." Does he ask, "Did Lewis and Clarke conclude a peace between them?" I again answer, "No." Does he enquire, "Can a solid peace be concluded between them, either by themselves, or by the influence of their traders?" I repeat, "No." Does he again enquire, "Is such a thing practicable, as a solid peace being concluded and observed between two savage nations, brought up in war?" I say, "No!" Such a thing is a perfect delusion. They must either be civilized or one of them extirpated, then there may be peace, but not till then.

As soon as the great conference of peace was over, our men were set to their work for the third time, and we now opened a trade with the natives which was carried on briskly particularly in provision and pack horses for the contemplated purpose of travelling, of hunting and exploring in the new and distant countries inhabited by the Snakes and other natives to the south. This brings us to the first Snake expedition.

The expedition was composed of fifty-five men of all denominations, one hundred and ninety-five horses, and three hundred beaver traps, besides a considerable stock of merchandise; but depending on the chances of the chace, they set out without provisions or stores of any kind. The season was too far advanced for the plan to be successful.

The party took their departure at the end of September in the full view and amongst the cheers of all the natives. Turning his back therefore upon the rest of his extensive charge, with all its ease and fruits of comfort, McKenzie without any second or friend in whom he could confide placed himself at the head of this medley, to suffer new hardships and face new dangers in the precarious adventures.

The charge of this important establishment with all its cares now devolved upon me, with the remnant of the people. And as we have already given a description of the place and noticed our reception among the natives, we shall here by way of variety present the reader with a brief list of the names of the tribes which inhabit this part of the country.

When the first traders arrived in the country they generally distinguished all the natives along this part of the communication indiscriminately by the appellation of "Nez Perces" or Pierced Noses from the custom practiced by these people of having their noses bored to hold a certain white shell, like the fluke of an anchor. The appellation was used until we had the opportunity of becoming better acquainted with their respective names. It was therefore from this cause that the present establishment derived its name.

The different tribes attached to Fort Nez Perces and who formerly went by that cognomen are the Sha-moo-in-augh, Ikam-nam-in-augh, E'yack-im-ah, Is-pipe-whum-augh, and In-as-petsum.[1] The tribes inhabit the main north branch above the forks. On the south

1 Groups now incorporated into the Yakima tribe.

branch are the Palle-to-Pallas, Shaw-ha-ap-ten, or Nez Perces proper, Pa-luck and Co-sis-pa[2] tribes. On the main Columbia beginning at the Long Narrows are the Ne-coo-im-eigh, Wiss-copam, Wiss-whams, Way-yam-pams, Low-him, Saw-saw and You-ma-talla bands.[3] And about the establishment, the Cayouse and Walla Walla tribes. It is to the two latter that appertain the spot on which the fort is erected, who are consequently resident in the immediate neighbourhood. The Shaw-ha-ap-ten and the Cayouse nations are, however, by far the most powerful and warlike of all these different tribes.

The two last mentioned regulate all the movement of the others in peace and war. And as they stand well or ill disposed toward their traders, so do the others. It is, therefore, the interest of the whites to keep on a friendly footing with them which is not at all times easy to do. They are however fast changing, and at times their conduct would almost encourage a belief that they are everything we could wish. Judging from these favourable intervals, a stranger would conclude that no part of the country could be more tranquil or peaceable than this quarter once so terrible; but a little knowledge of their history would soon convince him that although they often put on a fair outside, all is not right within. We hoped that things were getting gradually better, for the men of the place occasionally moved about with property in numbers of two or three at a time, and during my lonely strolls in the environs for the purpose of shooting, I fell in with bands who were suspicious looking; yet they never failed to accept me in the most respectful and best-natured manner. These circumstances augur favourable for the future. It will nevertheless be the work of years, perhaps of a generation, before civilization can manifest its influence over their actions.

The circumstances which caused our only uneasiness arose from the frequency of unpleasant rumours which obtained currency among the natives of the place that our absent friends had met with a total discomfiture from the Snake nation. Indeed so probable did

2 Palouse, Nez Percé, Potlatch, and Cayuse tribes.
3 Necootimeigh, Wasco, Wishram, Dalles, Cathlasco, Siuslaw, and Umatilla tribes.

their statements seem that they appeared no longer doubtful. These Indians being in the habit of viewing everything in that direction in the worst light, it was only natural they should place implicit belief in whatever they heard from these of their own nation about the frontiers.

At the time of these disturbing reports a man by the name of Oskononton, an Iroquois belonging to the Snake expedition, suddenly arrived at this place. His haggard appearance showed that he had suffered no ordinary hardships. After taking some refreshment and a little rest, for he was reduced to a skeleton, he related to me the story of his adventures. And I shall give it in his own words. "After entering the Blue Mountains," said Oskononton, "and we had got some distance into the Snake country, my comrades, to the number of twenty-five, kept teasing Mr. McKenzie to allow us to hunt and trap in a small river which appeared well stocked in beaver. At last he reluctantly consented, and we remained. Well knowing that if he had not done so, the Iroquois would have deserted. This was their plan. After the parties had separated and McKenzie and the main party had left us, we set to trapping and were very successful but had not been long there till we fell in with a small band of Snakes. My comrades began to exchange their horses, their guns, and their traps with these people for women! and carried on the traffic to such an extent that they had scarcely an article left, and being no longer able to hunt, abandoned themselves with the savages and were doing nothing!

"Unable to check their heedless conduct I left them and set out to follow the main party; but I lost my way, and getting bewildered turned back again to join my comrades. There I tried and tried again to persuade them to mind their hunting but in vain. So I left them again and set out on my way back to this place; but on the second day after leaving my associates, I observed at some little distance a war party and hid myself; fearing that my horse might discover my retreat to my enemies I resolved to kill it, a resolution I executed with the utmost regret. Although game was plentiful in those parts yet I dared not shoot, as the report of my gun might have led to my discovery in a place frequented only by enemies.

As soon as the war party passed on, I cut and dried part of my dead horse for food, and tying it up in a bundle, continued my journey.

"One day as I was entering the Blue Mountains I perceived several horsemen in full pursuit making after me, seeing there was not a moment to lose I thrust my bundle, provisions and all into a bush, ran down a steep bank, plunged into the water, a small river happening to be near, and hid myself beneath some driftwood, my head only out of the water, which fortunately was not very cold. The horsemen paraded up and down both sides of the little stream for some time, and then dismounting made a fire, had something to eat, and remained for more than two hours within fifty yards of my hiding place! They were Snakes. After dark I got out of the water, more dead than alive. I then went to look for my provisions, my bag and my little property, which I had thrown into the brush; but the night being dark, and I afraid to remain any longer, I set out as fast as I could on my journey without finding anything! Every moment I thought I heard a noise behind me, every branch that broke under my feet or beast of prey that started convinced me in spite of my senses that I was still pursued. In this state of alarm I passed the night but made very little headway, and in the morning took to another hiding plan. Tired and exhausted, I laid myself down to sleep without covering, without fire, and without either food or water! In this manner, travelling in the night and hiding during the day, I crossed the Blue Mountains, which took me three days and the most of that time without a shoe on my feet. Neither had I gun, fire steel, or anything to render travelling comfortable. By this time my feet had got swelled and blistered with walking, so that I took three days more between this and the mountains, making the seventh day, with the exception of a fine raw root, that I had not tasted food of any kind." This ended Oskononton's story.

I had no difficulty in believing the statement of the Iroquois. It was in accordance with their general character. Oskononton knew, as his story relates, nothing of the main party, so that I was still left in the dark as to its fate. After keeping the poor fellow upwards of three weeks to recruit his health and recover his strength I sent him on to Fort George, and this brings us to notice the passing events in that quarter.

Just at the time of Oskononton's arrival at that place, a party of his countrymen were fitting out for a hunting and trapping expectation to the Cowlitz quarter and he unfortunately joined it. The party however had not been long there before they got into trouble with the natives, and in an affray poor Oskononton in trying to rescue one of his companions got murdered. After this tragical affair, in which it was stated our trappers were the aggressors, the Iroquois had to make a precipitate retreat, abandon their hunting ground and make the best of their way back again to Fort George.

The Iroquois had no sooner got back than they gave Mr. Keith to understand that the Indians had without the least provocation killed one of their party and wounded two others. A deed so atrocious and a story so plausible had its effect at Fort George. Placing therefore implicit faith in the report of the Iroquois Mr. Keith with a view to investigate the matter, punish the murderers, and settle the affair fitted out without delay a party of between thirty and forty men, chiefly Iroquois, the very worst men in the world for such a business. And gave their charge to Mr. Ogden, an experienced clerk of the North West school. On reaching the Cowlitz all their enquiries were fruitless, they could find no offenders; until they got the assistance of How-How, one of the principal chiefs of the place, who conducted them to the very spot, little thinking that he would have cause to regret his friendly assistance.

In their approach to the Indians Mr. Ogden cautioned the Iroquois to be guarded in their conduct and do nothing until he first showed them the example, some then went one way, some another, making their way through the thicket and bushes; but a party of the Iroquois happening to make the Indian tents before Mr. Ogden, instead of waiting for orders or knowing whether those they had found were or were not the guilty persons, the moment they got within gun shot they fired on all they saw, and before Mr. Ogden or How-How could interpose, twelve persons, men, women and children were killed! Nor is it known to this day who were the guilty persons! Even after Mr. Ogden had arrived and tried to stop them, one more was shot and to crown their guilt, our people scalped three of their victims! The cause of the quarrel in which Oskononton lost his life arose from our trappers interfering with the Indian women, which brought down on them the vengeance of the men and ended in bloodshed.

The moment How-How saw the outrage committed on his people he wheeled about in disgust and left the party. The whites had now to make a hasty retreat before the neighbouring Indians had time to assemble and got back to headquarters with speed, carrying along with them several scalps which they exhibited on poles as trophies of victory, dancing with those trophies in the square of Fort George after their return! Anticipating no doubt a similar result from the Cowlitz quarter to that which followed the Wallamitte embassy the year before in a similar occasion, Mr. Keith was horror-struck at the cruelties committed on the natives by his people.

Every stratagem that experience could devise or hope inspire was now resorted to, in order to induce How-How the Cowlitz chief to pay a visit to Fort George, in order that footing might once more be allowed in the Cowlitz quarter. The Chinook to be sure were in his way, they were his enemies; but what of that, the whites were his friends. He was promised ample protection, and a safe return cordially pledged but he would listen to nothing. How-How was immovable.

At last however it was discovered that How-How had a daughter both lovely and fair, the flower of her tribe. Princess How-How was admired. Her ochre cheeks were delicate, her features incomparable! And yet her dress surpassed in lustre her person. Her robes were the first in the land. Her feathers, her bells, her tassels were unique, while the tint of her skin, her nose bob, girdle and girt were irresistible! A husband of high rank had to be provided for the Princess How-How, and Prince How-How himself formally acquainted with the wishes and anticipations of the whites. This appeal the sagacious and calculating chief could not resist! How-

How therefore with his fascinating daughter and train of followers arrived in their robes of state at headquarters. The bridal dress was beyond compare! Prince How-How now became the father-in-law of a white chief, and a fur trader became the happy son-in-law of Prince How-How.

We need scarcely mention here that the happy couple were joined together in holy matrimony on the first of April! After the marriage ceremony a peace was negotiated with How-How, this was the main point, the chief prepared for his homeward journey in order to pave the way for our trappers and hunters to return again to the Cowlitz.

But just as he and his followers were starting a sad blunder was committed by the whites, for it would appear that measures for their safety had either been overlooked or neglected and after all the courtesy that had been shown the great man, he left the fort unguarded; but had not advanced three hundred yards from the gate before he and his people were partially intercepted by some sculking Chinooks who waylaid and fired upon them. But How-How instead of retreating back to the fort for protection, boldly called out to his men to face their enemies and stand their ground. But the Chinooks being concealed, How-How's men could see nobody to fire at, so they immediately posted themselves behind trees. In the skirmish a ball happened to strike the fort, and whether a shot is fired accidentally or by design, the event is equally alarming. The moment therefore the ball struck the sentinel gave the alarm by calling out, "The fort is attacked! How-How and his men are in ambush!" In the confusion of the moment and seeing only How-How's party, the first impression, although exceedingly improbable, was that How-How himself had proved treacherous and on his departion fired upon the fort! Orders were therefore immediately issued to fire the bastion guns, by which one of How-How's men was severely and another slightly wounded. At the same time all the people who had been at work outside the fort came rushing in, and meeting parties in the square running to and fro in every direction collecting arms and ammunition, completed the confusion.

How-How and his party now stood between two fires! And apprehending treachery on the part of the whites was preparing to make a rush and force his way through the Chinooks and save himself and party, but by this time the people who had just entered the fort had time to set matters right by giving information that the Chinooks had been lying in ambush and first fired upon How-How, and that How-How was only defending himself; but in the bustle and uproar of the moment some time elapsed before men taken by surprise could reflect or understand each other. The moment the shots were fired from the bastion the Chinooks fled, thinking as a matter of course that they only had been fired at. As soon therefore as the whites ceased firing all was over, and the whole was only the work of a few minutes. How-How now was brought into the fort and the misunderstanding fully explained to him. But he was a changed man. On his part the habits of familiarity and friendship ceased, he was stern and sulky, and notwithstanding the praises that were bestowed on him; yet his pride was wounded and he remained sullen and thoughtful, and when he ultimately took his departure after receiving many presents and more promises, his fidelity was evidently shaken and his future support problematical.

An only field that now remained open for our trappers and hunters, as the Cowlitz could not be depended upon, was the Wallamitte! and to that quarter the thoughts of all were directed: notwithstanding a sufficient number of trappers and hunters were occupied there already; yet all those who had been driven from the northern quarters now bent their course to the southern, to join those already there. From the general conduct of the Iroquois among the natives it would have been better policy to have sent them all out of the country, distracting the natives, destroying the trade, and disgracing the whites.

The party numbering in all sixty men and headed by two halfbreed clerks from Canada proceeded up the Wallamitte until they had reached its source, and from thence, crossing some high ridges of land, hunted on the banks of the Umpqua and there they discovered many branches which promised a rich harvest of furs. Here our people fell in with numerous bands of the natives and who were all very peaceable; but from their shy and reserved manners and wishing to avoid the whites it was evident that they had never been much in the habit of trading with them; yet they had no objection to our people's hunting on their land. They wished to traffic and barter with them, they wished to play the same game with them as the Iroquois, according to Oskononton's story, played with the Snakes; but no inducement, no advances, could bring those natives into contact or familiarity with our people. The further therefore they advanced, the farther the Indians receded to avoid them. Seeing the natives timid and distant, our people resorted to threats!

One day while the Indians were raising camp, our people wished to detain some of their horses as hostages to ensure their return, the Indians resisted, when they in a moment of folly fired upon them! and it was found that no less a number than fourteen of the innocent and inoffensive Indians were shot dead in the affray, and that without a single arrow being shot in self-defence. The Indians fled, followed up by the hunters; but the number that fell in the flight was not ascertained.

Fear now seized the party, and a retreat followed. They fell back on the Wallamitte, and communicating their fears to the other trappers, all left the hunting ground in a panic and drew near to headquarters. From the Wallamitte Falls four men of their party and an Indian were dispatched to Fort George, with the accounts of what had happened; with a very plausible colouring of the whole affair in their own favor. These men while on their way thither had encamped at a place called Oak Point within twenty miles of the fort and were all, with the exception of the Indian, barbarously murdered one night while asleep! The deed was committed by five of the Class-can-eye-ah tribe,[4] the same band who murdered the three white men belonging to the Pacific Fur Company in 1811. This atrocious act of cruelty, taking place at the very gates of our stronghold, proved that the state of things was getting worse.

The whites called aloud for revenge, an example was necessary. Three parties were sent in pursuit of the murderers composed of a mixture of whites and natives. They were found out and laid hold

4 Cathlanahquiah tribe.

of. Four out of the five, after a trial of some length, were convicted and punished with death. The disasters of this year in the Fort George district alone it was supposed had reduced our annual returns four thousand beaver, equal to six thousand pounds sterling: and the dire effects produced on the natives by the heedless conduct of our people took years to efface.

Leaving Fort George, we now return to the Nez Perces quarter. We shall in the first place notice what effect the troubles at the former quarter had on the latter. The disasters in the Cowlitz had not only shut us out from that hunting ground but prevented our trappers from this place from proceeding across the ridge in the E-yack-im-ah[5] direction: for a party I had fitted out were frightened as soon as they crossed the height of land by the hostility manifested towards them, and they had in consequence to retrace their steps. They were nevertheless considering the short time they had been there very successful.

It is perhaps not generally known that the most direct line of communication from the Grand Forks to the ocean is by the river E-yack-im-ah, and although the portage across the dividing ridge from that river on the east to the Chick-ell-is River[6] on the west is considerable; yet the land carriage is no object in a place where the road is not bad and the means of transportation abundant, horses being everywhere plentiful.[7] All the resources of the interior might therefore with great facility be conveyed through this channel to Puget's Sound independent of the main Columbia, should the fate of war at any time offer obstacles to the free ingress and egress to the river itself. Or should the intricate and dangerous channel across the bar at its mouth yet choke up, as it sometimes does, to a very great degree with sand banks. By the E-yack-im-ah road the natives reach the ocean in ten days.

At this period of our anxiety and our declining hopes as to the fate of our friends in the Snake country, who should appear to remove suspense and give new vigour to our proceedings but Mc-

[5] The Yakima River.
[6] The Chehalis River.
[7] Probably along the White River to Puget Sound.

Kenzie from his voyage of discovery. He and six men reached Fort Nez Perces on snow shoes with their blankets on their backs, in good health and spirits, after a tedious journey of six months. The meeting was one of interest for McKenzie was no less cheered to find everything safe and our footing sure at this place than I was to witness his safe return under favourable circumstances, after so many discouraging rumours. The accounts McKenzie gave of the Snake country were flattering, the prospects encouraging; but the character of his people was the very reverse! we shall however let him speak for himself.

"After leaving this place last fall," said McKenzie, "we diverted our course across the Blue Mountains; but had not proceeded far into the country of the Snakes before the Iroquois began their old trade of plotting mischief; but being less numerous and more cowardly than their associates they did not avow their treacherous intentions publicly; I was however fully aware of their design and guarded against them but could not change their dispositions nor their heedless conduct, and fearing that they might desert or do something worse if in their power, I made a virtue of necessity and acquiesced in their wishes, thinking it better policy to do so than drag them along discontented to desert or abandon themselves with the Indians whenever an opportunity offered. So I put the best face on things I could, filled them out well in everything they required, and with the rest of the party proceeded on our journey, leaving them to work beaver in the rich little River Skam-am-naugh.[8]

"From this place we advanced, suffering occasionally from alarms for twenty-five days, and then found ourselves in a rich field of beaver in the country lying between the great south branch[9] and the Spanish waters,[10] but the natives in these parts were not friendly. In our journey we fell in with several bands of the Snake nation, and to each we communicated the welcome tidings of peace on the part of the Nez Perces; to which they one and all responded in the language of gratitude for anything new attracts their attention and

8 Indian Creek.
9 The Snake River.
10 The Green River.

the word 'peace' served as our letter of introduction among them. 'Our wishes,' said they, 'are now accomplished, nothing so desirable to us as peace.' I hope the impression may be a lasting one.

"After disposing of my people to the best advantage, trading with the natives and securing the different chiefs to our interest, I left my people at the end of four months. Then taking a circuitous route along the foot of the Rocky Mountains, a country extremely dreary during the winter voyage, till I reached the headquarters of the great south branch regretting every step I made that we had been so long deprived of the riches of such a country. Thence I steered my course for the river Skam-naugh, where I had left my Iroquois to hunt beaver in October last. During this part of my journey, I crossed and recrossed many parts I had seen in 1811. Instead however of finding the Iroquois together and employed in hunting or in the pursuit of hunting I found them by two's and by three's all over the country, living with the savages, without horses, without traps, without furs and without clothing! perfectly destitute of everything I had given them. I left them therefore as I found them. Iroquois will never do in this country. In fact, their introduction was the signal of our disappointments. On reaching this place, we found but little snow in the Blue Mountains. During the last two months we have travelled upwards of six hundred miles on snow shoes!" This account confirmed Oskononton's story.

Continuing the narrative of his journey, our enterprising adventurer next went on to describe the country, the resources, and animals they everywhere met with. "On our outward journey," said McKenzie, "the surface was mountainous and rugged, and still more so on our way back. Woods and valleys, rocks and plains, rivers and ravines alternately met us; but altogether it is a delightful country. There animals of every class rove about undisturbed. Wherever there was a little plain, the red deer were seen grazing in herds, about the rivers and round every other point were clusters of poplar and alder, and where there was a sapling, there the ingenious and industrious beaver was at work. The otters sported in the eddies, on the banks were seen the wolf and the fox sauntering in quest of prey; now and then a few cypresses or stunted pine were

VALLEY OF THE WILLAMETTE RIVER

A drawing by Henry James Warre

GREEN RIVER

A water color by Alfred Jacob Miller

to be seen on the rocky parts, and in their spreading tops, the racoon sat secure. In the woods the martin and black fox were numerous. The badger sat quietly looking from his mound. In the numberless ravines among bushes laden with fruits, the black, the brown, and the grizzly bear are seen. The mountain sheep and goat white as snow browse on the rocks and ridges, and the big horn species[11] run among the lofty cliffs. Eagle and vulture of uncommon size fly about the rivers. When we approached most of the animals, they stood motionless. They would then move off a little distance; but soon come back anew to satisfy a curiosity that often proved fatal to them.

"The report of a gun did not alarm them: they would give a frisk at each shot and stand again; but when the flag was erected being of a reddish hue, it was with apparent reluctance they would retire beyond the pleasing sight. Hordes of wild horses were likewise seen on the occasion; but of all the animals seen on our journey they were the wildest, for none of them could be approached. Their scent is exceedingly keen, their hearing also, and in their curiosity they were never known to come at any time within gun shot! One band of these contained more than two hundred. Some of them were browsing on the face of the hills, some were running like deer up and down the steps, and some were galloping backward and forward on the brows of the sloping mountains, with their flowing manes and bushy tails in the wind.

"Caverns without number are to be seen in the rocks on either side of the river. Many of them are of very great depth and dimensions, the shapes of the rocks are often picturesque. But on our way back the scene was changed, nothing to be seen but dreary and forbidding winter, the leafless forests and snow-clad hills with scarcely an animal to attract attention except a wolf or fox which now and then crossed our paths, or an eagle or vulture watching their prey about rapids when open water was still to be seen. All had now retreated for shelter to the thick woods, so that we were more than once on short allowance and on these emergencies had to regale ourselves on wolf's flesh, and even sometimes glad to get meat to

[11] Rocky Mountain sheep.

satisfy the cravings of nature. We required no stimulus to sharpen our appetites."

McKenzie had a three-fold object in view by leaving his people and returning to this place at such a season, to see some of the principal Snake chiefs, whom he had not seen with regard to the peace business between them and the Nez Perces, secondly to examine the country, and lastly, to ascertain the state of the navigation up the south branch, with a view of future operations. The two former of these objects was accomplished. The peace business as far as could be depended upon by parties living so much from each other. The results however must ever be doubtful.

After a short respite of only seven days at Nez Perces allowing him scarcely time to repose himself and recount his adventures, this indefatigable man set out anew through ice and snow to examine that state of the navigation into the Snake Country by the south branch. For this purpose he and his handful of Canadians, six in number, embarking on board of a barge, left Fort Nez Perces and proceeded up Lewis River.[12] The turbulent natives on both sides the stream, notwithstanding his late return from their foes, suffered him to pass through this channel unmolested. After a voyage of two months the boat with four of the men returned to this place, while McKenzie and the other two set out on the prementioned adventure of reaching the hunters, a distance of twenty days' travel through a country where it had often been asserted that "less than fifty men could not set a foot with safety!"

McKenzie's letter by return of the boat was elated. "Point Successful, head of the narrows,[13] April 15th, 1819." He then stated that "The passage by water is now proved to be safe and practicable for loaded boats with one single carrying place or portage. Therefore, the doubtful question is now set at rest forever. Yet from the force of the current and the frequency of rapids, it may still be advisable and perhaps preferable to continue the land transportation while the business in this quarter is carried on upon a small scale." He then goes on to observe that "We had often recourse to

12 The Snake River.
13 The Grand Canyon of the Snake River.

the line," and then adds, "There are two places with bold cut rocks on either side of the river[14] where the great body of water is compressed within a narrow compass, which may render those parts doubtful during the floods, owing to rocks and whirlpools; but there are only two, and neither of them are long." He then concludes his letter with these words, "I am now about to commence a very doubtful and dangerous undertaking, and shall I fear have to adopt the habits of the owl, roam in the night and skulk in the day to avoid our enemies. But if my life is spared, I will be at the river Skam-naugh with my people and return by the 5th of June. Hasten therefore the outfit with some additional hands if possible to that place. A strong escort will be advisable, and caution the person you may send in charge to be at all times both day and night on his guard."

After performing the annual trip to Fort George, the brigade on its return to the interior reached this place. I set about forwarding the Snake supplies. Accompanying the brigade was a small party of fifteen men intended for the Snakes, to strengthen McKenzie's party. Augmenting this small party to the number of twenty-six from my own establishment, I placed the whole under the charge of a Mr. Kittson,[15] an apprentice clerk from Canada, a novice in the country, but a smart fellow. With all possible haste Mr. Kittson and his men set off with the Snake outfit to meet McKenzie and his party at the river Skam-naugh, according to appointment. On the departure of the party I handed Mr. Kittson written instructions, as he was a new hand, and cautioned him in every possible manner against the thieving propensities of the natives along the lines.

But Kittson, full of confidence and life, thought all this caution unnecessary and swore that "all the Indians on the continent would neither steal the horses or anything else." "I am glad to hear it," said I. "Oh, I defy them," said he, and saying so we shook hands and parted. The task and responsibility of venturing into a new and dangerous part of the country, among hostile savages, with loads of property, was a risky undertaking for the most experienced

14 Part of the Grand Canyon of the Snake River.
15 William Kittson.

person, much more so was it for a person like Kittson, a perfect stranger and who had never received any charge of the kind before. Yet all went on well until the party had got to the territories of the Snakes, a ground which is ever exceedingly suspicious as lying between two contending nations. Too much care could not be had in keeping a sharp lookout and knowing when, or from which side, the danger might first show itself.

Seeing no traces of Indians Mr. Kittson allowed himself to be influenced by the opinion of his men, ever ready to despise danger in order to avoid watching at night. The whole party therefore in full confidence and security laid themselves down one night to enjoy the comforts of repose. In the darkness of the night however, hearing neighing and a noise among the horses the party started up half asleep, half awake, and rushing to where they had been feeding, discovered the thieves in the act of unhobbling them but in the darkness the villains got off, and in their retreat succeeded in carrying off twelve of them! The evil was now beyond remedy but not fatal to the expedition, as there still remained enough to carry the property; but the men as a just punishment for their heedlessness had to trudge it on foot.

From the encampment of the stolen horses the party advanced taking the utmost care to watch every night. One day however they found themselves in a beautiful open valley skirted by mountains, and not seeing any natives, for these sly marauders are never to be seen, and as their horses were fagged, they willingly let them graze for a few hours at large in the meadow around their little camp. The party being fatigued particularly those on foot very inconsiderately laying themselves down, in a few minutes they were over powered with that heavy sleep which their wearied travelling so much demanded. They had not been long in this state before the two short words "Hoo hoo! Hoo hoo!" sounding in their ears awoke them; but not to gladness for their horses were all gone!

Three of that banditti who at all seasons of the year infest the skirts of the frontiers on the Snake side had been, as they always are, watching from the adjacent hill the movements of all passengers, had crawled and concealed themselves among the long grass till they had reached the horses, then laying hold of one each, were beyond our people's reach before they could get their eyes well open!

No words can depict the anxiety of our little band, with the property on their hands, in an enemy's country, destitute of provisions, deprived of hope itself! Two days and nights passed and they had come to no decision: but on the third day about noon, while they were pondering on the steps that were next to take a cloud of dust was seen approaching from afar. Concluding they must be enemies, they made a hasty breastwork with their goods, and with their arms in their hands, waited their arrival in a state of anxious foreboding; but what must have been their joy on seeing a party of our own traders appearing driving before them the horses which had been the cause of their unhappiness.

McKenzie having arrived at the river Skam-naugh at the time appointed and not meeting with either men or supplies from this place, as he expected, dispatched ten men to ascertain the cause of the delay. Two days after these ten men had left their Bourgeois, in passing through a defile of the mountains they very unexpectedly met the thieves face to face, and recognizing the horses as belonging to the whites and seeing the Indians take to flight to avoid them they were confirmed in their conjectures, and they determined on taking after them. The chace lasted for upwards of two hours, when they overtook them. The thieves seeing their efforts to get off fruitless, turned round to sell their lives as dearly as possible. In such rencontres among themselves life is generally forfeited. They therefore boldly faced their pursuers, although three times their number. They fought desperately while they had an arrow remaining. One of them was shot by our people. Another was taken, and the third altho' severely wounded made his escape among the bushes. One of our hunters was wounded also. After the affray the party wheeled about and made for Kittson and his forlorn party driving all the horses before them, and arrived in safety. It was their approach that caused the cloud of dust already noticed. First so suspicious, and afterwards so pleasing.

Kittson's party now augmented to six and thirty men raised camp and set out once more with lightsome hearts. Two days had not however passed over their heads till they had another fright, for while they were encamped one night on a small river where everything around indicated serenity, two more horse thieves were detected in the night by the unhobbling their horses. In this instance the people on watch were more fortunate; they got hold of them and kept the rascals in safe custody till daylight, but the whites had suffered no loss, and therefore Mr. Kittson had the clemency to let them go unhurt. Each of the fellows had a quiver containing from fifty to sixty arrows, several pairs of shoes, and long lines for securing horses.

The party had now reached that inauspicious spot where some of the unfortunate men belonging to Reed's party were murdered in 1813.[16] There the cares of our party were not diminished at beholding some bands of the banditti of most suspicious appearance hovering about; but the whites being on their guard, they were allowed to pass unmolested.

Next day Mr. Kittson and party after all their mishaps arrived safe and in good spirits at the river Skam-naugh and joined Mr. McKenzie with his whole band, for he had contrived to assemble and bring together the greater part of his wayward and perverse Iroquois. Here Kittson delivered over his charge and receiving in return the Snake furs bent his course back again to this place, where he arrived on the 7th of July 1819. On his way back however, he had a very narrow escape from a war party; but got off with the loss of only two men, who fell a sacrifice at the first onset of the savages.

Had not the trouble in the Fort George department diminished the usual quantity of furs there we should have had, notwithstanding the defection of the Iroquois, a handsome augmentation to our returns this year. The Snake expedition turned out well, it made up for all deficiencies elsewhere and gave a handsome surplus besides.

McKenzie's party, now augmented by the addition of Kittson and his men who had no sooner delivered up the Snake furs at this

16 Near the site of Caldwell, Idaho.

place than they returned to join him, mustered strong. The natives and hunting ground, being also familiar to our hunters, were circumstances as far as we could judge that warranted our most sanguine anticipations as to the future. In his letter to me, McKenzie states that "Although the natives are at present in a very unsettled state yet if the contemplated peace succeeds, I hope that our success in this quarter next year will come up to the expectation of every reasonable man." With these remarks we shall close the narrative for the present year.

7. THE CENTRAL FORT

THE RESULT of the Snake expedition put an end to the sharp conduct which had for some years past divided the councils of Fort George.

No sooner was McKenzie's success in the Snake country known than his opponents were loud in his praise. It was pleasing to see this year the council of Fort George now enter so warmly and approve so strongly of our measures in having established Fort Nez Perces, and in gaining so promising a footing in the Snake country.

We have noticed Kittson's return to join the Snake expedition but before taking up the thread of our future proceedings we propose to give the reader a description and drawing of Fort Nez Perces, and then we shall conduct him to McKenzie's camp and give him a taste of Indian life in these parts.

For the purpose of protection as well as of trade among Indians, the custom is to have each establishment surrounded with an enclosure of pickets some twelve or fifteen feet high, and this enclosure is dignified with the name of fort, into which the natives have free ingress and egress at all times and within the walls of which all the business of traffic is transacted. A little more precaution was however necessary at the Nez Perces station, on account of the many war-like tribes that infest the country.

Instead of round pickets, the palisades of Fort Nez Perces were all made of sawn timber. For this purpose wood of large size and cut twenty feet long was sawed into pieces of two and a half feet broad by six inches thick. With these ponderous planks the establishment was surrounded, and on the top was a range of palisades four feet high which served the double purpose of ramparts and loop holes and was smooth to prevent the natives scaling the wall. The whole was supported by a strong gallery five feet broad all round. At each angle was placed a large reservoir sufficient to hold two hundred gallons of water as a security against fire, the element we most dreaded in the designs of the natives.

Inside of this wall were built ranges of stone houses and dwelling houses for the hands. And in the front of these buildings was another wall twelve feet high, of sawn timber also, with port holes and slip doors, which divided the buildings from the open square inside. So that should Indians at any time have got in they could see nothing but a wall before them on all sides, and they could have had no intercourse with the people in the fort unless by their consent, and would therefore have found themselves in a prison, and infinitely more exposed to danger than if they had been on the outside. Besides the ingenious construction of the outer gate, which opened and shut by a pulley, two double doors secured the entrance and the natives were never admitted within the walls, except when specially invited on important occasions. For all trade with them was carried on by means of an aperture in the wall only eighteen inches square secured by an iron door. This aperture communicated with the trading shop. We stood in the inside, and the Indians on the outside. Singular in this as in every other respect from all the other trading posts in the country.

Among other difficulties, it was not the least after the fort was built to succeed in bringing the Indians to trade in the manner we had fixed upon for the security of the place notwithstanding they had every convenience allowed them, a house at the gate, fire, tobacco, and a man to attend them at all hours. It was a long time before they got reconciled to our plan. "Are the whites afraid of us? If so," said they, "we will leave our arms outside." "No," said I, "if we had been afraid of you we should not have come among you." "Are the whites afraid we will steal any thing?" "No," said I, "but your young men are foolish." "That's true," said they. We persisted in the plan and they of necessity had to submit. Excluding the Indians, although contrary to Mr. McKenzie's opinion, ultimately answered so well that it ought to be adopted wherever the natives are either hostile or troublesome.

Our weapons of defence were composed of four pieces of ordnance from one to three pounds besides ten wall pieces or swivels, sixty stand of muskets and bayonets, twenty boarding pikes, and a box of hand grenades. The fort was defended by two strong wooden bastions and a culverin above the gate. It was therefore at once the strongest and most complete fort west of the Rocky Mountains and might be called the Gibralter of the Columbia.

To construct and finish in so short a time an establishment so strong and compact in all its parts was no ordinary undertaking. By industry and perseverance however, the task was accomplished. So that, in the short period of a few months, as if by enchantment, the savage disposition of the Indians was either soothed or awed, a stronghold had arisen in the desert, while the British banner floating over it proudly proclaimed it the mistress of a vast territory; it was an example of British energy and enterprise, of civilization over barbarism.

During the course of our proceedings a constant tide of visitors from quarters the most remote flowed in to satisfy their curiosity concerning our establishment. Among others were the turbulent lords of the falls;[1] but whether their barbarity was soothed by the compliment of a resource of this kind among them or whether they felt gratified by our embassy to conciliate their enemies and do away with the evils of war, it is difficult to say; but a visible reform was now very obvious in their deportment to the whites: for they invariably went and came in the most exemplary manner.

Having now given our readers a description of Fort Nez Perces and noticed the salutary effect our establishment had on the conduct of the natives, we now, according to promise, resume the narrative of operation in the Snake country. As soon as the annual supply of goods conveyed by Kittson had reached McKenzie's camp, knowing the character of his people, that they would, the moment they had their supplies in their own possession, be bartering and trafficking every article away with the natives, Mr. McKenzie in order to guard against this difficulty not only reserved the distribution among the party until the return of Kittson and the men who had to convey the furs to this place; but resolved on keeping the

1 Wishram Indians.

supplies entire until they reached their winter quarters, and then every man would have his equipment and winter supplies where it would be required. The conduct of the Iroquois last year had taught McKenzie this lesson. This measure was also a check against desertion, their supplies being before them encouraged zeal and stimulated all to a perseverance in well doing.

It was a plan however that subjected the person in charge to the risk of life as well as of property. Had the Snakes been of a character to respect property when once in their own hands, he might have distributed the whole and left every man to take care of his own; but the very reverse being the case, he was compelled to adopt the plan of taking care of it for them until they reached their winter quarters.

Therefore, as soon as Kittson and the men required to escort the furs to this place set off McKenzie was left with only three men! in charge of all the property, for although the Iroquois had returned to their duty, they were absent at the time collecting their horses and traps which they had left and squandered away among the Indians; but they were expected back hourly. Thus situated and the Iroquois not arriving at the appointed time McKenzie and his three men erected a small breastwork, secured their property, and accordingly waited with anxiety the arrival of succour.

Two days after this unavoidable division of our people, a very suspicious party of the mountain Snakes[2] appeared at their little camp. They were very importunate, and with the view of turning their barbarity into friendship McKenzie had given them some trifles, to get rid of them; but the kind treatment of our friends was construed into fear and only stimulated them to demand more. Soon after, other parties equally audacious arrived. But no Iroquois! The hostile attitude and threats of the natives were now beyond endurance. They attempted to get over the breastwork, to push our people back, and to steal all that they could lay hands upon! Up to this period our people stood on the outside of their property, but at this critical moment McKenzie and his men grasping their guns, sprang over the breastwork, lighted a match and

2 Bannack Indians.

placing a keg full of gun powder between them and their enemies, boldly determined to defend their property or die. At this decided moment the Indians, taken by surprise, fell back a little when Mc-Kenzie, with perhaps more courage than prudence, dared them to renew their threats!

While the fate of our little band hung as by a thread, the savages that menaced them took to flight, without a word! The first impression was that they were panic-struck from the dread of the powder. It was then apprehended that they meditated some stratagem, the respite however gave our friends time to reflect.

As soon as they considered it safe to look about them they perceived on the opposite side of the river a war party of the Shaw-ha-ap-tens consisting of two hundred men, all having fire arms and mounted on horseback. On their arrival they assembled in a tumultuous group on the beach. It was the Red Feather and his band who had been ill disposed at the peace. Our friends were now at no loss how to account for the sudden and mysterious departure of the Snakes! But still their situation was not the more secure, for they had as much to fear from the one party as from the other. For although the Shaw-ha-ap-tens have respected the whites on their own lands yet they had no mercy to expect in an enemy's country.

The appearance of this warlike cavalcade might have chilled the boldest heart. Their gestures, their yelling and whooping were truly terrible. The Indians called to our people to cross over and give them a smoke. At the same time it was evident they were making every preparation to take advantage of them while on the water. This invitation however not being complied with they held a council with a view, it was supposed, of crossing over themselves. Our people on perceiving this strengthened their little fortification, and having four guns to each man, they were determined at least on selling their lives dearly.

The natives in the meantime then plunged into the river with their steeds, but were forced back again. They plunged again and again but as often were compelled to return from the strength of the current. Their consultations were frequent, and the brandishing of their arms indicated their bloody intentions.

After capering along the bush on their chargers for some time, they at length disappeared and our party saw them no more. On their way back towards the Blue Mountains, however, they unfortunately fell upon the trail of Kittson and his party, and before he had time to get to a stronghold and concentrate his people the savages overtook his lead, shot and scalped two of his men. After the first onset, they wheeled about and got off clear.

No sooner had the war party disappeared than McKenzie and his men withdrew with their property to a hiding place. Crossing over a channel of the river they got upon an island, and took up their abode in the thick woods. From this retreat they could unperceived distinguish the savages passing and repassing in bands. They had however to avoid making a fire during the daytime, as its smoke would have discovered their retreat.

In this island our friends remained twenty-two days before Kittson and his party got back to them. And the very day, fifteen of the twenty-five prodigal Iroquois joined them. One had been killed in a scuffle with the natives, two deserted, and the other seven had abandoned themselves with the Snakes! The meeting of our friends was a joyful one, each party had its troubles and its adventures to recount. But such is the life of an Indian trader that these trying scenes are no sooner passed away than they are forgotten. Our friends now set about leaving the island to proceed on their journey.

Our trappers and hunters being now all mustered amounted to seventy-five men. And this was the number that composed the second adventure into the Snake country. Still twenty-five less than the number that had been promised to McKenzie. Advancing on their journey during the first few days they saw several parties of the banditti, and among others some of those very villains who had threatened to rob McKenzie and his three men were recognized! McKenzie therefore singled one out, and after addressing him at some length took hold of him and asked him if he was as brave a man that day as he was upon the former occasion! But the fellow was mute, then shaking him rather roughly he gave him a slap in the face and left him an object of derision to the bystanders!

The Indians now had changed their plan. In their progress they came to a very formidable camp of about eight hundred huts and tents. These Indians were engaged chiefly in fishing for salmon and being but indifferently disposed towards the whites, our party passed the night without sleep. And at dawn of day they left the suspicious ground to look out for a more desirable spot, as they were anxious to have a party with the chiefs, and on an island they again took up their position. From this secure spot it was thought imprudent to proceed further without having an interview with the chiefs of the different tribes as they advanced.

After the interview in which it was explained that the present visit of the whites among them was with the double object of making peace between themselves and the Nez Perces and of furnishing them with their wants. They were informed that the Nez Perces had made overtures of peace, they on their part, it was hoped, would not withhold their consent. When the word peace was mentioned one of the chiefs smiled, "Peace with the Shaw-ha-ap-tens," said he, then looking McKenzie steadfastly in the face and pointing to the current of the river, "Do you see that current?" said he. "Stop it then," exclaimed the great man. "That's impossible," rejoined McKenzie. "So is peace with the Shaw-ha-ap-ten, they are at this moment on our land and perhaps before night my wives and my children will be scalped by them!" McKenzie soothed the old chief and assured him that the whites would do their utmost to promote peace. That the whites were willing if encouraged to open a trade with the great Snake nation, a people whose land by lying so remote must at all times be ill provided with every necessary as well as the more essential part of their warlike implements. Adding to these professions a few trifling presents which left a favourable impression. This done, our friends prepared to change their quarters.

It was not McKenzie's intention on setting out to have visited these Indians or entered on the peace question at all, deferring these points until he had first conveyed and placed his men on the field of their labours; but having thus unexpectedly met with them and apprehending that he might not find them so conveniently at any other time, he now resolved on taking them tribe by tribe on his way and settling the business at once.

As our people advanced several bands were met and the same routine of peace-making gone through. One day as they journeyed they fell in with a friendly band of the Snakes, who gave them intelligence that a grand war party of the Indians inhabiting the east side of the mountains[3] were a short distance ahead of them. While these Indians and our people were in communication, a courier from behind overtook them with the news that five war parties of the Nez Perces men were also at their heels! and had killed several of the Snakes the preceding day. Verifying the words of the chief. Indian report is always to be received with great caution; yet our people thought it well to make a halt. Crowds of the banditti were emerging from all quarters and fleeing toward their stronghold in the mountains, a sure sign that some connection was apprehended. These manoeuvres convinced our people that there must be some truth in the reports. Under the circumstances they took up their stand in a small point of woods partly surrounded by the river, there resolving to wait for the present.

The friendly little band that had communicated the information to our people notwithstanding the most urgent entreaties would not remain with them but had turned off, preferring the security of the forests to the slender protection of the whites. Several other parties of the Snakes however came and encamped along with our people, depending on them for support. Other parties passed and repassed without stopping. The Nez Perces behind, the Blackfeet before, the hostile Snakes everywhere around; our people were completely surrounded. It was therefore beyond human foresight to see a way out of such a combination of evils as threatened them on all sides.

The Nez Perces finding that their enemies the Blackfeet intervened between them and the Snakes, wheeled about in another direction and our people heard nothing more of them. But the Snakes and Blackfeet had a severe battle which ended in favour of the

[3] Blackfeet Indians.

former. Thirty Blackfeet and more Snakes strewed the well-contested field. As soon as the vanquished retreated the Snakes paraded about, exhibiting their trophies within sight of our friends. Victory stimulated to revenge; the Snakes therefore assumed a high tone. They came in crowds from their hiding places and joining the victorious party in their scalp dancing and scalp singing, formed a host of at least five or six thousand. Their huts, their tents altogether resembled a city in an uproar, and their scattered fires and illumination during the nights exhibited rather an awful spectacle to our encircled friends. Their shouts and yelling, their gestures and frantic movements were no less terrifying.

After eighteen days' delay at Woody Point the natives moved off almost in a body, and from the spies which kept hovering about these Indians, we attained seasonable advice that the hostile tribes had retired: consequently, our party might pass on in all safety. So that by a combination of fortunate circumstances, they were again relieved from danger.

Having left their recent abode accompanied by a friendly chief and his band, our people marched through an open and delightful country. During this part of their journey they crossed the spot where the great battle had been recently fought and in many places saw putrid carcasses and human bones scattered about. And here the chief that accompanied our party pointed out the skulls of their enemies. "Look at these," said he to McKenzie. "The heads of the Blackfeet are much smaller than those of the Snakes, and not so round." They also crossed innumerable trails on which the tracks were still quite fresh; but at that period all appeared to be quiet. After thirty-three days' hazardous travelling, reckoning from the time Kittson joined the party on an island, they arrived at their hunting ground. Here the men were equipped for the winter and commenced hunting.

McKenzie intended, should the natives prove peaceably inclined, and the traffic get on smoothly among them, to spend part of the winter in examining the country further to the south. He was likewise anxious to have an interview with the principal chiefs of the Snake nation, not having hitherto seen them. In his letter to me

WILD HORSES

A water color by Alfred Jacob Miller

A NEZ PERCÉ INDIAN

A water color by Alfred Jacob Miller

dated "Black Bears' Lake,[4] Sept. 10th 1819," he remarked, "We have passed a very anxious and troublesome summer. War parties frequent. In danger often; but still we do not despair. Time and perseverance will do much. You will make no arrangements for forwarding our supplies, we have had enough of that already, I will accompany the spring returns and try to be at Fort Nez Perces by the 20th of next June." This letter was brought to me by an Indian of the falls at the latter end of October.

We have now given the reader some idea of an Indian trader's life in these parts, and by way of following up the subject a little further, we shall give an account of how trapping with a large party is generally carried on among Indians.

A safe and secure spot near wood and water is first selected for the camp. Here the chief of the party and property resides. It is often exposed to danger, or sudden attack in the absence of the trappers, and requires a vigilant eye to guard against the lurking savages. The camp is called headquarters. From hence all the trappers, some on foot, some on horseback according to the distance they have to go, start every morning in small parties in all directions, ranging the distance of some twenty miles around. Six traps is the allowance of each hunter, but to guard against wear and tear the complement is more frequently ten. These he sets every night and visits again in the morning sometimes oftener; according to the distance or other circumstances. The beaver taken in the traps are always conveyed to the camp, skinned, stretched, dried, folded up with the hair inside, laid by, and the flesh used for food. No sooner therefore has a hunter visited his traps, set them again, and looked out for some other place than he returns to the camp, to feast and enjoy the pleasures of an idle day.

There is however much anxiety and danger in going through the ordinary routine of a trapper's duty! For the enemy generally is lurking about among the rocks and hiding places watching an opportunity, the hunter has to keep a constant lookout. And the gun is often in one hand, while the trap is in the other; but when several are together, which is often the case in suspicious places, one half

4 Bear Lake.

set the traps, and the other half keep guard over them. Yet notwithstanding all the precautions some of them fall victims to Indian treachery.

The camp remains stationary while two-thirds of the trappers find beaver in the vicinity, but whenever the beaver gets scarce, the camp is removed to some more favourable spot: in this manner the party keeps moving from place to place during the whole season of hunting. Whenever serious danger is apprehended, all the trappers make for the camp. Were we however to calculate according to numbers, the prospects from such an expedition would be truly dazzling, say twenty-five men with each six traps, to be successfully employed during five months, that is, two in the spring, and three in the fall, equal to one hundred thirty and one working days, the result would be 58,950 beaver! Practically however the case is very different. The apprehension of danger at all times is so great that three-fourths of their time is lost in the necessary steps taken for their own safety! There is also another serious drawback unavoidably accompanying every large party. The beaver is a timid animal, the least noise therefore made about its haunt will keep it from coming out for nights together; and noise is unavoidable where the party is large. But when the party is small, the hunter has a chance of being more or less successful. Indeed were the nature of the ground such as to admit of the trappers moving about in safety at all times, and alone, six men with each six traps would, in the same space of time and at the same rate, kill as many beavers, say 4716, as the whole twenty-five could be expected to do! and yet the evil is without a remedy. For no small party can exist in these parts. Thence the reason why beaver are so numerous.

Having conducted McKenzie and his party to their hunting ground, we shall take our leave of them while we notice the occurrences at Fort Nez Perces, and then in due time, we will take up the subject of the Snake expedition again. Our last entry of this place was the effect our establishment had on the conduct of the Indians. Yet with all their submission it was more apparent than real, for I have never experienced more anxiety and vexation than among these people. Not an hour of the day passed but some insolent fellow, and frequently fifty at a time, interrupted us and made us feel our unavoidable dependence upon their caprice. "Give me a gun," said one. "I want ammunition," said another; a third wants a knife, a flint or something else. Give to one, you must give to all! Refuse them, they immediately get angry, tell us to leave their lands, and threaten to prevent our people from going about their duties. Their constant theme, "Why are the whites so stingy with their goods? They hate us or they would be more liberal." A fellow raps at the gate, calling out, "I want to trade," when you attend his call, he laughs in your face, and has nothing to sell! In short, they talk of nothing but war, think of nothing but scalp dancing, horse racing and gambling: and when tired of these, idling is their delight. On every little hill they are to be seen all day in groups, with a paper looking glass in one hand, and a paint brush in the other. Half their time is spent at their toilet, or sauntering about our establishment. In their own estimation they are the greatest men in the world. The whites, who labour, they look upon as slaves and call them by no other name! I had therefore to lay down a rule in all my dealings with them. However sudden the call might be, I never obeyed it until I first walked backward and forward across the fort twice. Nothing then surprised me or ruffled my temper, and I often found the benefit of the plan.

These Indians with all their independence are far from being a happy people. They live in a constant state of anxiety. Every hostile movement about the frontier excites alarm and sets the whole country on the qui vive.

We have already noticed that a band of the Shaw-ha-ap-tens, on its return from a new expedition against the Snakes, killed Detorme and Icanvene, two of Kittson's men, on their way to this place with the Snake returns. They also killed several of the Snakes. One evil often leads to another, for the Shaw-ha-ap-tens had no sooner got back than a Snake party were at their heels; but happening to fall in with a few stragglers frolicking among the bushes gathering berries, belonging to the Walla Walla camp, not three miles from our fort, they killed one man, four women and five children, then recrossed the mountains and got off clear, carrying along with them the scalps of their victims and two young women and a man as slaves.

The two captive women as well as the man being of some rank caused a tremendous commotion at this place. The first intimation we had of this sanguinary affair was the next morning after the deed had been committed. Going on the gallery as soon as I got up, according to usual custom, I perceived at no great distance a dense crowd of people, some on foot, some on horseback, making for the fort in the most frantic and disorderly manner and filling the air with shrieks and commotions. It struck me the instant I saw them that it was a war party, calling therefore all hands together every man was placed at his post, and we anxiously awaited their approach. Having only ten men about the fort at the time.

As they drew near, the more frantic and tumultuous they became. I inspected the men's arms and finding one fellow named Quinze Sous, pale and agitated and his gun still unloaded, and fearing his cowardly conduct might influence others, for they were all more or less panic-struck, I drew the iron ramrod out of his gun and giving him a rap or two over the head with it, drove him off the gallery and locked him up in one of the stores, then returning, I promised a reward to every one of the others that would behave well. By this time the crowd had reached the fort gate and I saw for the first time that it was no war party but our own Indians! Yet seeing them carry a number of dead bodies, the affair appeared still more mysterious. And as Indians often carry false colours to decoy the unwary, we were determined to be on our guard. Friend or foe we were prepared to receive them. The number might have been four hundred in all. But they were a mixture of men and women. It may be asked where were all our guns, our bastions, and strong fort if a rabble of Indians gave us so much anxiety? Our object, we answer, was not merely defence but peace and friendship; we could have, few as we were, easily dispersed the crowd; but one shot from our guns would have sealed our ruin and that of our friends in the Snake country. The whites never oppose force to force but in the last extremity.

The crowd no sooner reached the fort gate than the seven bodies were laid on the ground, the weather being sultry the bodies were much swollen and extremely offensive. This was no sooner done than the savage habit of cutting themselves, mingled with howling and shrieks of despair, commenced. The scene was horrible. Under such circumstances sympathy for the living as well as the dead was excited, because their pain and suffering must have been acute, and this as a matter of course increased their inclination to violent mourning.

To have seen those savages streaming all over with blood, one would suppose that they could not have survived such acts of cruelty inflicted on themselves; but such wounds although bad are not dangerous. To inflict those wounds the person takes hold of any part of his skin between his forefinger and thumb, draws it out to the stretch and then runs a knife through it between the hand and the flesh which leaves, when the skin resumes its former place, two unsightly gashes resembling ball holes out of which the blood issues freely. With such wounds and sometimes others of a more serious nature the near relatives of the deceased completely disfigure their bodies.

As soon as the bodies were laid on the ground with their crimson dyed garments, one of the chiefs called by the Canadians, Gueule Plat[5] called out to me with an air of effrontery, "Come out here." The moment this call reached me, I felt a conflict between duty and inclination. Refuse the call I could not, yet I obeyed it with reluctance, and almost wished myself with Quinze Sous in the store, rather than perforce where I was. Turning round to the sentinel at the door I told him to lock the gate after me and keep a sharp lookout. The moment I appeared outside the gate so horrible was the uproar that it baffles all description. Intoxicated with wrath and savage rage, they resembled furies more than human beings. Their hasty, wild and forbidding looks were all directed towards me, as if I had been the cause of their calamity.

Tum-a-tap-um, the chief, then coming up to me and pointing to one of the dead bodies, said, "You see my sister there," then uncovering the body to show the wounds, added, "That is a ball hole!

5 Broad Feather.

The whites," said he again, "have murdered our wives and our children! They have given guns and balls to our enemies. Those very guns and balls have killed our relations." These words were no sooner uttered than they were repeated over and over again by the whole frantic crowd, who hearing the chief believed them to be true. Enthusiasm was now at its height. Their gestures, their passionate exclamations, showed what was working within and I expected every moment to receive a ball or an arrow! one word of interruption spoken by me at the critical moment in favour of the whites might have proved fatal to myself. I therefore remained silent watching a favourable opportunity and also examining closely the holes in the garments of the dead bodies. The holes, I was convinced, were made by arrows and not by balls as the chief had asserted; but it remained for me to convince others when an opportunity offered.

Every violent fit of mourning was succeeded, as is generally the case among savages, by a momentary calm, as soon therefore as I perceived the rage of the crowd beginning to subside, nature itself beginning to flag, I availed myself of the interval to speak in turn: for silence then would have been tacit acknowledgement of our guilt. I therefore advanced, and taking the chief by the hand said in a low tone of voice, as if overcome by grief, "My friend, what is all this? Give me an explanation. You do not love the whites! you have told me nothing yet!" Tum-a-tap-um then turning to his people beckoned to them with the hand to be silent, entire silence was not to be expected. He then went over the whole affair from beginning to end. When the chief ended and the people were in a listening mood I sympathized with their misfortunes, and observed that the whites had been undeservedly blamed. "They are innocent," said I, "and that I can prove. Look at that," said I, pointing to an arrow wound which no one could mistake. "The wounds are those of arrows, not balls." Nor were the Snakes themselves so much to blame as we shall be able to show.

At these accusations the chief looked angry, and there was a buzz of disapprobation among the crowd; but I told the chief to listen patiently until I had done. The chief then composed himself, and

I proceeded. "After your solemn acquiesence in a peace between yourselves and the Snakes, through the influence of the whites, the Shaw-ha-ap-tens violated the sacred pledge by going again to war across the Blue Mountains; and not content with having killed their enemies they killed their friends also! They killed two of the whites! The Snakes in the act of retaliation have therefore made you all to mourn this day, they have made the whites to mourn also! But your loss is less than ours, your relations have been killed; but still you have their bodies, that consolation is denied us. Our friends have been killed; but we know not where their bodies lye!" These facts neither the chief nor the crowd could gainsay. And the chief with a loud voice explained them to the listening multitude. When they with one voice exclaimed, "It is true, it is true." Leaving the chief I then entered the fort and taking some red cloth, laid six inches of it on each body, as a token of sympathy, then told them to go and bury their dead but a loud fit of lamentation now closed the scene. The bodies were taken up, and the crowd moved off in a quiet and orderly manner.

But the satisfaction we enjoyed at the departure of the savages was of short duration, for they were scarcely out of sight and I scarcely inside when another band related to those that had been killed arrived at the fort gate and the loud and clamorous scene of mourning was again renewed.

Among the second crowd of visitors was a fellow dignified by the name of Prince, and brother to one of the young women who had been carried off by the Snakes. Prince encamped within fifty yards of the fort, and his tent was no sooner pitched than he began to chant the song of death. When an Indian resorts to this mode of mourning it is a sure sign that he has thrown his body away, as the Indians term it, and indicates self destruction. Being told of Prince's resolution, I went to his tent to see him and found him in a standing position, with his breast leaning upon the muzzle of his gun, his hair dishevelled, and singing with great vehemence. He however never raised his head to see who I was. I knew all was not right, and spoke to him but received no answer, so I went off to return to the fort; but had scarcely advanced twenty yards from his tent before I heard the report of a gun behind me, returning back again I found the unfortunate fellow lying on the ground weltering in his blood, his gun partly under him. He was still breathing. The ball had entered his left breast below the nipple and come out near the backbone. The wound was bleeding freely, and he disgorged great quantities of blood. I went to the fort for some assistance, but on our return I expected that every moment would have been his last; yet we dressed his wound and did what we could to allay his suffering.

The Indians now assembled in great numbers, and were noisy and violent. In the first instance they threw all the blame of the unfortunate affair on the whites; but in their rage and violence they quarreled among themselves, and this new feature in their policy removed the odium in some degree from the whites and threw the tide of popular fury into another channel. During the affair one of those unfortunate wretches called medicine men happened to be sitting at the fort gate when a brother of the man who had shot himself went up to him, saying, "You dog you have thrown your bad medicine on my brother and he is dead, but you shall not live," and in saying so shot him dead on the spot! The ball in passing through his body went more than three inches into one of the fort palisades. I was standing on the gallery at the moment he was shot, and, had it been on any other occasion but in the midst of a quarrel between the Indians themselves, we certainly should have revenged his death on the spot for he was an excellent Indian and a sincere friend of the whites.

The scene now assumed a threatening aspect. Guns, bows, arrows, and every missile that could be laid hold of came in requisition. Robes, feathers, bells, belts, and trinkets of every description were rattling about in true savage style. The fellow who had just shot the medicine man was shot in turn, and before the chiefs arrived or could get a hearing three others were shot. The place appeared more like a field of battle than anything else: beside the five bodies that lay lifeless on the ground, twice that number were desperately wounded.

As soon as the deadly quarrel began, not knowing the intent of the Indians nor how it might end, I shut the gates and kept as clear of the quarrel as possible. In the midst of the confusion the Indians kept pouring in from all quarters, adding fuel to the flame, and some of them in approaching the place, thinking it was a quarrel between the whites and themselves, fired a shot or two at the fort before they were aware of their mistake, which made us take to our bastions. Our matches were lighted, guns pointed and we ourselves watching the manoeuvres of the savages around us. For one unguarded shot would have involved us in the quarrel, and that it was our intent to avoid as it would have put an end to all our prospects, both in the Snake as well as the Nez Perces quarter.

As soon as the chiefs could get a hearing, peace was gradually restored. The five dead bodies were removed to the Indian camp at a distance from the fort, but such a scene I should never wish to witness again. This affray happening at our very door gave us much uneasiness, and to keep the balance of good will at all times in our favour was a task of more than ordinary difficulty.

The day after, the different tribes assembled at Fort Nez Perces, and I had my hands full; the Shaw-ha-ap-tens arrived, the Cayouses, the Walla Wallas, and many others. The affairs of the preceding day; the subject of our adventures in the Snake country, and the peace business were discussed. A thousand questions were put and answered. Each chief betrayed impatience, one and all had to be satisfied. The whites were indirectly taxed with all the late troubles. They threatened to disregard the peace, and the late disasters furnished them with a cause. They were bent on going to war with the Snakes again. As this step might have proved fatal to our intercourse in that quarter, I tried every plan to divert them from it. I invited them into the fort to smoke. There matters were talked over again, and they smoked and talked during several meetings. A whole week was spent in this business. At last however we came to terms, we all smoked the calumet of peace once more! And the chiefs solemnly promised not to renew hostilities until at least our friends had left the Snake country.

As soon as our troubles were over and matters had settled down to their ordinary level, I took Prince, the man who in cool despair had shot himself, under my care as he still survived and showed symptoms of returning strength, kept him, and nursed him from July until December following, when he was so far recovered as to be able to ride on horseback. At this stage, he accompanied his relations to their wintering ground: but as he was still unable to undergo the fatigue of hunting or endure much exercise, I fitted him out with the means of passing the winter comfortably and we parted.

In the spring on the return of the Indians to the fort, I was much pleased to see Prince, strong and hearty as ever! "I am sure," said he to me, when we met, "you are glad to see me well." I told him I was very happy to see him recovered, and hoped he would be a good man and love the whites. He appeared thankful, and promised he would. "But," said he to me again, "You must give me a new gun, you know my relations destroyed my gun when I got wounded." "I know they did," said I; "but I have no gun to spare." "I have been long sick," said he, "and am poor. I have nothing to buy one myself, and I cannot hunt without a gun." "You have plenty of horses," said I, "why don't you buy one?" On my saying so, he hung down his head. I saw however that my refusal did not please him, and that my telling him to sell his horses and buy a gun pleased him less. But I thought I had done enough for him, and the more I gave him the less he would hunt. So I told him again I had no gun to spare. That I had nursed him for half a year and saved his life, and that now as he was well he must try and provide for himself.

"What," said he sharply, "do you love a gun more than you love me?" "No," said I, "but I have no gun to spare." On my saying so he got rather sulky and held down his head, the first indication of an Indian's displeasure, for he had been telling his friends, as I heard afterwards, that I would refuse him nothing. All this however passed between us without remark, and as I thought, of good will on both sides. I took no further notice of what he said but turned round to another Indian, to settle some little business I had with him. While doing so Prince suddenly started up, saying, "Since you are so stingy, and love your gun so well, keep it: and give me an axe, perhaps you will refuse me that too!" I was rather nettled at the fellow's impertinence, so I refused him; "What my friend," said I, "are you really angry with me?" "Yes," said he abruptly, "The white people have two mouths, and two words. You said you liked me, and yet you refuse me a gun; but give me an axe, and keep your gun, since you prefer to see me like a squaw with an axe, rather than like a man with a gun." "What, my friend," said I to him, "have I not done enough for you? Have I not done more for you than all your own people put together? Have I not saved your life? Have I not supported you all the winter? Yes, my friend, I have done so. And now that you are well, you must do for yourself. I cannot let you have an axe or anything else, unless you pay for it as others do; nor does your present conduct merit any more favours at my hand," and saying so, I turned round to the Indian I had been speaking to a little before.

But the moment I turned round from him he caught hold of a gun and made an attempt to shoot me in the back; but it fortunately missed fire, and before I had time to turn around the gun was taken out of his hands by one of the chiefs, who holding it up in the air, fired off the shot! and it was fortunate that it missed fire the first time.

After this Prince stood sullen and motionless. "Is it because I saved your life, that you wished to deprive me of mine?" but to this he made no reply. Taking therefore a ball out of one of his comrade's pouches close by I offered it to him, saying, "let me see now if you really wish to kill me, there is a ball, load your gun again," and then stood before him. But he would neither take the ball nor reload the gun. This scene took place in the presence of more than fifty Indians, who remained silent spectators. I then entered the fort leaving Prince still standing; but a few minutes afterwards he sneaked off and left the place: for the savages could not forbear reproving him for his conduct.

The reader has now a specimen of the gratitude which a trader often meets with among the barbarous people. But we must follow Prince a little further.

After leaving the place, he happened to meet at a little distance from the fort, one of my men, a Canadian by the name of Meloche, coming home from a hunting trip. Prince therefore went up to him with a smiling countenance. After shaking hands and talking a little with Meloche, Prince said to him, "Let me see your gun," he made no hesitation but handed it to him, for he looked upon Prince as one of ourselves, being so long about the place. And Meloche often helped to take care of him during his sickness. No sooner however had he got the gun into his own hands than he, as Indians generally do, examined whether or not it was loaded, and finding it was, leaped on his horse, drew to one side, and began to quarrel with Meloche and reproach the whites, alluding to my having refused him a gun and axe. But Meloche was not a man to be frightened by mere words, and Prince, to prevent his getting hold of him, turned round, shot Meloche's horse, kept the gun, and scampered off!

Meloche arrived at the fort enraged, got a horse and gun and would have pursued after Prince at all hazard had I not prevented him, intending rather to adopt some milder plan for the recovery of his gun and the loss of his horse; but time was not allowed us to put this plan into execution. Not many days afterwards, Prince exchanged the gun with another Indian for a horse. The Indians going out to hunt one day Prince in approaching an elk was accidentally shot dead by a ball out of the very gun he took from Meloche! The fellow who had it happened unluckily to be approaching the same animal as Prince but in an opposite direction, when on firing the ball missed the elk, glanced from a tree, and proved fatal to Prince! With these remarks we hasten to close the present chapter, reserving for our next the proceedings in the Snake country.

8. COUNCIL OF THE SNAKES

THE BUSINESS of the year being ended, we resume the subject of the Snake expedition. McKenzie in following up his first intention disposed of his trappers to the best advantage, and taking with him three men and an Indian chief left his people and set out on a trip of discovery towards the south; but had not proceeded far before he met with the main body of the great Snake nation headed by the two principal chiefs Pee-eye-em and Ama-qui-em. An interview with these two great men in reference to the peace was McKenzie's chief object, in the trip he had undertaken. He therefore lost no time but returned back to where he had left his people, the Indians accompanying him.

The regularity and order of these people convinced the whites that they were under a very different government to any other they had yet seen in the country, even preferable to the arrangements of the whites, the influence of the two great chiefs being at all times sufficient to restrain and keep the whole in subordination, and our friends free from annoyance. Not so was it among our own trappers: for although McKenzie had only been absent from them ten days, on his return he found that the Iroquois had commenced their old tricks of trafficking away their hunting implements with the natives, and their familiar and criminal intercourse had already drawn down on them the contempt of the Indians.

To rectify therefore the follies and the animosities which had been engendered between both parties by the conduct of the thoughtless Iroquois, was difficult and well nigh brought the whites into a disagreeable scrap, but the good sense and conduct of the chiefs on this occasion was in the highest degree praiseworthy, so that matters were soon amicably adjusted. This done, McKenzie turned his attention to the Indians and the peace; but before we

165

enter upon that subject we shall give some account of the Snake Indians as a nation.

The great Snake nation may be divided into three divisions, namely the Sherry-dikas, or Dog-eaters, the War-are-ree-kas, or Fish-eaters and the Ban-at-tees or Robbers.[1] But as a nation, they all go by the general appellation of Sho-sho-nes, or Snakes. The word sho-sho-ne means in the Snake language "Inland." The Snakes on the west side of the Rocky Mountains are what the Sioux nation is on the east side, the most numerous and the most powerful in the country. The Sherry-dikas are the real Sho-sho-nes, and live in the plains hunting the buffalo. They are generally slender but tall, well made, rich in horses, good warriors, dressed well, clean in their camps and in their personal appearance bold and independent.

The War-are-ree-kas are very numerous; but neither united nor formidable. They live chiefly fishing and are to be found along all the rivers, lakes and water pools throughout the country. They are more corpulent, slovenly, and indolent than the Sherry-dikas. Badly armed, badly clothed, they seldom go to war. Dirty in their camps, in their dress, and in their persons, and differing so far in the general habits from the Sherry-dikas that they appeared as if they had been people belonging to another country. These are the defenseless wretches the Blackfeet and Piegans from beyond the mountains generally make war upon. The foreign mercenaries carry off the scalps and women of the defenseless War-are-ree-kas, and the horses of the Sherry-dikas; but are never formidable nor bold enough to attack the latter in fair and open combat.

The Ban-at-tees, or Mountain Snakes live a predatory and wandering life in the recesses of the mountains, and are to be found in small bands, or single wigwams among the caverns and rocks. They are looked upon by the real Sho-sho-nes themselves as outlaws. Their hands against every man, and every man's hands against them! They live chiefly by plunder. Friends and foes are alike to them. They generally frequent the northern frontiers and other mountainous parts of the country. In summer they go almost naked

[1] These tribal subdivisions are the present Shoshones, Snakes, and Bannacks.

but during winter they clothe themselves with the skins of rabbits, wolves, and other animals.

They are complete masters of what is called the cabalistical language of birds and beasts, and can imitate to the utmost perfection the singing of birds, the howling of wolves, and the neighing of horses, by which means they can approach, day or night, all travellers, rifle them and then fly to their hiding places among the rocks. They are not numerous, and are on the decline. Bows and arrows are their only weapons of defence.

The country, then, that the other Snake tribes claim as their own and over which they roam is very extensive. It is bounded on the east by the Rocky Mountains, on the south by the Spanish waters.[2] On the Pacific or west side by an imaginary line beginning at the west end or spur of the Blue Mountains behind Fort Nez Perces and running parallel with the ocean to the height of land beyond the Umpqua River, in about north Lat. 41. This line never approaches within one hundred and fifty miles of the Pacific. And on the north by another line running due east from the said spur of the Blue Mountains and crossing the great south branch or Lewis River at the narrows, till it strikes the Rocky Mountains two hundred miles north of the Stone Pilot Knobs,[3] or the place hereafter called the "Valley of Troubles."[4] The Snake country therefore contains an area, on a rough calculation, of about 150,000 square miles. For an Indian country it may be called thickly inhabited, and may contain 36,000 souls or nearly one person to every four miles square.

With all their experience our friends possessed but a very confused idea of the Snakes, both as to their names or numbers. One would call them Ban-nacks, and another Warracks, while a third would have them named Dogs! Nor was it till I had subsequently gone to their country, travelled, traded and conversed with them that I could learn anything like facts to be depended upon, and even after all I can state, it cannot be fully relied upon as entirely correct.

2 The Colorado River drainage.
3 The Grand Tetons.
4 The southern end of the Bitterroot Valley.

It was from the chiefs, who it would appear were very intelligent men, that McKenzie and his people, by indirect questions, came to the conclusion that the Snake nation numbered as stated; which of course is only our approximation to truth; to direct questions he could get no satisfactory answer, and that is the case with almost all the savages. Ask an Indian his name and he will hesitate to tell you! Ask him his age and you will receive an evasive answer! And when McKenzie put the direct question to the great chief Pee-eye-em, "How many Indians were there in the Snake nation?" he said, "What makes you ask that question?" "I should like to know," said he, "in order to tell our father, the great white chief." "Oh! oh! tell him then," said Pee-eye-em, "that we are as numerous as the stars."

In that part of the country where our friends had taken up their winter quarters the buffaloes were very numerous; thousands covered the plains. In this land of profusion the Indians likewise pitched their camp. The novelty of the presence of the whites and the news of peace soon collected an immense crowd together. Sherry-dikas, War-are-ree-kas, and the Ban-at-tees: so that before the end of a month there were, according to their statements, more than ten thousand souls in the camp! This immense body covered a space of ground of more than seven miles in length, on both sides of the river: and it was somewhat curious as well as interesting to see such an assemblage of rude savages observe such order.

The Sherry-dikas were the centre of this city. The War-are-ree-kas at one end, the Ban-at-tees at the other, forming as it were the suburbs. But in this immense camp, our people were a little surprised to see, on each side of the Sherry-dikas or main camp, nearly a mile of vacant ground between them and their neighbours the War-are-ree-kas and Ban-at-tees. This mysterious point was soon cleared up; for in proportion as the other Indians came in they encamped alongside the Sherry-dikas, till at last the whole vacant space was filled up, and the same of the War-are-ree-kas and Ban-at-tees. Each clan swelling its own camp, so that each great division was in a manner separate; and yet the whole was governed while thus assembled together by the voice of the two great chiefs, Pee-eye-em and Ama-qui-em. These two chiefs were brothers, and both fine-looking middle-aged men. The former was six feet two inches high, the latter above six feet, and both stout in proportion. Mc-Kenzie, himself the stoutest of the whites, was a corpulent heavy man, weighing 312 lbs. Yet he was nothing to be compared with either in size or weight to one of the Indian chiefs! His waist was too narrow by fourteen inches to button around Pee-eye-em!

Having now presented our readers with a brief outline of the Snake Indians, we next remark on that all-absorbing topic the peace. As soon as all the natives were assembled together, McKenzie made known to the chiefs his views as to the establishing of a general and permanent peace between themselves and their enemies on the northern frontier. Besides Pee-eye-em and Ama-qui-em there were fifty-four other dignitaries at the council board, six of whom were War-are-ree-kas; but not one Ban-at-tee! The rest were all Sherry-dikas and others belonging to the same class. After stating that the Nez Perces had agreed to the peace, and that it now depended solely upon them to have it finally ratified, McKenzie also signified to them that if the peace met with their cordial approbation and was once established throughout the country, the whites would then open a profitable trade with the Snake nation, and that henceforth they might be supplied with all their wants.

On hearing the concluding part of the proposition, the approbation was universal. All seemed to hail peace with their enemies as a most desirable object. Here the great Sachem, Pee-eye-em rose up, and was the first to speak. "What have we to do with it," said he, "We never go to war on the Nez Perces, or any other tribe in that quarter nor do they ever make war on us. These," said he, pointing to the War-are-ree-kas, and Ban-at-tee camps, "These are the people who disturb and wage war with the Nez Perces, and plunder the whites when in their power; but we have no hand in it. And for us to run after and punish the Ban-at-tees every time they do evil would be endless. It would be just as easy for us to hunt out and kill all the foxes in the country as to hunt and punish every Ban-at-tee that does mischief. They are like the mosquitoes, not strong but they can torment, and by their misdeeds and robberies, the War-are-ree-kas often suffer from the inroads of the northern tribes."

169

"The Blackfeet and Piegans,"[5] continued Pee-eye-em, "are our only enemies, a peace with them would be more desirable to us than a peace with the Nez Perces; but still, as it is the wish of the whites, the interest of the War-are-ree-kas, and to get our wants supplied, we cordially agree to it." Ama-qui-em spoke next and gave his consent. And then Ama-ketsa, one of the War-are-ree-kas, a bold and intelligent chief, spoke at great length in favour of the peace: and denounced the Ban-at-tees as a predatory race, and the chief cause of all the Snake trouble with the Nez Perces.

A whole week was spent in adjusting this important business, and our people were heartily tired of it. At last, when all the chiefs had given their consent, four of the Ban-at-tees were invited and their approach was marked by fear. The peace was fully explained to them, and they were distinctly told by Pee-eye-em and Ama-qui-em that if they did not regard the peace and live like the other Snake tribes, they would be punished with death.

In uttering these words, Ama-qui-em got quite enthusiastic. "Yes," said he to the trembling Ban-at-tees, "you are robbers, and murderers too! You have robbed the whites, you have killed the whites!" After this declaration he made a pause, as if regretting what he had said, and went on, "But why should I repeat a grievance, it is now past; let us utter it no more; go then home to your wives and your children. Rob no more! and we shall all be friends. You see the whites before you, they are our friends, you must be their friends. We must enforce the observance of peace, tell your people so, and forget it not."

The poor Ban-at-tees stood trembling and silent before the council, like criminals; but the moment Ama-qui-em sat down they all called out in the Snake language, "Kackana tabeboo, Kackana tabeboo." "We are friends to the whites, we are friends to the whites."

The business over, McKenzie presented Pee-eye-em and Ama-qui-em moccasins beaded with the emblem of peace. And at their request, one was given a blanket, a belt, and a skillet.

[5] The Blackfeet tribe is divided into the Blackfoot, Piegan, and Blood subtribal groups.

As the council broke up, our friends were anxious to know the truth of Ama-qui-em's assertion "that they, the Ban-at-tees, had already killed the whites," and therefore sent for that chief and enquired into the matter when Ama-qui-em, after some little hesitation, explained it by telling McKenzie that it was the Ban-at-tees that plundered and murdered Mr. Reed and his party in the autumn of 1813.

Our readers will no doubt have observed that we have omitted the customary ceremony of smoking during the present treaty of peace. Our reasons for so doing arose from the fact that the Snakes prefer their own tobacco to ours: and they are perhaps the only Indian nation on the continent that manufacture and smoke their own tobacco. Several of them were however seen with bits of our tobacco in their medicine bags; but scarcely any of them were seen to smoke. As to the ceremony of smoking at their councils, no Indians indulge in it more freely than the Snakes do.

The peace business was no sooner concluded than a brisk trade in furs commenced. In their traffic the most indifferent spectator could not but stare to see the Indians, chiefly War-are-ree-kas and Ban-at-tees, bringing large garments of four or five long beaver skins each, such as they use during winter for warmth, and selling them for a knife or an awl! and other articles of the fur kind, in proportion. It was however so with the Columbia Indians in our first years; but they soon learned the mystery of trade, and their own interest. So will the Snakes, for they are not deficient in acuteness. Horses were purchased for an axe each. And country provisions, such as dried buffalo, was cheap. Our people might have loaded a seventy-four gun ship with provisions, for buttons and rings!

But it was truly Indian-like to see these people dispose of articles of real value so cheap while the articles of comparatively no value at all, at least in the estimation of the whites were esteemed highly by them. When any of our people through mere curiosity wished to purchase an Indian headdress composed of feathers, or a necklace of bear's claws or a little red earth or ochre out of any of their mystical medicine bags, the price was enormous. But a beaver skin worth twenty-five shillings in the English market might have been purchased for a brass finger ring scarcely worth a farthing. A dozen of the same rings was refused for a necklace of bird claws not worth half a farthing.

Beaver or any kind of fur was of little or no value among these Indians, never having any traders for such articles among them. Nor could they conceive what our people wanted with their old garments. "Have the whites," said a chief one day, smiling, "not better garments themselves than ours?" Such garments however were not numerous, and were only used by the poorest sort. The Sherry-dikas were all clothed in buffalo robes and dressed deer skin; but no sooner had one and all of them seen European articles than they promised to turn beaver hunters; and this disposition was of course encouraged by our people. Axes, knives, ammunition, beads, buttons and rings were the articles most in demand. Clothing was of no value. A knife sold for as much as a blanket: and an ounce of vermilion was of more value than a yard of fine cloth! With the exception of guns which they might have got from other Indians, they had scarcely an article among them to show that they had ever mixed with civilized man, although it is well known they had of late years occasionally seen the whites.

Trade was no sooner over than Ama-qui-em mounted one of his horses, rode round and round the camp, and that of itself was almost the work of a day, now and then making a halt to harangue the Indians, remind them of the peace, their behaviour towards the whites, and to prepare them for raising camp. Three days successively this business was performed by the chief, and in the morning of the fourth all the Sherry-dikas decamped in a body and returned in the direction they had come. Although these people were very peaceable and orderly; yet our friends got heartily tired of the crowd, and were no less anxious than pleased to see them move off. The War-are-ree-kas and Ban-at-tees remained behind and were very annoying, they soon began to assume a haughty tone, even the Ban-at-tees began to hold up their heads and speak, after the Sherry-dikas had left us. "We now," said our friends, "often wished the Sherry-dikas back again." At the end of a couple of weeks more, however, they all went off but not without stealing three of the hunters' best horses and some beaver traps. So much for the peace! but the loss was less felt than the annoyance of the thieves who had stolen them: and our people were glad to get clear of them.

When the Indians had left the ground our hunters were divided into parties throughout the neighbourhood: and with the others, three of the Owhyhees went along a small river to trap, where no danger was apprehended. Our people were now left to pursue their business of hunting: and they trapped with great success for some time; but as soon as the winter set in, some of the banditti kept hovering about their camp with the intention of carrying off their horses, which subjected them to constant watching day and night. Our people therefore took advantage of a snow storm and removed some distance in order to be out of their reach.

During bad weather, which lasted ten days, their want of a guide, and their ignorance of the best passes through the mountains brought them into imminent peril of losing all their horses. At length however, they were fortunate enough to get a place of shelter where their animals could feed and they encamp in safety. Every one now felt that their horses were secure and themselves relieved from watching. And that they had outwitted the Indians! The very next morning after they had arrived, six of their horses were stolen! and a gun and two steel traps, which had been at the door of a hunter's tent, were carried off! The Indians had dogged them all the way and played them this trick at last. So that they had to adopt the same plan as before and watch all winter.

To those who had never travelled in these wilds, it may be interesting to know how the trapper's horses are fed and stabled during winter.

No fodder is provided for them; there is no stable nor shelter but the canopy of heaven above them. In snow up to their bellies and often a crust on the top as hard as ice, the horses beat down the crust, scrape off the snow with their forefeet, and feed on the dry and withered grass at the bottom, and passing the winter without a drop of water except from the icicles and snow they happen to eat with their dry and tasteless food. After passing the night in this manner they are bridled, saddled and ridden about by the hunters all day; and when they arrive at night, covered with sweat, tired and hungry, they are turned out again to dig their supper in the face of the deep snows, and in a cold ranging from 20 to 50 below zero of Fahrenheit's thermometer. The exercise may keep them in some degree warm; but the labour necessary to procure their food during night is full as fatiguing and laborious as their labour by day! and yet, these hardy and vigorous animals are always in good condition!

But to return to our subject. During the storm, while our people were on their journey one of the hunters named Hodgens, getting separated in the drift and snow from the party, was lost. In his wanderings he lost his horse, and from cold and hunger almost lost his life for the lock of his gun got broke, so that he could not make a fire, and during two days and two nights he had to weather the storm without any! but on the fourteenth day while scarcely able to crawl he had the good luck to fall on the main camp of the War-are-ree-kas. Then recognizing the chief's tent from the manner in which it was painted, he advanced towards it more like a ghost than a living being. On his entering, Ama-ketsa, surprised at his unexpected arrival and still more surprised at his emaciated appearance, stared him in the face for some time and could scarcely believe either his eyesight or his senses, that it was a white man; but as soon as he was convinced of the reality and made acquainted with his forlorn state, he ordered one of his wives to take off his shoes and put a new pair on his feet, gave him something to eat, and was extremely kind to him.

There he remained for eleven days in the chief's tent, nursed with all the care and attention of a child of the family until his strength was recovered. As soon as Hodgens was on his legs again, Ama-ketsa furnished him with a horse, some provisions, and sent one of his own sons to conduct him to the whites, and although Hodgens could give him no clues as to where the hunters were encamped, yet on the eighth day they arrived safe and sound at their friends', and as straight as if they had been led by line to them; which convinced our people that the Indians knew well the place of their retreat. Indeed in those parts to avoid the Indians would be to avoid themselves!

A party of our people had been out a whole week in search of Hodgens, found his dead horse, but despairing of finding him they returned to their campsite, all hopes of ever finding Hodgens alive vanished: and he did arrive. The pleasing and moreover the friendly conduct of Ama-ketsa toward him was a strong proof of that chief's good will towards our people. During our friends' stay in this place they had several surprises from the Indians, but they managed matters so well that no more of their horses were stolen.

There our friends passed a winter of five months, before the fine weather broke in upon them. Then removing to some distance commenced their spring hunt in a part of the country rich in beaver. While here they were visited by several bands of the Snakes, chiefly Sherry-dikas, and among others by Pee-eye-em and Ama-qui-em with a large squad of followers. The astonishment of these people was great on the day of their arrival at seeing two hundred and forty beaver caught by the hunters and brought into camp all at once.

These two great men were very anxious to know from McKenzie whether any of his people had been killed by the Indians during the winter, and being answered in the negative, they appeared much pleased. They were however told that one had been lost but was found. Little did our friends then think what had really happened, or what had invited the Indians to be so inquisitive. It will be remembered that three of the Owhyhees, as well as others had been fitted out on a little river to hunt beaver, and our people had not then heard any tidings of them. The three unfortunate men had all been murdered; this was what the chiefs had heard and were so anxious to know.

As our people were about to start on their homeward journey, the two friendly chiefs expressed an ardent wish to accompany them. "We wish," said they, "to see the Shy-to-gas," exclusive of seeing the Nez Perces, they thought by accompanying our people it would ensure their return to their lands again. Our people however did not discourage them from so tedious and hazardous a journey, and so embarrassing to our people. McKenzie however assured them of his speedy return. After spending about ten days with our people, they set out to return homeward. Both parties therefore took leave of each other with feelings of regret. As soon as the chiefs went off our people prepared to start and in the meantime, a party with an Indian guide was sent off to pick up and bring to the camp the three Owhyhees already mentioned. They found the place where they had been hunting, and where they had been murdered! The skeleton of one of them was found but nothing else. The fact that one of their horses had been seen in the possession of the banditti left no doubt in the minds of our people that they were the murderers.

The season being now well advanced our people had no time to lose, loading therefore one hundred and fifty-four horses with beaver and turning their faces towards Fort Nez Perces, the whole party commenced its homeward journey over hills, dales, rocks and rivers for twenty-two days' travel until they reached the long wished-for Blue Mountains again. There they spent a couple of days to rest and refresh their fatigued animals.

Various had been the reports brought to us by the Indians as to the fate of our friends in the Snake country, and as the time of their expected arrival drew near the more anxious of course we became, when one day a cloud of dust arose in the direction they were expected and by the aid of a spy glass we perceived from four to five hundred horses, escorted by as many riders, advancing at a slow pace in a line of more than two miles in length resembling rather a caravan of pilgrims than a trapping party. It was our friends! accompanied by a band of the Cayouse Indians, who had joined them as they emerged from the defiles of the Blue Mountains and soon after McKenzie, in his leather jacket, and accompanied by two of their chiefs, arrived at the fort. And this brings our subject up to the 22nd of June 1820. Nothing could exceed the joy manifested by all parties, and the success attending the expedition surpassing even our most sanguine expectations.

After a year's absence and laborious toil our friends required some rest, and while they were enjoying the interval of repose, we propose to employ ourselves in collecting from their conflicting and imperfect details some further notes and remarks on the Snake country, a country now become the centre of attraction to all parties connected with the trade.

The general features of the Snake country presents a scene incomparably grateful to a mind that delights in varied beauties of landscape and the manifold work of nature. The soft Blue Mountains whose summits are above the clouds and the wide extending plains with the majestic waters in endless sinuosities fertilizing with their tributary streams, a spacious land of green meadows. The towering hills and deep vallies, with their endless creeks and smiling banks, convey an idea that baffles all description.

The Rocky Mountains skirting this country on the east soon deviate from their stupendous heights into sloping ridges, which divide into a thousand luxurious vales giving rise to as many streams which abound with fish. The most remarkable heights in any part of the great backbone of America are three elevated insular mountains or peaks. They are seen at a distance of one hundred and fifty miles and the hunters very aptly designate them the Pilot Knobs.

In these parts are likewise found many springs of salt water, and large quantities of genuine salt, said to be as strong as any rock salt. South of Lewis River at the Blackfeet Lake[6] this article is very abundant and some of it six inches thick, with a strong crust on the surface. Near the same lake our people found a small rivulet of blue sulphurous water bubbling out from the base of a perpendicular rock more than three hundred feet in height. It was blue as indigo, and tasted like gun powder.

Boiling fountains having different degrees of temperature are very numerous, one or two were so very hot as to boil meat. In other parts among the rocks hot and cold springs might alternately be seen within a hundred yards of each other, differing in their temperature.

In passing many considerable rivers the Indian path or footway, instead of leading to a ford, would tend to a natural bridge. In-

6 Blackfoot Lake.

stances of this kind were very frequently met with. One of those bridges was arched over in a most extraordinary manner from one precipice to another, as if executed by the hand of man. It was no uncommon thing to fall in with rivers issuing suddenly out of the earth in the level plains, continuing a serpentine course for several miles, and then as suddenly enter the earth again. In one of these openings our people set their traps and at the first lift caught thirty beavers and one or two otters!

Some considerable streams were likewise observed to gush from the faces of the precipices some twenty or thirty feet from their summits, when on the top no water was to be seen! In two or three instances our people heard the noise of water under their feet, as if rapids, yet for several miles could neither get a drop to drink nor see any. That this country contains minerals there can be but little doubt; many indications of copper, iron, and coal were seen by our hunters.

In many parts the soil is composed of a rich black loam with indications of marl, this is the case in all the valleys but more frequently in the higher parts the eye is wearied with the sight of barren plains and leafless rocks.

It had been noticed how abundantly the natives of this quarter of the world are supplied with various kinds of food. The many nutritious roots, berries, and all kinds of uncultivated vegetables suited to the Indian palate which the country produces sets starvation at all seasons of the year at defiance, unless through the negligence of the natives themselves.

The War-are-ree-kas are expert and successful fishermen and use many ingenious contrivances in catching the salmon but the principal one is that of spearing: for this purpose the fisherman generally wades into the water often up to his waist and then cautiously catches the ascending fish, the water being clear, he poises and balances his fourteen-foot spear so well and throws it so adroitly that he seldom misses his aim. Others again erect scaffolds, while many stand on projecting rocks with scoop nets and in narrow channels they make weirs and form barriers.

With all these methods and many more in full operation and on almost every point the fish, except those in deep water, seldom escape the cunning and dexterous men.

From fifty to one hundred persons may be seen within a short distance of each other, all being employed in their own particular way. At the same time, the youngsters are not idle but employed in carrying home the fish to the camp, while the women, old and young, are each at their post, cleaning and preparing them for future use and particularly to meet the urgent demands of a long winter.

It seems the salmon is not terrified by noise, for in all these instances the fishermen call out loudly to each other. The immense quantities of this delicious and serviceable fish caught at even one of these great fish camps might furnish all London with a breakfast! and although many hundred miles from the ocean, our people affirmed that it still retains its richness and flavour. From the skill of the natives in curing them they continue at all seasons of the year sweet and in good condition. They are dried slowly in sheds covered above to exclude them from the rays of the sun.

Yet with all this profusion of salmon, buffalo in great profusion, and of vegetables before them, so depraved is the appetite of the savage, that he has often recourse by way of change or variety to the most nauseous and disgusting articles of food. Yet they are perhaps not more pernicious to health than many of the highly seasoned and deliterious dishes used among ourselves, and are no doubt just as delicious and palatable to the taste of the rude savage as the others are to the taste and palate of the polished member of civilized society. The Snakes feast on the most loathsome reptiles: such as serpents, mice, and lice! The curiosity of our people was often attracted by their singular mode of diet. Beneath the shade of the bushes is found an enormous kind of cricket. Skipping in the sun is a good-sized grasshopper, and gigantic mounds of pismires of enormous growth are likewise very frequent: all these insects are made subservient to the palate of the Snake Indian.

These delicacies are easily collected in quantity and when brought to the camp, they are thrown into a spacious dish along with a heap of burning cinders, then tossed to and fro for some time, until they are roasted to death. Under this operation they make a crackling noise like grains of gun powder dropped into a hot frying pan. They are then either eaten dry or kept for future use, as circumstances may require. In the latter case, a few handfuls of them are frequently thrown into a boiling kettle to thicken the soup.

One of our men had the curiosity to taste this mixture and said that he found it most delicious! Every reptile or insect that the country produces is after the same manner turned economically to account to suit the palate of the Snake Indian. But then in the accounting for taste I have seen the whites, in a camp teeming with buffalo, fowl, fish and venison of every kind, longing for horse flesh, purchase a horse and make a feast! Nor is it uncommon in these parts to see the voyageurs leave their rations of good venison and eat dogs' flesh! But the reader will cease to be surprised at these things when we mention the fact that people in this country, habituated as they are to such things, live almost as the Indians, eating everything at times that can be eaten. Some from choice, others from necessity.

Various herbs, shrubs, and plants are to be found: some of them highly estimated by the natives for their healing qualities. We have seen that the Snakes prefer their own tobacco to ours, and now speak of that plant more particularly. The Snake tobacco plant grows low, is of a brownish colour and thrives in most parts of the country, but is a favourite of sandy or barren soil, grows spontaneously and is a good substitute for tobacco, having the same aromatic flavour and narcotic effect as ours; it is weaker than our tobacco, but the difference in strength may be owing to the mode of manufacturing it for use. For this purpose their only process is to dig it and then rub it fine with the hands or pound it with stones until it is tolerably fine. In this state it almost resembles green tea. In smoking it leaves a green taste or flavour in the mouth.

Our people however seemed to like it very well, and often observed that with it they would never ask for any other; yet with all their fondness for the Snake tobacco, I observed that the moment they reached the fort the Snake importation was either bartered away or laid aside; one and all applied to me for good old twist! The Snakes would often bring it to our people for sale; but generally in small parcels, sometimes an ounce or two, sometimes a quart, and sometimes as much as a gallon. In their bartering propensities, however, they would often make our friends smile to see them with a beaver skin in one hand and a small bag containing perhaps a pint of the native tobacco in the other: the former they would offer for a paper looking glass worth two pence; while for the latter they would often demand an axe worth four or five shillings!

There is a fabulous story current among these people and universally believed, that they were the first smokers of tobacco on the earth! and that they have been in the habit of using it from one generation to another since the world began. That all other Indians learned to smoke and had their tobacco first from them. That the white people's tobacco is only good for the whites: and that if they would give the preference to the white people's tobacco and give up smoking their own it would then cease to grow on their lands and instead, a deleterious weed would grow up in its place and poison them all.

Although these people show a very absurd degree of ignorance in trade, they are nevertheless very ingenious. Their ingenuity in many instances show them to be in advance of their Columbia neighbours. As an example their skill in pottery. The clays to be found all over their native soil are of excellent quality, and have not been overlooked by them. They of all the tribes west of the mountains exhibit the best, if not the only specimens of skill as potters in making various kinds of vessels for their use and convenience. Our people saw kettles of cylindrical forms, a kind of jug, and our old-fashioned jars of good size, and not altogether badly turned about the neck, having stoppers. This last serves to carry water when on long journeys over parched places. These vessels although rude and without gloss are nevertheless strong, and reflect much credit on Indian ingenuity.

With travelling in the Snake country our friends were often at a loss how to get across the different rivers that barred their way, even about the Indian camps, from the singular part that the Snakes never made use of canoes, and they are the only Indians we know of that derive their living chiefly from the waters that are without them. Nor could our people assign any reason or learn the cause. Among all other fish tribes the canoe is an article considered indispensable. When the natives had occasion to cross any rivers a machine constructed of willows and bullrushes was hastily put together in form of a raft. This clumsy practice is always resorted to, although a dangerous mode of conveyance. Our people had frequently narrow escapes. At one time in crossing the main river on a raft of this description they happened to get entangled and were in the utmost danger of perishing, when some Snakes plunged in to their relief, and disentangling them swam the raft to shore, existing for more than an hour beyond their depth, notwithstanding it was at a period of the year when the river was partly froze over.

It was amusing to listen to the miraculous tales of our people of the manner in which the Snakes would elude their grasp. Passing through the meadows and flats of long grass, they would often perceive at distance a person walking. On these occasions they ran to see who it was; but after reaching the place and looking for some time around he would perceive to his astonishment the object of his search, as far from him in an opposite direction; not satisfied, he would start again; but to no purpose. The object would again and again show itself in another direction like two persons playing hide and seek.

The moment a Snake perceives a person pursuing him, he squats down among the grass; but instead of running forward to avoid his pursuer he runs backward, as if to meet him: taking care however to avoid him; so that by the time his pursuer gets to where he first saw the Snake, the Snake is back at the place from whence his pursuer started! In the art of instantaneous concealment and of changing places they are very remarkable. They are very appropriately called Snakes, the name they bear. This applies to the Bann-at-tees.

The trappers consisting of seventy men being fitted out anew, McKenzie was again at his post, and turning their faces once more towards the Snake country they left Fort Nez Perces on the fourth of July, after a short stay of only twelve days.

We now continue with another portion of our narrative, and in doing so we must in order to link together and under our subject as intelligibly as possible, take a retrospective view of the scenes that took place between the two rival companys in 1816.

The Courts of Justice having jurisdiction over all criminal offenders in this country as those of Canada, consequently all parties guilty or suspected of being guilty belonging either to the North West or to the Hudson's Bay companies during the hostile feuds were sent thither for trial. We now lay before our readers the result of those trials.

As soon as it was echoed abroad that an investigation into the rights of parties or the safety of individuals was about to take place, many of the North West managers were much perplexed. Expedients were found out, and every artifice that could have been devised was put in requisition to defeat the ends of justice, or rather screen themselves from guilt.

The chief outrages that had been committed were affected not by the ruling power but by their subordinates, many of whom were in consequence hastily got out of the way. And the more remote posts of the North as well as the Columbia had the benefit of their company. Those who could not be conveniently disposed of in this way were sent off among the Indians for a time: so that, when the various indictments were exhibited in the courts of law against individuals no evidence could be found to convict or prove any of them guilty: and this has and always will be the case in a country so remote from civilization and the seat of justice.

When all was done in Canada that could be done the main feature of the case remained just as it was, without being advanced or bettered, after a protracted investigation of four years! The Hudson's Bay Company still held their right of sovereignty over Rupert's Land, and the North West Company still disputed that right: for the lawyers, equally eminent on either side, claimed the victory. And this was the only result and it proved an abundant harvest to them, while it ruined their clients: costing the North West Company alone the enormous sum of fifty-five thousand pounds sterling! This conflict was the last expiring effort of the North West Company!

From litigation the parties had recourse to mediation, and the result of the negotiation was a union of the two companies into one by a "deed poll," bearing date the 26th day of March 1821. The deed poll provides among other things that the trade theretofore carried on "by both parties separately shall in future be carried on exclusively in the name of the Governor and Company of Adventurers of England Trading into Hudson's Bay," or in other words, "the Hudson's Bay Company." By this arrangement the North West Company merged into the Hudson's Bay Company. The deed poll may be very good, as well as the Charter; but we should have liked it much better, after all the evils we have witnessed arising from doubts and disputes, had the charter itself been renewed and stamped with the authority of the three estates, King, Lords, and Commons. And this would have most effectually set the question at rest forever and put all doubt as to the legality or illegality of the charter out of question. Monopoly saved Rupert's Land from anarchy in the day of troubles.

The downfall of the North West Company cast gloom over its numerous train of retainers and Canadian dependents and over the whole savage race from Montreal to the Rocky Mountains, and from the Rocky Mountains to the frozen ocean. A range of country greater in extent than the distance from Canada to England. The company of which we are now speaking was, during its day, the life and soul of the French Canadians. And the French Canadians were always great favourites with the Indians, no wonder then that a deep sympathy should be manifested on its ruin!

All those persons connected with the late North West Company when promotion was prior to the date of the "deed poll" were therein provided for, whereas all those expectant till time of promotion ran beyond that period were excluded; but some of the latter party were provided for by a pecuniary remuneration and among this last class it was my lot to fall, for my promotion did not

184

SNAKE INDIAN CAMP

A water color by Alfred Jacob Miller

Courtesy Walters Art Gallery

A WOMAN OF THE SNAKE TRIBE AND A WOMAN OF THE CREE TRIBE

A drawing by Charles Bodmer

come on till 1822. On this occasion, a letter from the Honourable William McGillivray put me in possession of the fact "that five hundred pounds sterling had been placed to my credit in their books." But I never received a penny of it!

Being thus released from the North West Company, I had to begin the world anew, making the third time in the course of my adventures. Still following however the irresistible propensity of my inclination to see more of the Indian country, I immediately entered the service of the Honourable Hudson's Bay Company; but for two years only.

My prospects in the Pacific Fur Company were but short lived, and my hopes vanished like dreams! In the North West Company, seven more years of my life had gone by, and with them my prospects, and there is a singular coincidence between both disappointments for had the American Company not failed in 1813 my promotion had taken place in 1814, so in like manner had not the North West become extinct in 1821 I had reached my expectation in 1822.

The high standing of the late North West Company induced all those in any way connected therewith to deposit their savings in the house of McGillivray Thain and Company, the then head of the concern, and every one having money there considered it just as safe as if it had been in the Bank of England. But the wild and profuse extravagances indulged in by keeping a horde of retainers during the law contest of four years sunk the house in debt, the firm became insolvent, which unfortunate circumstance involved all and deprived many individuals of all their hard earnings. I lost fourteen hundred pounds, which left me almost pennyless!

While these changes were passing on who should arrive in health and high spirits at Nez Perces after another year's absence but Mc-Kenzie from the Snake country, on the 10th of July 1821, with an increase of returns and the good fortune not to lose a man. At this period his contract of five years had expired, and the object of his mission was fully accomplished; but being too late in the season to get out of the country he passed the winter with me at Fort Nez Perces and crossed the Rocky Mountains in the autumn of 1822.

Although somewhat foreign to our subject, we may be permitted to follow this enterprising and indefatigable adventurer a little further. The man that but a few years before was only fit to eat horse flesh and shoot at a mark was now from his perseverance and success in recovering a losing trade become so popular among all parties in the fur trade that we find him snugly placed in the new "deed poll" as a Sachem of the high chiefs! Consequently instead of winding his way to Canada, after crossing the mountains, he shaped his course to the council at York factory:[7] nor had he been long there before he was raised a step higher by being appointed governor of Red River Colony,[8] the highest post in the country next to the Governor-in-chief. Which honorable station he held with great credit to himself and satisfaction to the public for a period of nearly ten years.

Availing himself of his rotation at the end of that period he made a tour through the United States, and during that tour, purchased a small estate delightfully situated near Lake Erie, called Mayville: then returning to Red River for his family he retired from the service and left the country altogether and went to spend the remainder of his days at his rural seat of Mayville, in the State of New York.

Mr. McKenzie was eminently fitted, both in respect of corporeal and mental qualities, for the arduous and very often dangerous labour of conducting the business of his employers in regions hitherto but rarely trodden by the foot of the civilized man, and among tribes as fickle in their manners. Capable of enduring fatigue and privations, no labour appeared too great, no hardships too severe. Bold and decided in the presence of danger, he was peculiarly adapted to strike awe into the heart of the savage, who has instinctive reverence for manly daring. Nor was he destitute of those less striking qualities that gain but do not awe mankind. Intimately acquainted with the disposition of the savages he had to deal with, he could adopt measures amongst them which to oth-

[7] Located on Hudson's Bay, at the mouth of the Hayes River.

[8] The Red River Colony was situated in the area between Lakes Manitoba and Winnipeg on the north, and the present international boundary on the south.

ers appears only extreme folly, and whose successful issue alone could evince that they had been prompted by the deepest sagacity and knowledge of human nature. The instance already recorded of his distributing his property among the Indian chiefs and finding it untouched on his return, after a considerable interval of time, is a sufficient proof of this. But Mr. McKenzie, notwithstanding his liberal endowments and education, for he had been designed for the ministry, had a great aversion to writing, preferring to leave the details of his adventures to the pen of others.

To travel a day's journey on snowshoes was his delight; but he detested spending five minutes scribbling in a journal. His travelling notes were often kept on a beaver skin written hieroglyphically with a pencil or piece of coal, and he would often complain of the drudgery of keeping accounts. When asked why he did not like to write his answer was, "We must have something for others to do." Few men could fathom his mind, yet his inquisitiveness to know the minds and opinions of others had no bounds. Every man he met was his companion: and when not asleep, he was always upon foot strolling backward and forward full of plans and projects, and so peculiar was this pedestrian habit that he went by the name of "Perpetual Motion."

9. JOURNEY OF A BOURGEOIS

T HE LAST CHAPTER closed the career of
the North West Company, McKenzie's adventures in the Snake
quarter, and placed the trade of the country in possession of the
Hudson's Bay Company. But before we take our leave finally of the
North Westers, there are yet a few fragments left which we propose, to make the reader thoroughly to comprehend his subject,
and we propose devoting the present chapter to these details.

The branch of mercantile pursuit which confines the trader to
a residence for a series of years among savages in the far distant
wilds of North America may appear in the light of banishment
more than an appointment of choice, in search of that competency
which in a variety of ways fortune places more or less within our
reach.

Yet of persons who have spent any portion of their years in these
countries few or none are known who do not look back with a
mixture of fond remembrance and regret on the scenes they had
passed, preferring the difficulties and dangers of their former precarious but independent habits to all the boasted luxuries and
restraints of polished society. There they spend a long and health-
ful life. The table groans with every species of venison, wild fowl,
and with every kind of wild fruits, while the simple element in its
purest state is their harmless beverage.

In the frequency of their voyages, the diversity of landscape
brings ample food for contemplation and delight. The indispensable discharge of duties in the thronged fort, or in the bustling
camp. Domestic endearments, the making provisions for the passing day, and the sport of the gun, together with the current events
among the tribes, furnish unbounded variety to banish unhappiness and ennui. At the very commencement of the fur trade, advan-

tages of the nature were never in the reach of the daring adventurer whose hazardous strides first traced out the futile paths of the Far West.

Their strength often proved unequal to their task; yet they had to push on ignorant of dangers before them, or what obstructions barred their retreat. They had no settled habitations or fortified holds to shelter them from the tempest or from the phrensy of the natives. They were ignorant of the languages, customs and manners of the tribes, whether they were well or ill disposed to them, or lived at peace or war with their neighbours. Without experience, it was not possible always to avert the storms ready to burst over their heads. Neither was it possible to enjoy tranquillity of mind and as for comforts, they were unknown. They had in fact everything to dread and guard against. But it must be admitted that in proportion to the well-known increase in the more essential points of gain, the secondary objects of security, convenience, and comfort have had due attention paid them. And where establishments of any standing (such as Spokane House was in its day) they are by no means wanting in the principal requisites of comfort; it may be said that the trader of this period has only to reap, in each successive year, at ease, the harvest planted for him by those who went before him. It is so now on the Columbia, and with all that range of country lying between the Rocky Mountains and the Pacific. The roads are pointed out to all new-comers, the paths known, the Indians more or less civilized, so that the leaders of this day have little left them to do.

From a terror of the hardships endured in the Indian countries, it was seldom that the first adventures could persuade any persons to follow them who were able to live decently at home. Their associates were consequently taken from the common hands, who did not either read or write. But the number of independent fortunes amassed in the Indian trade at length attracted the attention of creditable mercantile houses. Companies were formed, inducements were held out to young men of respectable families, and many of these instead of embarking as had been customary for the West or East Indies preferred the road to Canada, in order to join the association which had by this time assumed the title of the North West Company.

These young men did not hesitate to sign indentures as clerks for the period of seven years, and to these were generally attached twice seven more, before such situations became vacant as were to crown their ambition. Hence ordinary men were weeded out of the country, and it is not now strange to find the common Canadian, the half-breed, the civilized Indian, the native of the land, and the man of gentle birth and education at their respective duties in the same establishment, along the immense chain of communication which extends as far as the frozen ocean, and from the Atlantic to the Pacific Ocean.

The nature of their trade has a mixture of the mercantile and the military. The clerks have charge of trading posts, according to their merits and abilities, some upon a very considerable scale. They are first taught to obey, afterwards they learn to command. At all times much is expected of them. It sometimes happens to be long before they receive charge of a first-rate establishment; but when the general posture of affairs is propitious to their employers, it is not very often that their laudable prospects are disappointed. They at length arrive at the long wished goal of partners, and are entitled to a vote in all weighty decisions, and are henceforth styled Esquires.

The Bourgeois lives in comfort. He rambles at his pleasure, enjoys the merry dance or the pastime of some pleasing game. His morning ride, his fishing rod. His gun and his dog, or a jaunt of pleasure to the environs in his gay canoe. In short, no desires remain unfulfilled. He is the greatest man in the land. The buildings belonging to the Company are both neat and commodious, each class is provided with separate abodes. The apartments are appropriately divided into bedrooms, ante-chambers and closets. Here is seen the counting room, the mess room, the kitchen and pantry, the cellars, and Indian hall and there are handsome galleries. Nor can we pass over in silence one chief object of attraction. Even in this barbarous country, woman claims and enjoys her due share of attention and regard. Her presence brightens the gloom of the solitary post, her smiles add a new charm to the pleasures of the wilderness. Nor are the ladies deficient in the accomplishments that procure admiration. Although descended from aboriginal mothers, many of the females at the different establishments throughout the Indian countries are as fair as the generality of European ladies, the mixture of blood being so many degrees removed from the savage as hardly to leave any trace; which at the same time their delicacy of form, their light yet nimble movements, and the penetrating expression of the "bright black eye" combine to render them objects of no ordinary interest. They have also made considerable progress in refinement, and with their natural acuteness and singular talent for imitation, they soon acquire all the ease and gracefulness of polished life. On holidays the dresses are as gay as in polished countries and on these occasions the gentleman puts on the beaver hat and the ladies make fine show of silks and satins, and even jewelry is not wanting.

It is not surprising therefore that the roving North Wester, after so many rural enjoyments under residence of twenty years, should feel more real happiness in these scenes than he can in any other country. Gentlemen from their constant intercourse with Indians make a free use of tobacco, mixing it as the Indians do with a certain herb, this with their favourite beverage of strong tea constitutes their chief luxury, and agrees well with their mode of life. But whether it be the food, mode of living, or climate, it certainly happens that great longevity is seldom known among them on returning to civilized society even when they return from these parts in the prime of life!

It is therefore to be lamented that people who spend their better days in search of a precarious fortune should be so very unfortunate in the enjoyment thereof; very few indeed of them, outlive their means! And we may ask among the hundreds who have left the country during the last quarter of a century, some with competencies, some with fortunes, where are their means at this home now? Is there one in the full enjoyment of his health and means! If the trade here has made little advancement of late years, it has unquestionably been rapidly successful in the more softening considerations of comfort and refinement.

191

Canadians it is admitted are best calculated for the endurance of hardships and expedition in the business of light canoe men, it is seldom that other men are employed in such arduous labour. Indeed the Canadians considered as voyageurs merit the highest praise.

Another class however remain who merit less praise. They are in this country styled freemen, because they are not amongst the hired servants of the Company. These are generally Canadians or others who have spent their better days in the quality of canoe men in the company's service but who, deficient in provident sagacity to save part of their earnings for the contingencies of old age, have to bend to necessity and sooner than proceed to their own country to live by hard labour, resolve in passing the remainder of their days among the natives. It often happens however that young men of vicious and indolent habits join them, lost like the others to all the ties of kindred blood, country and Christianity.

They may be considered a kind of enlightened Indian, with all the imperfections but none of the good qualities of their countrymen. Their similarity to the Indians in their vagrant mode of living brings on them their contempt, and they are likewise despised by the whites because they become savages. Indeed they are more depraved, designing, and more subtle than the worst of Indians. They instruct the simple natives in every evil to the great detriment of traders, with whom in consequence they are never on a friendly footing. They live in tents, or in huts like the natives: and wander from place to place in search of game, roots and herbs.

Sometimes they live in the utmost abundance; but as they are not always expert hunters they have at times to undergo the extremities of want. In this case they are objects of commiseration, and the traders not unfrequently administer to their wants; but such is their ingratitude that they are seldom known to make them a cordial return.

On account of their rapacity, they do not always secure a perfect understanding with the tribe to which they are attached; but Indians are so friendly to whites of every description when they throw themselves upon their mercy that an instance of cruelty to the free man is seldom or never heard of. They fall victims sometimes to the fury of an opposite or adverse native at war; but otherwise they are by no means an unhappy race, and they commonly live to an advanced age. But there cannot be a better test for knowing the worthless and bad character in this country than his wishing to become a freeman; it is the true sign of depravity, either in a wayward youth or backsliding old man. They seldom agree with one another and consequently scatter amongst the natives by ones and twos only. Collectively they may be at present about fifty or sixty on the Columbia. But in all other parts of the Company's territories they are far more numerous.

The next class we have to notice are natives of the Sandwich Islands. It was from this people that captains in their coasting trade augmented their crews in steering among the dangerous natives from the Columbia River to Bering's Straits, and from the precedent, the inland traders adopted them when their complement of Canadians happened to come short of their demands. They are submissive to their masters, honest and trustworthy and willingly perform as much duty as lies in their power; but are nevertheless exceedingly awkward in everything they attempt. And although they are somewhat industrious they are not made to lead but to follow, and are useful only to stand as sentinels to eye the natives or go through the drudgery of an establishment.

It has often been found however, that they are not wanting in courage; particularly against the Indians, for whom they entertain a very cordial contempt. And if they were let loose against them, they rush upon them like tigers. The principal purpose for which they were useful on Columbia was as an array of numbers in the view of the natives especially in the frequent voyages up and down the communication, and doubtless they might have been found more serviceable had not a dullness on their part and an impression of their insufficiency on ours prevented both sides from any great degree of intercourse. Being obtained however, for almost their bare victuals and clothing the difference in expense of them and Canadians forms a sufficient consideration to keep up the custom of employing more or less of this description of men.

The contrast is great between them here and in their own country where they are all life, all activity, for when I saw them there I thought them the most active people I had ever seen. This difference in their habits I am inclined to attribute to the difference of climate, their own being favourable to them in a high degree. When we consider the salubrity of the Sandwich Islands it is hardly to be wondered at that the unhappy native, when transplanted to the snows and cold of the Rocky Mountains should experience decay of energies. From exposure to the wets and damps prevalent at the mouth of Columbia many of them become consumptive and find their graves in the stranger's land.

The Owhyhees however are such expert swimmers that little of our effects are lost beyond recovery which accident now and then consigns to the bottom of the water in our perilous navigations: and it is next to impossible for a person to get drowned if one or more of them are near at hand: in that element, they are as active and expert as the reverse on dry land, on every occasion they testify a fidelity and zeal for their master's welfare and service.

There are at this time only about a score of these men in the country.

Among the people employed in this trade are a set of civilized Indians from the neighbourhood of Montreal. These are chiefly of the Iroquois nation, at the period they form nearly a third of the number of men employed by the Company on the Columbia.

They are expert voyageurs but especially so in the rapids and dangerous runs in the inland waters, which they either stem or shoot with the utmost skill. The object of introducing them into the service of the traders was to make them act in the double capacity of canoe men and trappers.

They are not esteemed equal to the ablest trappers, nor the best calculated for the voyage. They are not so inoffensive as the Owhyhees, nor to be trusted as the Canadians. They are brought up to religion, it is true, and sing hymns oftener than paddling songs; but those who came here, and we are of course speaking of none else, retain none of its precepts. They are sullen, indolent, fickle, cowardly and treacherous. And an Iroquois arrived at the manhood is still as wayward and extravagant as a lad of other nations at the age of fifteen. Iroquois have been found uniformly to deceive without fail.

We shall now draw the attention of our readers to another class, the last we propose to notice, Indian women and the half-breeds of the country. About the different establishments there are some of the natives employed in the capacity of servants. Some as outdoor drudges, some as cooks, some as fishermen, and some as couriers. They are often found useful among their own tribe, or those in the neighbourhood.

In the establishments belonging to the whites in the Columbia are many Indian women as wives to the different classes of people in the employ of the Company. There may be in all about fifty. Some of them have large families: and the tenderness existing between their husbands and themselves presents one great reason for that degree of attachment which the respective classes of whites cherish for the Indian countries. The vigilance of these women has often been instrumental to the safety of the forts, when the most diabolical combinations were set on foot by the natives.

As it frequently happens that their husbands go home to Canada with the means of living at their ease these women must of necessity rejoin their respective tribes, where they generally remain in a state of widowhood during a year or two, in expectation of their return. If the husband does not return, she then bestows her hand on one of his comrades who has the good fortune to please her fancy the best.

Habituated to the manners of the whites, they prefer living with them for the rest of their lives and generally prove faithful to their husbands. They are likewise much attached to their families, a disposition inherent in all Indians. Nor are they wanting in many other qualities necessary to the good housekeeper; they are tidy, saving and industrious. And when they must rejoin their tribe the whites find them very friendly, and they never fail to influence their connexions to the same effect. By these means, a close alliance is found between the leaders and the aborigines of the country and might, by means of their offspring, be instrumental in bringing civilization among the Indians were some wise policy adopted for the government and care of half-breeds, whose destiny it is to be left in indigence by poor parents in this far-distant region of the earth.

Some benevolent society would no doubt, if set on foot, meet with all due encouragement. Ways might be devised by appointing an agent or guardian to each district of the country for the due superintendence, maintenance, clothing and education of all such poor children as are left in the Indian countries. I am convinced from my own experience in these parts that nothing of the kind could ever work well, unless the Hudson's Bay Company were to take the management; that alone would insure its success.

For the promotion of the benevolent design an appeal is here made to the philanthropic disposition of the Honourable North West Company who now preside over that great family of mankind, inhabiting a vast tract of Indian country from the Atlantic to the Pacific and from the Pacific to the frozen ocean.

Half-breeds, or as they are more generally styled, brules, from the peculiar colour of their skin, being of a swarthy hue, as if sunburnt, as they grow up resemble, almost in every respect, the pure Indian. With this difference that they are more designing, more daring, and more dissolute. They are indolent, thoughtless, and improvident. Licentious in their habits, unbounded in their desires, sullen in their disposition. Proud, restless, and clannish, fond of flattery. They alternately associate with the whites and the Indians, and thus become fatally enlightened. They form a composition of all the bad qualities of both.

But the more unfortunate part of these are those born of wealthy parents or men holding the rank of gentlemen in the service such as Bourgeois and clerks. These men have often been remarkable for indulging their children. In lieu therefore of teaching their offspring industry and frugality they allow them to run about the establishment learning among Indians, freemen, voyageurs and others every vice that can degrade human nature. The father however is a gentleman. The son forsooth must be a gentleman too! None so great as he, he can race horses, run dogs, smoke tobacco, and shoot arrows. He must not degrade himself with labour. While in the service all this does very well; but when the father leaves the service, so does the son too. They are no longer in the service, but in civilized life. The son looks about and is disgusted with the drudgery of labour. Still hangs about his father. Knows nothing, can do nothing. Bows and arrows are more congenial than the spade or the hoe, and longs to get back to the scenes of his boyhood. To get rid of the gentleman son, therefore, the father sets him up in business, and gives him a portion of his goods; but business he does not understand. His thoughts are still upon bows and arrows. He fails, falls back again upon his more than half-ruined father. The father dies. The son gets his hands on the root of all evil, flourishes for a time in wasteful extravagance. The father scarcely yet cold in his grave the last shilling is gone, and the son soon outcast is idle again, in want again. A sort of outcast from society.

It sometimes happens that a promising youth is sent home. Five hundred pounds are spent on his education, and the accomplishments of drawing, music, and dancing added. He returns to the country again for they must all get back again to the land of their nativity. He tries his fortune one way, tries it another; but business and the restraints necessary to succeed in business are disagreeable, he gets tired, descends from respectable society. His learning becomes useless. Tries his bows and arrows again, forgets even that aboriginal accomplishment, gets lost in the crowd. Many bad consequences from the customary mode of abandoning half-breed children. It degrades white men in the eyes of the natives. By far the greater part of those who are employed in this quarter from Montreal are in reality nothing else but half-breeds, with this difference however, that they are more knowing in mischief but less skilled than the others in the requisite occupations of the land.

We shall now bring to view their better qualities. Half-breed children, instructed in the principles of religion and morality, and taught at an early age some useful trade, would doubtless prove an ornament to society. They are frequently endued with the most lively apprehension, naturally ingenious, hardy and enterprising. They are by far the fittest persons for the Indian countries, the best

197

calculated by nature for going among Indians: they are insinuating and not unfit instruments to mollify their countrymen and teach them the great end of civilization. They are naturally of an acute understanding, are expert horsemen, active woodsmen, noted marksmen, able hunters. They surpass all Indians at the chace. They are vigorous, brave; and while they possess the shrewdness and sagacity of the whites, they inherit the agility and expertness of the savage.

It is a misfortune that those who might otherwise be calculated to shine in various spheres of civilized life should thus be lost to their country: and the most deplorable, since it is in our power to make them useful. And for aught we know, these may be Nelsons, these may be Wellingtons whose talents lye buried in the listlessness and obscurity of the dreary waste. Of this class the first child, a male, was born at Columbia on the 24th day of January 1812; I notice it now, as the circumstance may in a new country like this become on some future day matter of history.

Children from the Indian countries do not generally turn out well in civilized society. Those however brought up among the lower classes seem to thrive the best. Their genius, their habits, and their ideas it would appear correspond best with that sphere of life.

We now come to notice the last relic of the North West Company, the universal idol of its day, the light canoe being the chief gratification to a North West proprietor, the person of highest rank in the Indian countries. The Canadians or voyageurs dignify their master by the name Bourgeois, a turn handed down from the days of the French in the Province of Canada.

The Bourgeois is therefore carried on board his canoe upon the back of some sturdy fellow generally appointed for this purpose. He seats himself on a convenient feather bed, somewhat low in the centre of his canoe, his gun by his side, his little cherubs fondling around him, and his faithful spanial lying at his feet.

No sooner is he at his ease then his pipe is presented by his attendant. He then puffs the Indian leaf in curling clouds. His silken banner undulates over the stern of his painted vessel. Then the bending paddles are plied, and the fragile craft speeds through the currents with a degree of fleetness not to be surpassed. Yell upon yell from the hearty crew proclaims the prowess and adroitness.

A hundred miles performed, night arrives, the hands jump out quickly into the water and their Nabob and his companions are supported to terra firma. A rousing fire is kindled, supper is served. His honor then retires to enjoy his repose. At dawn of day they set out again, the men now and then relax their arms and light their pipes; but no sooner does the headway of the canoe die away than they renew their labours and their chorus, and a particular voice is ever selected to lead the song. The guide conducts the march.

At the hour of breakfast they put ashore on some green plot. The tea kettle is boiling. A varigated mat of no ordinary kill is spread, and a cold collation set out. Twenty minutes and they start anew. The dinner hour arrives, they put aground again, the liquor case accompanies the provision basket. The contents of both are set forth in simple style and after a refreshment of twenty minutes more off they set again, until the twilight checks their progress.

When it is practicable to make way in the dark four hours constitute the allowance of their rest, and at times on boisterous lakes and bold shores they keep days and nights together on the water, without intermission and without repose. They sing to keep time to their paddles. They sing to keep off drowsiness caused by their fatigue, and they sing because the Bourgeois likes it.

Through hardships and dangers, wherever he leads they are sure to follow with alacrity and cheerfulness. Over mountains, over hills, over valleys, over dales, and woods, and creeks, and lakes and rivers. They look not to the right, nor to the left. They make no halt in foul or fair weather. With skill they venture to sail in the midst of waters like oceans, and with aptitude no less amazing they shoot down the most frightful rapids. All comes well to them, and they generally come off safe.

When about to arrive at the place of their destination they dress with neatness, put on their plumes and a chosen song is raised, they push up against the break as if they meant to dash in splinters, but most adroitly back their paddles, whilst the foreman springs on shore to arrest his vessel, like a fiery courier curbed in his speed.

On this agreeable occasion every person advances to the waterside, great guns are first to announced the Bourgeois' arrival. A grand shaking of hands takes place as it often happens that people have not met for years, even the Bourgeois goes through this mode of salutation, with the meanest. There is perhaps no country where the ties of affection are more binding than here. Each addresses his comrades as his brothers. All address themselves to the Bourgeois with reverence as if he were their father.

From every distant department of the company's concerns, a special light canoe is fitted out annually to report their transactions. The one from the Columbia sets out from the Pacific Ocean the first of April, and with the regularity and rapidity of a steam boat it reaches Fort William on Lake Superior the first of July: remaining there till the 20th of that month, takes its departure back, and with an equal degree of precision arrives at Fort George, mouth of Columbia River, on the 20th of October.

A light canoe likewise leaving the Pacific reaches Montreal in a hundred days, and one from Montreal to the Pacific in the same space of time: thus performing a journey of many thousand miles, without delay, stoppage, or scarcely any repose, in the short period of little more than six months.

Having now concluded our remarks on the different class of whites, or half-breeds, and others connected with the trade of this country, we resume the subject of Fort Nez Perces quarter.

The different Indian tribes inhabiting the country about Fort Nez Perces often go to war on their southern neighbours, the Snakes: but do not follow war as a profession. They likewise frequently go to the buffalo, as the Flatheads and others west of the mountains do. They are inhabitants of the plains, live by the chace, and are generally known and distinguished by the name of "black-robes" in contradistinction to those who live on fish. They are easily known from their roving propensities, their dress, cleanliness and independence. They are rich in horses, seldom walk on foot, expert hunters, good warriors, and are governed by far more powerful and influential chiefs than any of the other tribes on the Columbia.

WANDERING ROOT DIGGERS, CALLED SHOSHOCOES, OF THE SNAKE TRIBE

A water color by Alfred Jacob Miller

MOUNT BAKER LOOMING OVER "PUGET'S SOUND"

A drawing by Henry James Warre

And although we do not intend to follow them through all the varied scenes of their warlike exploits, for that has already been more or less done in our remarks on the Snake country: yet that the reader may have a more correct idea of their habits and general appearance on such occasions we shall first present him with a short description of a warrior and his horse, both ready accoutred for a war expedition, and next point out to him their general treatment of slaves taken in war, and lastly conclude the subject of our remarks in this chapter with a brief accounting of their language.[1]

The tribes of Fort Nez Perces we enumerated already: on the present occasion, we shall more particularly direct the reader's attention to the Walla Walla, the Cayouse, and the Shaw-ha-ap-ten tribes. The last mentioned is the Chapunnish of Lewis and Clarke. First then as to the war chief's head-dress, a matter of great importance. It consists of the entire skin of a wolf's head, with the ears standing erect, fantastically adorned all over with the tawdry ornaments of bear's claws, bird's feathers, resembling a ruff or peacock's tail which is entwined round the cranium, hangs down like a banner to the ground, but when on horseback it floats six or seven feet in the air. The loss of this is the loss of honour. The price of a first-rate war head-dress is two horses. On his body is simply a shirt or garment of thin draped leather, cut and chequered into small holes, painted or tattooed with a variety of devices. Strapped tight round the waist a black leather girdle binds the garment and holds the mystical medicine bag and decorated calumet, articles, in the chief's estimation of no ordinary value. Then gun, the lance, the scalping knife, a bulky quiver, are all in their places. Although thus accoutred, he appears no ways embarrassed. You must actually see a warrior to believe with what dexterity and ease he can use each weapon, and how nimbly he can change one for another, as occasion may require.

Next comes the favourite war horse, and a description will convey but a faint idea of the reality. Although horses are generally cheap and easily purchased by the natives; yet there is no price will

---

[1] At the end of this chapter Ross added an Indian vocabulary of about three hundred words.

induce an Indian chief to part with his war horse. Those entirely white are preferred. Next to white, the speckled or white and black are most in demand. Generally all horses of those fancy colours are claimed by the chiefs in preference to any other and therefore double, triple, the value of others. And as much pains is bestowed to adorn, paint and caparison a war horse as a warrior himself. On the occasion I am now describing, the horse was a pure white. After painting the animal's body all over and drawing a variety of hieroglyphic devices, the head and neck were dappled with streaks of red and yellow. The mane black, the tail red, clubbed up in a knot and tied short. To this knot was appended two long streamers of feathers served to a strong leather thong by means of sinews which reached the ground, forming as it were two artificial tails which, in addition to ornament, served the rider to lay hold of while in the act of crossing rivers. A bunch of feathers as big as a broom standing some twenty inches above the ears ornamented the head; the rider as well as the horse was so besmeared with every sort of colour in red, blue and yellow ochre that no earthly being could tell what their colour was.

Five or six hundred men thus mounted and armed have a somewhat grand and imposing appearance. But the most interesting part of the scene is not yet told. A few days before setting out on these expeditions the whole cavalcade parade and manoeuvre about their own camp. On the one occasion I went purposely to see them. One of the principal chiefs at the commencement mounted on horseback, took up his stand on an eminence near the camp, while at the same time the whole troop mounted in fighting order assembled in a group, and from a gallop to a full race, the cleverest fellow in front. In this manner they whirl round the tents. During all the time silence prevails within the camp, while the horsemen all the time keep shouting, yelling, and go through all attitudes peculiar to savages.

This moment throwing themselves to the right, the next moment to the left side of the horse, twisting and bending their bodies in a thousand different ways. Now in the saddle, out of the saddle, and nothing frequently to be seen but the horses, as if without riders, parrying or evading according to their ideas the onset of their assailants, and I could very easily conceive that the real merit of the manoeuvers was not who could kill most of his enemies; but who could save himself best in battle! So dexterous and nimble were they in changing positions and slipping from side to side that it was in the twinkling of an eye. As soon as the manoeuvring was over they were again harangued and dismissed.

The subject next to be considered is the treatment of the slaves taken in war. On their return from an expedition of this kind the warparty keep in a body and observe the same order as at starting, until they reach home. And if successful their shouting, yelling and chanting the war song fill the air. The sound no sooner reaches the camp than the whole savage horde, young and old, male and female, sally forth not however to welcome the arrival of their friends but to glut the desires of implacable revenge by the most barbarous cruelties on the unfortunate captives.

The slaves, as is customary on such occasions, are all tied on horseback, each behind a warrior. But the squaws no sooner meet them than they tear them down from the horses without mercy, and then begin by trampling on them, tearing their hair and flesh, cutting their ears and maiming their bodies with knives, stones, sticks, or other instruments of torture. After thus glutting their revenge, they are driven to the camp.

It is then settled unalterably what the slaves are doomed to suffer. Every afternoon, some hours before sunset, the camp makes a grand turnout for dancing the scalps. For this purpose two ranks or rows of men, a hundred yards long or more, arrange themselves face to face, and about fifteen feet apart. Inside of them are likewise two rows of women facing each other, leaving a space of about five feet broad in the middle for the slaves, who arranged in a line occupy the centre in a row by themselves. Here the unfortunate victims, male and female, are stationed with long poles in their hands and naked above the waist, on the ends of these poles are exhibited the scalps of their murdered relations. The dancing and chorus then commence, the whole assemblage keeping time to the beating of a loud and discordant sort of drum. The parties all move sideways, to the right and left alternately, according to Indian fashion, the slaves at the same time moving and keeping time with the others. Every now and then a general halt takes place, when the air resounds with loud shouts of joy and yell upon yell proclaim afar their triumph.

All this is but a prelude to the scenes that follow. The women placed in the order we have stated, on each side of the slaves, and armed with the instruments of torture, keep all the time jeering them with the most distorted grimaces, cutting them with knives, piercing them with awls, pulling them by the hair and thumping them with fist, stick or stone, in every possible way that can torment without killing them. The loss of an ear, a tooth, the joint of a finger or part of the scalp torn off during these frantic fits are nightly occurrences. And if the wretches thus doomed to suffer happen not to laugh and huzza, which in their situation would almost be contrary to the efforts of human nature, or fail to raise or lower according to caprice the scalps in regular order, they are doubly tormented and unmercifully handled.

On these occasions a termagant often pounces upon some victim, who not unfrequently falls senseless to the ground under the infliction of wounds. And if any of them happens from a sudden blow, to start back a little out of line, another in the rear instantly inflicts another wound, which never fails to urge the same victim as far forward. So that they are often kept pushed backward and forward, till at last they are insensible.

The men however take no part in these cruelties but are not silent spectators. They never interfere, nor does one of them, during the dancing, menace or touch a slave. All the barbarities are perpetuated by the women! These are the only examples I have ever witnessed among savages wherein the women out-do the men in acts of inhumanity: and where sympathy is not regarded as a virtue by that sex. But then we must take into consideration that it is part of the law of the land. It is a duty the females, according to the customs of war, are bound to perform.

When these acts of savage life happen near the establishments, curiosity occasionally induces the whites to attend. On one occasion

I stood for some time looking on, but as I could do nothing but pity, I soon withdrew from the heartrending scene. At dusk the dancing ceases, and the slaves henceforth conveyed to the camp, washed, dressed, fed and comfortably lodged, and kindly treated, until the usual hour of dancing the following day arrives, when the same routine of cruelties is gone through. This course is generally persisted in for five or six days without intermission, and then discontinued altogether. From that time, they are no longer regarded in the camp as common property but placed under the care of their proper masters, and subject only to them. Their treatment ever after is quite as good as could be expected, and is often according to their own merit. They are nevertheless at all times subject to be bought, sold, and bartered away in the same manner as any other article of property belonging to the owner.

10. VALLEY OF TROUBLES

H AVING in the preceding chapter given a brief account of the people employed in the fur trade west of the mountains, I will henceforth confine the narrative to my own adventures in the Snake country.

In the spring of the year 1823 I drew up a statement on the subject of the trade in the Snake country which after submitting to the gentlemen superintending the company's affairs on the Columbia, I forwarded to the Governor and Council at York factory. In the meantime however, as several of the trappers and hunters had on Mr. McKenzie's retiring been left without much employment a party was fitted out for the Snake country and placed under the direction of a Mr. Finan McDonald, a veteran of the North West school now in the Hudson's Bay Company's services.

Soon after McDonald's departure however, John Warren Dease Esq., a titled clerk of the new company, arrived from Rupert's Land, informing me that I had been named to succeed Mr. McKenzie in the charge of the Snake country, and that he had come to relieve me and take charge of Fort Nez Perces. I observed that the charge of the Snake country was more befitting a chief factor than a clerk, and would suit him better than me, and that besides I had made up my mind to leave the country. This avowal took my friend by surprise as my departure might have placed himself in the Snake country, a quarter much dreaded by all North Westers.

My arrangements however for the two years having expired,[1] and being prepared for leaving the country, I left Fort Nez Perces in charge of Mr. Dease and set out with my family for the Rocky Mountains;[2] but on my arrival there, I met Governor Simpson's

1 McKenzie had departed in 1821, at about the time that Ross had agreed to stay on for two years under the Hudson's Bay Company.

letter in reply to the statement I had transmitted in the spring. This letter was dated "York factory 13th July 1823" wherein the Gov. observed "We have given the subject of your communication in reference to the Snake country mature consideration, and have resolved to fit out an expedition to that quarter, whereof we tender you the management for three years." This proposal was accompanied by the offer of a liberal salary. Yet having set out with a view of leaving the service, I hesitated to accept the proposal. My inclinations prompted me to continue my journey and yet a desire to meet the Governor's views inclined me strongly to close with the offer, and my further opinion was supported by my friend P. S. Ogden Esq. who living on the spot did everything in his power to persuade me to accept the appointment.

Never did my mind undergo such a conflict as on this occasion, and two days passed in anxious suspence before I could determine. Ultimately however I resolved to go back on, being promised eighty men; but for one year only. Embarking therefore with my family, we took the current for Fort Nez Perces, and on arriving at Kettle Falls, I was astonished to learn that on McDonald's return from his Snake trip he and his men, instead of being as expected at Fort Nez Perces, were all at Spokane House! Hither of course I had to shape my course, and I reached that place at the close of October. But had I known that I should have required to start from Spokane instead of Fort Nez Perces no consideration would have made me return, for this report disarranged all my plans, and was a departure from the Company's views which threw the Snake trade again into the old channel.[3]

No step could have operated more to the detriment of our Snake affairs than the falling back again upon Spokane as a depot for carrying on the trade of that quarter: and if the reader refers to

2 That is, he had begun his return to the Canadian settlement of Red River.

3 Ross had planned to leave from Fort Nez Perces, travel along the Snake River, and thus gain his objective. Instead, he had to begin from Spokane House, gain the Pend Oreille waterway, move east along the Clark Fork River to Flathead House, proceed east and south through the Jocko area to Hellgate, travel south through the Bitterroot Valley, cross the Continental Divide, travel farther south, and then recross the Divide.

the fourth chapter, he will very naturally ask the question "Why did McDonald, instead of going to Fort Nez Perces, return to that place!" We have already noticed that he was a veteran of the North West school; he had passed many years among the fascinating pleasures of the far-famed Spokane House, and the moment that McKenzie had turned his back on the Columbia old prejudices were revived.

Before leaving this part of our subject, we might make a remark or two on McDonald's late trip to the Snakes. Everything considered, the trip was as successful as would have been expected in this for McDonald was a zealous and faithful servant; but in other respects, it was rather an unfortunate trip. In a conference with a war party of the Piegans one of his men, named Anderson, got treacherously shot! In a pitched battle which took place between his party and the Blackfeet, he lost seven more of his men! and in a squabble with the Iroquois of his own party, he got badly wounded from an accidental discharge of a gun.

At Spokane House I remained but a few days. Instead however of my complement of eighty men, I could only muster forty, and of that small number, many of them were questionable. With these however, I left on the 12th of November and proceeded up Flathead River to the post of that name,[4] situated at the foot of the mountains. There I remained for some time and picked up fourteen more making my party, including myself, in all 55 persons, each of which had to be fitted out according to his capacity as a hunter with a gun, from two to four horses, and from six to ten steel traps besides clothing and ammunition, and generally on credit. With this number I made preparations for setting out on my expedition.

On assembling my people I smiled at the medley, the variety of accents of dresses, habits, and ideas; but above all, at the confusion of languages in our camp in which were two Americans, seventeen Canadians, five half-breeds from the east side of the mountains, twelve Iroquois, two Abanakee Indians from Lower Canada, two natives from Lake Nepissing, one Saultman from Lake Huron, two

4 Flathead House, located on the site of Eddy, Montana.

Crees from Athabasca, one Chinook, two Spokanes, two Kouttan-nois,[5] three Flatheads, two Callispellums,[6] one Palooche,[7] and one Snake slave! Five of the Canadians were above sixty years of age, and two were on the wrong side of seventy. The Iroquois were good hunters but plot wars, often killing and faithless. From five to ten of the more trusty and resolute would always be required as a guard on the camp and horses, and could therefore be but seldom employed in trapping beaver. And as for the nineteen natives, they were only of use, as far as members went, in taking care of our horses, in these respects however they proved very serviceable. So that upon the whole I could scarcely count on more than twenty trappers at any time.

In summing up however, we must not forget that twenty-five of the party were married and several of the youngsters carried guns: so that in our camp there were exclusive of the men twenty-five women and sixty-four children. The rest of the equipment consisted of seventy-five guns, a brass three pounder, two hundred and twelve beaver traps, and three hundred ninety and two horses, together with a good stock of powder and ball and some trading articles. I now observed to my men that the journey would be long and not at all times perhaps exempt from danger, but that we might with industry and perseverance anticipate a successful trip. Yet if there were any among the party who preferred remaining at home to going on the journey, the choice was now offered them; this I stated as a bar to grumbling on the journey but the whole with one voice exclaimed, "We prefer going." This point being settled, I next warned them that our safety and success would very much depend upon our unanimity and care, and that all would be little enough to guard against surprise and preserve our horses, on which the success of the undertaking depended. Hence, I said, a night watch would be established rigidly and enforced during the journey upon every one in turn. This met their approbation.

The council of Fort William did every thing that could be done

5 Kootenai Indians.
6 Kalispell Indians.
7 Palouse Indian.

to render the trapping system in the Snake country during McKenzie's time as efficient as possible, but their instructions had to travel 3000 miles and to pass through the hands of many subordinates, each of whom according to the nature of things in this country had a voice, which influenced the final arrangement and not unfrequently stripped it of its usefulness! And the same remarks are true in reference to the Hudson's Bay Company, for the council of York factory is as far removed from the scene of action as the council of Fort William was. McKenzie had to combat the evil, so had his successors; but all to little purpose, for the system instead of improving by experience is getting worse every day.

One half, perhaps two-thirds of the people I had under my command were more expert at the bow and arrow than at the use of the beaver trap, more accustomed to indolence and free will than to subordination.

This party being now ready, we left the Flathead and proceeded on our journey. By starting in the depth of winter less difficulty was experienced in providing for so many people. Our camp with all its defects appeared at a little distance somewhat formidable. The whole cavalcade when in marching order presented a line of a mile or more in length. Having made about eight miles and killing only one deer for we had to depend upon our guns for our supper, that small animal proved but a slender repast for a hundred thirty-seven hungry mouths. We encamped at a place called Prairie de Chevaux,[8] and next day at Prairie de Camass,[9] where our hunters had a little better luck, killed six deer, so we had a better supper and we required it for we had passed two days on only one light meal.

The day following we passed the crossing place where I picked up several pieces of the best iron ore I had seen in the country: and a short distance from that are the forks. There we left the main branch of the Flathead River, where it makes a quick bend to the N.W. to the lake of that name. Then following up what is called Jacques Fork,[10] we encamped at Riviere aux Marons[11] or Wild Horse River. Our travelling went on but slowly owing to the scar-

8 Horse Prairie.   9 Camas Prairie.
10 The Jocko River.   11 Finley Creek.

city of provisions for we had nothing with us. In the course of this day's travel we made a halt and smoked our pipes at a spot on which some faint traces of civilization were to be seen. A Mr. Howes, an entertaining individual belonging to the Hudson's Bay Company established himself here in 1810; but after passing part of the winter, he recrossed the mountains again, and never returned: we believe this is the first and only instance in which any of the servants of that company had penetrated so far to the west prior to the country falling into their hands in 1821.

Soon after encamping the Iroquois began to sing hymns, as soon as I heard that I doubled the watch and gave strict orders to watch their motions as the singing of sacred music by these hypocritical wretches is a sure sign of disaffection. As I expected, early next morning I found the Iroquois in a body, with old Pierre and John Grey at their head, standing at my hut door. Knowing their character, this did not surprise me. I was however anxious to know the cause, and addressed myself as a matter of course to the head man. "What now Pierre?" said I. "Oh nothing," said he, "The Iroquois merely wish to see their accounts." This being a reasonable demand, although somewhat out of place, I of course complied; although I well knew that such a request was but the introduction to some other more unreasonable demand, for they had all of them seen their accounts before starting. But this is the way they generally introduce all subjects. After explaining their accounts I asked them their motives, as this was neither the time nor place to be inquiring about accounts nor discussing arrangements. After several remarks Pierre observed, "Our debts are heavy, and we are never able to reduce them in a large party, allow us to go off by ourselves and we shall do much better." Here I reminded them of their conduct when left by McKenzie at the river Skam-naugh, and of course resisted their intention. I pointed out to them the consequences, that the party was already too small, and that further division would put an end to the expedition altogether. "Why," continued I, "did you not express yourselves before starting, when I offered you either to come or to remain? It is now no longer time, and I hope such a request will not be made again. The Company place great confidence in your exertions and I shall do everything in my power to make your undertaking comfortable and profitable." With these assurances they seemed satisfied, and we proceeded.

The Iroquois however lagged behind, and arriving some time after we had put up encamped on one side; this being an unusual step I suspected all was not right, and that they were still bent on playing us a trick. I therefore sent for Pierre and explained matters fully to him and learned for the first time, from Pierre, that Grey was a plotting busybody. Confidence was restored, the Iroquois reconciled once more. In consequence of deep snows and bad weather, we remained for several days in the same encampment. Here I assembled the people and made some new regulations.

I observed to them that there appeared to be a great and unnecessary waste of ammunition in the camp. That hitherto when the party was travelling half of the people, the ignorant as well as the experienced hunters, were occupied in pursuit of game, by which the animals were more frequently frightened than killed, the duties of the journey and camp both neglected, and provisions scarce; a change of system was therefore necessary. To this end it was settled that four hunters in turn should precede the camp daily, and all the rest attend to other duties: and it was anticipated that we should be always better supplied with provisions, other duties better attended to, and not a third of the ammunition spent.

In observing the effect produced by guns of different calibres, it was found that the rifles of small bore taking from 60 to 70 balls to the pound very frequently did not kill, although they might hit: while rifles taking from 30 to 40 to the pound seldom missed killing on the spot. The former out of twenty shots seldom kills more than seven or eight animals, whereas the latter, of twenty shots fired fifteen are generally deadly. It was therefore settled that the rifles of larger calibre should be used in all places where animals proved scarce.

Our party consisting of four classes of people differing in almost everything but the human form, Canadians, half-breeds, Iroquois, and natives of different nations, it was agreed with the consent of all that I should appoint the person of most influence in each party as a head over the rest. This arrangement would relieve me of much trouble and promised to work well. In all difficult cases I was to call these head men together to hold a council, so that things might go on smoothly.

From Riviere aux Marons we raised camp and proceeded on our journey up what is called the Valley of Racine aux Mere, or Spet-lum country,[12] along the base of the mountains until we reached a defile of the dividing ridge called Hell's Gates, a distance from Flathead Fort of about 70 miles, general course S.E. This place is rendered notorious as being the great war road by which the Pie-gans and Blackfeet often visit this side of the mountains; by the same pass the Flatheads and other tribes cross over to the Missouri side in quest of buffalo. The spot has therefore often been the scene of many a bloody contest between these hostile nations.

This being the usual and only place known to the whites for passing the mountains, I hesitated for some time between two opinions, whether to cross there or proceed in hopes of crossing somewhere else to more advantage. Difficulties presented themselves in either case: by adopting the former, we should have been exposed to the Blackfeet and other tribes during a journey of three weeks, the time we should have taken before we could have reached a pass either to get clear of those tribes, or back into the Snake country; by the latter the road was virtually unknown to the whites, and the mountains lofty and abrupt; yet we decided on the latter, and determined to continue our course.[13]

Here again the Iroquois wished to go off, saying they would make good hunts in the recesses of these Alpine ridges; but I knew them too well to be duped by their artifices. They would have either sneaked back or lurked about among the Flatheads and gone with them not to hunt the beaver nor pay their debts, for that never

12 The Bitterroot Valley, which they had not yet reached. Hellgate Canyon opens upon the site of Missoula, Montana.

13 Here Ross had to decide whether to pass through Hellgate Canyon and enter the relatively known though dangerous country of the Blackfeet, or to avoid the Blackfeet by traveling south along the Bitterroot River, a region entirely unknown.

troubled them, but to feast on buffalo. I therefore got them brought round again, thinking that if I once succeeded in getting them back into the heart of the Snake country, all would be right and they would not be so anxious to be off by themselves.

In this encampment we remained for a day or two, and our hunters killed four wild horses. Just at the time we were starting one morning, and in the act of crossing a deep ravine not far from our camp, about twenty of those beautiful and hardy tenants of the mountain came dashing down from a neighbouring height, with their shaggy manes and long bushy tails waving in the wind; but with all their keen scent, the rifles of our hunters brought four of them to the ground, before they had time to turn round! It is a rare thing for them to be either entrapped or approached and our hunters were more delighted with their success in this little adventure than if they had killed a hundred buffalo. We also got 27 elks and 32 small deer at this place, which secured the party for a while from hunger.

On leaving our encampment at Hell's Gates, I discovered that one of my Iroquois named Jacob had deserted; to have gone in pursuit of him would have been in vain, if he wished to keep out of our way, so we continued our journey but had not proceeded far, when the advanced party called out "Enemies! Enemies! Blackfeet!" As soon as the word "enemy" is uttered, everyone looks at the priming of his gun and primes anew, which in the present occasion was no sooner done than a party mounted on horseback advanced at full speed. We were soon prepared to receive them either as friends or foes. On our getting up to them we found eight Piegans squatted down at the corner of a thicket with their snowshoes and other travelling necessaries at their side.

On our approach they manifested a good deal of uneasiness, so that not one of them got up to shake hands with us, a custom peculiar to most Indians; but sat still, each having his bow and arrows lying between his legs ready for action; but as soon as we spoke to them, their fear vanished and they became cheerful. In answer to our queries they said, "We have been a month on our journey, in search of the whites to trade." But seeing scarcely anything with them, I asked them what they had to trade. Which rather puzzled them; for they kept looking at each other for some time, without giving an answer. I took them to our camp, gave them a smoke, and then warned them not to follow us nor attempt to steal our horses; for if they did I would shoot them.

Trade however was not their object, they were scouts on the lookout from some large camp. On putting up at night I was informed that several of the Iroquois had followed the Piegans and traded away all their ammunition for a few useless Indian toys, one of which was a headdress of feathers! On inquiring into the particulars, I found the report to be true. I spoke to Pierre the head man and reproved them for their conduct; elk and small deer now became abundant, so that our hunters had no difficulty in keeping the pangs of hunger at a distance. Our traps brought us twelve beaver; being our first successful attempt since we started.

The second day after passing the Piegans,[14] two of the Iroquois, named Laurent and Lizard, deserted the party and turned back; it was some hours before I had notice of the circumstance. Now that they had begun there will be no end to desertion, thought I, if a stop is not speedily put to it; because Jacob got off clear, others think to do so. Losing no time, I took four men with me and pursued after the fugitives. It was a leap in the dark for they might have hid themselves so well in a few minutes time that we could never have found them out; but we came upon the fellows as they were making a fire at the distance of sixteen miles off, and so surprised were they that they took no steps to get out of the way: so we at once laid hold of them but could not by fair means prevail upon them to return. We therefore had recourse to threats, being determined, since they gave us so hard a ride, not to deal too softly with them. Lizard in particular would neither lead nor drive, and we threatened to drag him back at one of the horse tails before he consented to go. Back however we brought them; but having to sleep on the way, we had to keep watch on the rascals all night. On the next day we got back to the party early, raised camp and proceeded, but we had not got far before the cry of "Enemies! Ene-

14 The party was now traveling up the Bitterroot Valley.

mies!" sounded in our ears, a party immediately pushed on ahead, when the supposed enemies turned out to be friends. It was six Nez Perces whom we supposed to be horse thieves, none of them had saddles and yet they were driving horses before them.

Although we had no danger to apprehend from these people yet their presence annoyed us, for it still kept a door open for some of our party to desert, so we got clear of them as soon as possible and hastened on our journey. Before parting however, Pallade, one of the Spokane Indians belonging to our party wished to accompany them. Pallade was a good fellow in his way; but not being accustomed to long journeys he got faint-hearted, so I gave him his discharge and he turned back.

As we left the Indians however, four of the Iroquois kept in the rear and exchanged with the Nez Perces two of their guns for horses! If they had not guns to defend themselves, they had a relay of horses to carry them out of danger! Such improvident and thoughtless beings as Iroquois should always be restricted to their hunting implements: all the rest goes in traffic among the natives, to no purpose. During some days past, the weather had been very severe so that many of the old as well as young got severely frostbitten on their fingers, noses, cheeks, and feet. At every encampment more or less beavers were caught daily. Elk, deer, and mountain goats became very numerous: so that our new regulations made us fare well in the way of provisions. Had it been our lot to pass here in summer instead of winter, there are many level spots and fertile valleys from the appearance of the country that might invite the husbandman and the plough.

After putting up one evening the uncommon noise made by wolves about our camp annoyed us. At last it struck me that it might be wolves on two legs imitating the animal and as the place was very suspicious, I doubled the watch that night and we lay down in our clothes but passed a restless night. In the morning however all was safe, and we were early on our journey. In no place of our trip, scarcely Hell's Gates itself excepted, did we meet with such a gloomy and suspicious place. At every bend of the river wild and romantic scenes opened to view. The river alone preventing the hills and cliffs from embracing each other, and we had to cross and recross twelve times in half as many miles, until we reached a rocky and slippery path on its margin, on which grew a few pine trees, through which the narrow and intricate path led.

Out of one of the pines I have just mentioned,[15] and about five feet from the ground is growing up with the tree, a ram's head with the horns still attached to it! and so fixed and embedded is it in the tree that it must have grown up with it. One of the horns and more than half of the head is buried in the tree; but most of the other horn, and part of the head, protrudes out at least a foot. We examined both. The tree was scarcely two feet in diameter. Here we put up at an early hour and called the place Ram's Horn in compliment.

Our Flathead Indians related to us a rather strange story about the ram's head. Indian legend relates that as the first Flathead Indians that passed this way one of them attacked a mountain ram as large and stout as a common horse, that on wounding him, the fierce animal turned round upon his pursuer, who taking shelter behind the tree, the ram came against it with all his force, so that he drove his head through it, but before he could get it extracted again the Indian killed him and took off the body but left the head, as a memento of the adventure. All Indians reverence the celebrated tree, which they say by the circumstances related conferred on them the power of mastering and killing all animals. Hunters therefore, in passing this way, sacrifice something as a tribute to the ram's head! And one of the Iroquois, not to incur the displeasure of the god of hunters hung a bit of tobacco to the horn, to make his hunting propitious!

Late in the evening when our hunters, who had been in advance of the camp, arrived, they had a sad story to tell. "We have been," said they, "at the head of the river, our travelling in this direction is at an end: the mountains ahead surround us in all directions, and are impassable, the snows everywhere beyond the banks of the river from eight to ten feet deep! and that without a single opening or

15 The Ram's Head or Medicine Tree is close to the bank of the East Fork of the Bitterroot River, near the mouth of Medicine Creek.

pass to get through; so that we may turn back without going further, for we shall have to go by Hell's Gates at last!" Discouraging as these remarks were, we made preparations to advance; for I was determined not to turn back while I could advance. Leaving therefore Ram's Horn encampment, we proceeded in various directions, after making several traverses through ice and snow, we then left the river and crossed what we named the Little Mountain, the ascending and descending of which occupied us many hours, in putting two miles behind us! Regaining the river again, we continued our journey, till we reached a little fork, where two small streams crossed each other at right angles, in the middle of a deep valley, hemmed in by lofty mountains,[16] the appearance of which seemed strongly to confirm the opinion of the hunters, that we could proceed no further in the present course! Here we made a pause and all gazed in wonder at the bold and stupendous front before us, which in every direction seemed to bid defiance to our approach! This gloomy and discouraging spot we reached on the 12th of March 1824, and named the place "The Valley of Troubles."

March 13th. Our situation and the hopeless prospect before us made me pass a sleepless night; but on going through the camp this morning I found many others and the Iroquois in particular with a smile of gratification on their countenances at the idea of their having to turn back. And the very idea of such anticipations on their part aggravated the evil on mine. After putting the camp in a position of defense, for we now had to consider ourselves in an enemy country, I took six men with me and proceeded in the direction our road lay, in order to reconnoiter the passes in the mountains. We set out on horseback and finding in one place an opening out of which opened a small rivulet,[17] we followed it about four miles or more till we reached its source, the source of the Flathead River.[18] But not finding a pass to advance further with horses, we

16 The small valley in which Sula, Montana, is now located. The "little fork" was formed by the juncture of the East Fork of the Bitterroot with Cameron Creek on the north and Camp Creek on the south bank.

17 Camp Creek.

18 The Bitterroot joins the Clark Fork River near Missoula, Montana. Ross considered the Bitterroot to be the main river and therefore thought himself to be at

tied them and proceeded on foot. At the head of the rivulet or creek we ascended one of the mountains,[19] for more than a mile till we reached the top of it where it was level ground; but the snow there was seven feet deep! nor could we form any idea as to the nature of the country further on, it being thickly covered with timber. So we returned, took our horses, and got back to the camp late in the evening, to pass another comfortless night.

March 14th. During this day I got six of my most trusted men ready, with snowshoes and four days' provisions, and sent them across the mountain to ascertain the depth of snow, the nature of the pass, and the distance to the other side. Their instructions led them to follow the road along the creek where I had been on the thirteenth. We shall now leave them to pursue their journey while we notice the occurrences about the camp.

The men I had dispatched were no sooner started than I sent off four others to see if any other more favourable opening could be discovered in a different direction, while myself and a few others proceeded in another quarter; but both parties proved unsuccessful. So we all returned, hungry, fatigued, and discouraged and none more so than myself, although I had to assume cheerfulness to encourage others.

March 15th. The sun had scarcely appeared over the mountain ridges, before some of our people called out, "Indians! Indians!" when we beheld, crossing from the woods, five solitary wretches on snowshoes coming towards our camp. On their arrival I was rejoiced to find that they were Snakes, as I expected to get some interesting information from them respecting the mountain passes and other matters. They were however anything but intelligent; we could neither understand them nor they us, consequently we could learn nothing from them.

These strangers were the very picture of wretchedness, and had a singularly odd appearance. They were wrapped up in buffalo hides with the hair next to their skin and caps of wolfskin, with the

the headwaters of the Flathead system, a succession of rivers and lakes debouching into the Columbia some ten miles south from Trail, British Columbia.

19 Saddle Mountain, not more than a mile from present-day Gibbon Pass.

ears of that animal as erect as if alive. They resembled rather walking ghosts than living men! Their condition however excited com-
passion. They belonged, if we could judge from the jargon they
spoke, to the mountain Snakes. Yet with all their ignorance, I intended attaching them to our party had not an unforeseen circumstance prevented it.

The day after the five Snakes arrived, two of the hunters came
running into camp almost breathless, calling out, "A war party, a
war party!" This announcement rather surprised me to think
where a war party could come from at the season of the year, and
in such a part of the country as we were in, as Indians seldom go
on war expeditions during the winter. We however got our big
gun ready, match lighted, and all hands armed in a few minutes
when I observed at a short distance, a large body of Indians coming down the slope of a hill, having every appearance of a war party.
On their approaching our camp, not knowing what might happen,
I immediately ordered the Snakes off to the woods; but told them
to join us again as soon as the storm passed over; but we never saw
them afterwards.

When the Indians who were approaching us had got within two
hundred yards of our camp they made a halt, and collecting in a
group, stood still. To this group we pointed our gun. Taking then
a flag in my hand and one man with me we went up to them; I telling my people at this time that if there were danger or the Indians
attempted anything to us, I would wave a handkerchief as a signal
for them to fire off the gun at once. They however proved to be a
mixture of Nez Perces and Shaw-ha-ap-tens,[20] eighty-four in number, headed by two of the principal chiefs. We then all joined the
camp.

Although not a war party nor our declared enemies; yet they are
not at all times friendly when abroad and I could have very well
disposed with their visit, under existing difficulties they were
hailed with a heartfelt welcome by most of my people, particularly
the Iroquois.

It will be recollected that some time ago we fell in with six Nez

[20] Both are names for the same tribe.

Perces with whom two of my Iroquois had to exchange their guns for horses, which horses it would appear did not belong to the fellows who had sold them. They belonged to our visitors, and the chiefs claimed them as soon as they arrived, mentioning the six Nez Perces and the place where they had stolen the horses. The Iroquois had therefore to deliver them up and I was not displeased at it. When the Indians were going off however, I interposed in their behalf and the chiefs consented to give them two old guns in lieu of the new ones they had given for the horses!

On this occasion, the head chief told me that since we had passed Hell's Gate the Blackfeet had stolen at two different times 135 of the Nez Perces and Flathead horses. He also informed me that five of the Snakes had been at the camp of the former on an embassy of peace, succeeded in the object of their mission, and returned loaded with presents. It was not likely however that the five wretches we had seen were the delegates spoken of! In reference to the pass through the mountains, the absorbing question with me, the chief observed that we could not possibly pass before the month of May! and then the only practicable road was in the direction my men had gone.[21] This information was not calculated to cheer us in our present situation. At the expiration of two days all the Indians left us but not before they had rifled the unprincipled Iroquois of almost every article they possessed, in exchange for Indian toys.

Expecting hourly the return of the six men I had sent across the mountain on the fourteenth, I had been revolving in my mind the best plan to be pursued. In the meantime however, as I expected their report would be such as would discourage any further advances and as such might have a decided effect on the conduct of my people, I resolved on going to meet them in order to prepare their report before it reached our camp, and to place it before the people in its most encouraging features. So I set off under the pretence of going to hunt; but after proceeding some five or six miles[22] and waiting all day I returned at night unsuccessful, telling my

21 The route suggested by the chief is present-day Gibbon Pass.
22 The distance from the camp site to Saddle Mountain is about ten miles.

people of course that I had seen plenty of game; but failed in killing any.

I passed a sleepless night, and getting up early the next morning
and telling my people I was going off again to hunt I set out to wait
with anxious forebodings, the arrival of my men; but had not been
long at my station before I was agreeably relieved by their arrival
and the more so by their having loads of buffalo meat on their
backs, a very welcome article to us in our situation, for animals had
become very scarce about the camp, and our hunters had to go a
long distance before finding any. The men had been six days on
their journey and two of them were almost snow-blind, a grievous
and painful malady which often affects people travelling on snow
in the spring of the year. We however sat down on the crust of the
snow, struck a fire, and made a meal on the flesh they had brought
with them. During all the time Grand Paul, the chief man, related
the story of their journey which we will give the reader in his
own words.

"From the head of the creek we proceeded across the mountain
in a south-east direction. The first three miles were thickly wooded,
and the snow from six to eight feet deep with a strong crust on the
top. Afterwards the country became more open with occasional
small prairies here and there, the snow however keeping the same
depth with the crust still harder and harder on the top as we advanced for about three miles further, till we had reached fully the
middle of the mountain. From there all along to the other side, a
distance of six miles more, the snow ranged from five to six feet
deep with the crust very strong, till we got to the open prairies. The
distance therefore across is twelve long miles, a distance and depth
of snow that can never be passed with horses in its present state.

"Beyond the mountain is a large open plain over which the snow
is scarcely a foot deep, and there we found plenty of buffalo, sixteen of which we killed; but for want of wood and other materials
we could not make stages to preserve the meat but had to abandon
it to the wolves, excepting the little we have brought with us."
Here, then, is a description of the mountain pass as related by those

who had examined it. So that we knew now something of the extent of the difficulties before us. Country generally pretty level.

According to the plan in my own mind I instructed the men how they were to act on getting to the camp in order that they might not discourage the people, who at the time required but the shadow of an excuse to turn back. "Pass we must," said I to them! "You will therefore proceed to the camp without, however, letting any-one know that you have seen me, and the story that you will tell there will be thus: That the mountain is only eight, instead of twelve miles," for it appeared to me very possible that the men themselves might have exaggerated the distance, "that after the first three miles the snow gets less and less, and that a south wind with a few fine days, which we may now hourly expect, would soon reduce the quantity of the snow. The difficulty of passing will be easily overcome, and that once on the opposite side buffalo for our-selves and grass for our horses will be abundant. That a few days' exertions will put all our troubles and difficulties behind us, and in plenty of beaver we shall soon forget our toil and make up for the lost time."

The men went off to the camp and did just as I told them. I re-turned late in the evening; but without having killed any game! So that my people of course, marked me down in their own mind as a blundering hunter. On reaching the camp I of course pre-tended not to know of my men's arrival, went up to them, asked the news of their trip, when Grand Paul, in the presence of all, re-peated the story I had put into his mouth, respecting the road, the snow, and the distance. With all the difficulties of the undertaking pressing on my mind, I assembled the head men of the different parties and several others together, and we held a council on the steps to be taken in order to cross the mountains.

But our council was very discordant; some began by observing that the undertaking was utterly impossible, others smiled at the folly of such an attempt, while some thought it even madness to attempt making a road over such a field of snow. Nettled at their obstinacy, I instantly checked their remarks by observing that I did not call them together to decide on the possibility or impossibility of making the road, that I had settled that point already in my own mind; but simply to have their opinions on what they might consider the easiest and best way of doing it for do it we must: and the sooner they became unanimous the better.

This sudden check caused such a long pause that I got alarmed that they would not speak at all. After some time however old Pierre broke silence by observing that "We might try horses." Others remarked that "It would be easier done on foot." While some said nothing at all, but observed a sullen silence. The general view however was for turning back. Here I had to interrupt them again. I told them turning back was out of the question. Some then observed that we might remain where we were until the fine weather would make the road for us. Old Pierre again spoke in favour of trying the road, some others spoke to the same effect! On this occasion, I had every reason to be satisfied with the conduct of old Pierre the Iroquois while on the other hand John Grey and his confederates opposed those who were for making the road. And on this occasion the disaffected were the most listened to. Grey opposed everything but turning back. At last however they all agreed to try the road any way I wished.

I then presented to them the necessity of our persevering in the direction we were in and that without a moment's delay, that according to Paul's report there were only eight miles and that would scarcely be 300 yards to each. That the joint efforts of so many men and horses would soon remove the trifling difficulties before us. My opinion therefore was, that we should set about making the road the following day; and to this they all agreed, and we parted in good spirits.

I began to think that all would go on well; but I soon found out to my great disappointment that what was settled within doors was soon forgotten out of doors for when our meeting broke up our negotiations fell to the ground. Old Pierre began to waver, and for everyone that was for making the road ten were against it, and to add to our other perplexities there unfortunately fell, during the night, more than a foot of snow!

March 20th. Notwithstanding the conflicting opinions regarding the road and the unlooked-for fall of snow, I ultimately succeeded in getting 45 men to start, with 80 horses, to begin the road and never did I set out on any undertaking with less hopes of success than I did on this. On arriving at the place, we were at a loss for some time how to begin; but after a good deal of manoeuvering, one man on snowshoes took the foremost horse by the bridle, while another applied the whip to urge the animal on; when it had made several plunges forward, it got fatigued so there we left it in the snow, but the head and ears above the surface.

A second was then whipped up along side of the first, and urged forward, making several plunges, still farther on, and then it lay in the snow, some six or seven yards ahead of the other. The third did the same, and soon till the last: when nothing was to be seen of our eighty horses but a string of heads and ears above the snow! We then dragged out the first, then the second, and so on, till we had them all back again; the difficulty of getting them extricated was greater than that of urging them forward: but we were partly recompensed by the novelty of the scene and the mirth and glee the operation diffused among the people. All this was very well for a while, but the men as well as the horses soon got tired of it. This single operation, for we only went over all the horses once, occupied us nine hours and we got only 580 yards of the road half made, and returned to camp after dusk!

Our first attempt, although an arduous one, produced no very flattering result, scarcely a quarter of a mile, although I represented to the people that it was far beyond any expectation; but in my own mind the task appeared beyond our means of accomplishing it, and one of the most discouraging undertakings I had ever attempted. And when so hopeless under shelter of the woods what would it be out in the open plains, when it would be liable from every blast of wind, drift or snow to be filled up in as many hours as we should spend days in opening it? I however put the best face on things, and did everything in my power to cherish that hope which was so necessary to encourage my people to persevere and finish that which we had begun.

March 21st. After some hesitation among the people, we again resumed our labours at the road; but out of forty men and eighty-five horses which had set out in the morning twenty-eight of the former and fifty of the latter were all that reached the ground, so that after eight hours' hard toil in much the same way as the day before we only made the distance of 370 yards, and dark night brought us back to our quarters. With various degrees of success and much anxiety and labour we continued doing more or less each day till the 27th, when we reached the extremity of the woods; but in the open plains our progress promised to be exceedingly slow and discouraging: both on account of the additional distance we had to travel backwards and forwards, as well as the uncertainty of the winds and drift, which kept filling up the road nearly as fast as we could open it. Nor had we after eight days' harassing labour got over more than one-third of the distance! Although if anything the depth of the snow had got less; yet in no place was it under seven feet. There were also other inconveniences. The mornings were cold as in winter; but during the day the sun melted the snow on our clothes and made them uncomfortable, and in the evening they froze and got stiff on our backs. The task was so disheartening that on the last day I found myself left at the task with only four of that number! I alone worked with heart and hand. After smoking our pipes, we turned our faces towards the camp but not to enjoy pleasure, for a dark and discouraging gloom had now spread its influence from one end of the camp to the other.

Still trying however to show a cheerful countenance I began to praise our actions and admire the progress we had made, in order to draw from the better affected portion of my people a full disclosure of their feelings on the subject of the road, although I could read their feelings and their thoughts as well as I knew any man. For disappointment now appeared inevitable, and I had soon to regret that I had given them the opportunity of expressing themselves, for their looks without an expression might have convinced any man that nothing was working within, but a determined stand against any more road making. I therefore changed the subject as quickly as possible. This conversation took place at some little distance from the camp.

In this perplexing situation, I saw something must be done without delay. I therefore began to mention to them the advantages that we would derive from changing our plan of proceeding altogether. Not that I really thought we could better it; but because I foresaw that without something new to divert their present feelings we should never advance. We again joined the camp.

But if discouraged before, I found but little to cheer or console me in the camp. Provisions were scarce, neither did our horses, more than ourselves fare too well. Everything in fact seemed to set against us.

The greatest difficulty however was the treachery of the Iroquois, in proportion as other troubles embarrassed me, never failed to take advantage of them: at this very time, it was assumed that they were trying to diffuse disaffection through the whole party. Perceiving a storm fast gathering, I prepared to meet it.

I immediately convened not only the four principal men as they were called, for their influence as well as their fidelity was at an end, but all hands. After stating the great progress we had made in so short a time, and the praise that was due to their unwearied exertions, I proposed as an improvement that there should be a week's respite from labour in order to lay in a stock of provisions and give time for the snows to decrease in the mountains and at the other side, and then, with a few fine days, we should be able to finish the road in a short time. That the horse plan did not succeed well, that we should adopt a more efficient and expeditious plan of proceeding. We should get mallets and wooden shovels made. This done, two men would break the crust, the shovel men would follow, while the greater part would keep packing down the snow with their feet behind. That twenty men, day about, would be employed, and the others would guard the camp, provide provisions, and we would make short work of it. Having thus stated my plan in a few words, I paused for their answers. Their silence was enough.

Here I found, but too late, that I had committed a blunder on assembling all the camp together, for it is always easier to gain on the few than on the many. At last they broke silence, and twenty voices spoke at once. I was mortified to find that my private instructions to Grand Paul respecting the length of the road had got among them; which by no means mended the matter. John Grey stated, that "the road across the mountain was twenty miles, and the snows nearer twenty feet deep than seven!" Old Pierre and others observed, "We had no provisions for ourselves, and our animals were starving," while many swore against making any more of the road. "We will neither work with mallets nor shovels." In short, the universal cry was for turning back, and relinquishing the road as impossible. "Where are the provisions," was the general cry, "our families are now starving." I told them if we had no provisions we had hunters, we had guns and ammunition. "I will answer for provisions," said I, "let there be but a good understanding and unanimity among ourselves, secure that, and I will answer for the rest. Besides," continued I, "in accomplishing the task before us, we can boast of having done what was never equalled by man in this country before!"

After some time and a great deal of speechifying a few of them began to come round and expressed themselves as friendly to the plan of making the road, simply I supposed, because it was new; among the first were some of the Iroquois: we must give every one his due. And had I not known their character too well I might have been led to believe that they were in right good faith. Even John Grey seemed to adopt my views. This man, an Iroquois half-breed from Montreal and educated, had no small degree of influence over his countrymen but he was unfortunately a refractory and base character. After stating however my views to them, they all agreed to continue the road, after a week's respite. I began once more to entertain some hopes of success. We then smoked our pipes together, and parted for the night in the most friendly manner.

Notwithstanding the apparent good understanding, I soon heard that Grey had been very busy in trying to poison the minds of the Iroquois, and of the others by strongly advising them to turn back and not submit to any more road-making. That I was but one man, and could not force them to it. That they had dug long enough in snow, and they would have a summer's work of it, and he doubted if they could do it in one summer! he swore. Back he was determined to go, and he would wish to see the man that would prevent him; reasoning among people already tired and disaffected had its influence. I knew Grey was disseminating this feeling in the camp and was of course preparing, in the feeble position I stood, to counteract it. Nothing however declared itself openly till the second day in the evening, and I was in hopes his machinations would have fallen to the ground; but in this I was mistaken, for a little before sundown he came to my tent, saying he wished to see me, I told him to come in. After sitting down for a few minutes he told me that "he was deputed by the Iroquois and other freemen to let me know that they regretted their promise made at the council and could not fulfil it, that they were all resolved on abandoning the undertaking and turning back!"

He said that by remaining to make the road they would lose the spring hunt, and besides, that they were tired of remaining in the large party and wished to hunt apart, moreover that they did not come to this country to be making roads: they came to hunt beaver. "As for myself," said Grey, "others may do what they please, but I shall turn back. I am a free man, and I suppose I can do as I please." John having proceeded this far, I got out of all patience and interrupted him by observing, "Whatever you have got to say, John, on your own behalf, I am ready to hear; but not one word on behalf of any one else. The present," said I to him, "savours very much of a combination to defraud the Company and disappoint me. You have all taken a weary view of things. Every rose," continued I, "has its thorn, John: so has the hunting of beaver. You say that by remaining to make the road you will lose the spring hunt. You will do no such thing; but by turning back you will lose not only the spring but the fall hunt. The spring here is later by a month than in any other part of the country. Your plan is a bad one, even were it at your choice, which is not the case. You follow my advice John, I alone am answerable for your hunts. Since you dislike large parties you should have remained at home and not have come to this country at all. Small parties cannot hunt here. And as to your digging in snows and making roads, it is of two evils perhaps the least. It is better for you to be making roads for a few days than to have had for as many weeks to contend with a more powerful and dangerous enemy: which would have been the case, had we passed through Hell's Gates and had to fight our way among the Blackfeet.

"We have all embarked," said I to him, "on a sea of troubles; great quantities of furs are not to be secured in these parts without fatigues, cares, hardships, and perils. My advice therefore to you and to all is to submit to circumstances, abandon the idea of turning back."

John however persisted in his opinion, and swore that neither fair words nor anything else would alter his mind, that "back he would go." "You are a most unreasonable man," said I to him, "you gave your consent two nights ago and things are not worse now than they were then, and you now withdraw that consent. But I did wrong in asking your consent, I ought rather to have commanded, and for the future I am determined to ask no man's consent in such matters, and if you attempt to turn back I shall certainly try to stop you or any one else." On my saying so, John abruptly got up, bade me good night, and went off.

Grey's conduct made me pass an anxious and uncomfortable night; but as usual I got up early in the morning and soon afterwards, sure enough as he had said, John collected, saddled, and loaded his horses ready for a start, and every eye in the camp was directed to witness his departure. The affair had now come to a crisis, the success or failure of the expedition depended on the issue. I went up to him with a cocked pistol in my hand, and ordered him either to pay his debt or unsaddle his horses and turn them off with the others, or he was a dead man. John seeing no person interfere thought better of it, unsaddled his horses, and I returned to my tent, not another word was spoken, and here the affair ended.

Although I had now succeeded in settling the knotty point with Grey, yet I was not altogether without my fears that something might take place to disturb our arrangements, it was evident from the sullen conduct of the Iroquois that if left together they would still be plotting mischief. To divide them as quickly as possible was my only plan. I therefore fitted out and dispatched a party of ten men to cross the mountain in pursuit of buffalo, not forgetting to place four of the Iroquois among them. The other hunters were dispersed in every direction in quest of smaller game; my friend John Grey I kept in the camp with myself.

The small deer had become very scarce, and in my anxiety to get a stock of provisions laid up that we might proceed with the road, I offered a reward of a new gun to the hunter who should prove himself most deserving, this had a good effect but as the valleys furnished but little, they had to proceed to the mountains in search of the big horn, or mountain sheep as they are called, and a third party took to the woods for mallets and shovels, so that I had them all divided the next day and the distribution promised fair to preserve peace and good order for a time.

Scarcity of provisions troubled me greatly, and to ensure success as far as possible I studied to make such a distribution of the people that neither plots nor travelling could well be carried on without detection, and with strict economy in the camp and an equitable distribution of everything that came with it, we hoped to guard against the worst. The big horn party had good luck during several days; but those animals are smaller in size than I had been in the habit of seeing elsewhere with very disproportionate heads for the size of their bodies, and still more disproportionate horns to the size of the head. The average weight of these animals was 70 lbs. The head of the male generally weighed as much as a third of the body, and the horns were twice the weight of the head without them. One of the ram's horns brought into our camp measured 49 inches in length, following the curve or greatest side round the convex side, and the circumference in the thickest part, 28 inches. This horn weighed eleven pounds. On the seventh day after starting, the buffalo hunters from across the mountains arrived successful and our supplies from all quarters put us in possession of eight days' provisions in advance, with which we prepared to resume our labours at the road.

April 3rd. At six o'clock in the morning after an interval of seven days, I set out with forty men and seventy horses with shovels and mallets for each, John Grey among the number, to resume our labours at the road. After reaching the place however, the weather turned out so bad with sleet and snow that we were forced to return home without doing much. And what was still worse, many parts of the road already made were filled up again, this was a very discouraging circumstance, and caused a good deal of murmuring. Indeed the distance from our camp to the scene of operation being not less now than nine miles and the return another nine was of itself, without any other labour, a day's work. Many hints were given by the Iroquois about rum, that had I now and then a dram to give them, my road would soon be made. I knew myself that a little in our present state would have done more towards hastening on the road than all the powers without it, and I would at this time have given twenty guineas for as many pints of rum, had it been in my power to get it!

April 4th. At an early hour this morning we were again at work with the same number of men as yesterday. But whether from the novelty of our shovel operations or that the new plan was better than the old one I could not say, but we made in the usual depth of snow and same number of hours eight hundred and ten yards; but were so tired at night as to be hardly able to mount our horses.

On the 5th with the same number of men as the day before, we only made about four hundred and fifty yards, although we laboured the same number of hours.

On the 6th. We did nothing at all. I attempted to start in the morning, but the attempt proved fruitless: there being a good deal of reluctance and altercation among the parties so that I had at last to yield to circumstances and there was no road-making that day, I was rather apprehensive that as the conflicting opinions were marked with a good deal of bad feelings they would have resulted in a second break-up; but fortunately we got all our differences arrayed and closed the day in harmony.

April 7th. Early this morning I started with thirty-five men, and happening to fall on a small ridge part of the way, we succeeded in opening rather more than a mile in length, in almost bare plains. This was cheering, and greatly revived our sinking spirits; but we were kept in constant alarms for fear the wind and drift should rise, for had it blown but an hour it might have destroyed the labour of days. Our hopes now rested on calm weather, and to labour day and night, till we should accomplish the task before us. Six of the men volunteered to work all night! Some encamped on the ground. Others went home and I among the latter number, for I could not venture to sleep out one night lest new troubles arising in the camp should disarrange all my plans.

April 8th. At sunrise I set out this morning with every man and boy I could muster, leaving only five men to guard the camp, and not a murmur was heard, our success now depending on dispatch. Several of the women were in attendance with horses to carry us back at night. During last night the six men who volunteered their services had only made about fifty yards. This day to our annoyance there fell a good deal of drizzling rain, which wet us to the skin, and in the evening our clothes froze on our backs and became stiff, but the people notwithstanding encamped at the edge of the woods instead of going home, so as to begin early in the morning, I and another man only returning to the camp.

April 9th. At an early hour, and before a single man of the party who had slept out had got his eyes open, I was on the ground to rouse them up. And although we began to work somewhat later in the day than usual yet before night, our day's labour proved the best we had made, having with our shovels, our mallets, our feet, and the additional assistance of fifty-eight horses beaten down a distance of nearly two miles in length! After this day's labour, and not until then, did my people entertain a hope of success. From that time we all indulged the anticipation of accomplishing our task in spite of every obstacle. The wind alone, over which we had no control, was all I now dreaded. The two next days, the tenth and eleventh, our task was that of slaves.

April 12th. At 5 o'clock in the afternoon of this day I and four others, after a day of severe toil, reached the other side on horseback! but being too late, and our horses too tired to return, we encamped there. The dread of the wind blowing kept us from all rest, and when I did slumber a little after the fatigue of the day, it was only to dream of fine roads and pleasant walks and then awake to blame my fancy for having deceived me. Nor was it till we had reached the other side that I was fully aware of my situation, for had it come on to blow the road through which we had forced our way would have been rendered impassable and I should then have found myself completely separated from my people for days, when all our labour and anxiety would have been to no purpose had my people taken advantage of the opportunity thus offered to return back. But fortunately the night was calm and I got back and joined my people on the thirteenth.

On the 14th. We raised camp, and bidding farewell to the Valley of Troubles, where we had been kept in anxious suspense for thirty-three days, put up for the night at the head of the creek, or foot of the mountains, prior to our crossing it. And an anxious night we passed.

The spot on which we now encamped forms the extreme point of Flathead River, which may be considered a distance of 345 miles from its entrance into the main Columbia a little above Kettle Falls, of which some two hundred and fifty are navigable for craft of moderate size, and the rest for loaded canoes.

On the top of the mountains before us, and over which our road leads and not more than a mile from our present camp, is a small circular spring of water issuing out of the ground, and over which I stood for some time smoking my pipe with a foot on each side of it. This spring is the source, as far as I can learn, of the great Missouri River,[23] which after meandering through the mountains nearly parallel with our road crosses the grand prairie, where after uniting with several other smaller streams, a river fifty feet broad and about two and a half deep is formed which then flows in the direction of east.

---

[23] This spring is only one of a number feeding the Big Hole River, which becomes the Jefferson. The Jefferson joins with the Madison and the Gallatin to form the Missouri. Ross knew the country to where he stood, and had heard of the Missouri. By combining knowledge and hearsay he concluded that the Missouri was not far off.

April 15th. Long before daylight we were all on foot, in order to profit by the crust in passing the mountain. When all were ready I took my stand on the side of the road as they began to ascend, to see that all passed. As soon as we reached the summit of the mountain the string, a mile and a half in length, began to form. Six men with about thirty of the light horses led the van. The loaded horses were next, the families followed, and I with four of the men brought up the rear. But every now and then a halt unavoidable took place. A load would get upset or disarranged, a horse ingulphed, or some of the families entangled in the snow. So that it was one constant run forward and backward lifting, adjusting, and encouraging all day.

It was a new scene in the wilderness. Nothing appearing above the surface of the snow, of all that was moving, but the heads and shoulders of the riders! Children calling out with hunger, men with thirst, women affrighted, dogs howling, a scream here and a scream there; yet amidst all this bustle, anxiety, and confusion we pressed forward and got safely across after fifteen hours' exertion just as the sun was setting, and without loss or accident to either man or beast. And my first prayer was that a snowstorm might render the road behind us impassable to both man and beast, so as to prevent the Iroquois or anyone else from attempting to turn back or give us further annoyance.

But the struggle was over, not the distance however of eight miles as was stated, nor yet of twelve, as Paul had given us to understand, but eighteen! and perhaps few men in the ordinary routine of their lives in this country ever suffered more anxiety or laboured harder to accomplish a task they had undertaken than was our lot during the month past.

Making the road took the united labour of fifty men and two hundred and forty horses, with all the other available means within our power, twenty-one days! and it must be allowed to have been an arduous undertaking with such a medley of people, and the more so, where it is taken into consideration that our supper at night depended on the good or bad luck of our hunters during the day. To their exertions and perseverance however no small merit was due.

11. LAND OF THE PIEGANS

T HE MOUNTAIN with all its perplexities and difficulties being now behind us, we considered ourselves on hunting ground and also on enemy's ground, both incidents requiring additional care; for these reasons new and stringent regulations became absolutely necessary. It was therefore settled as to the night watch that all the horses should in future be collected into one band close by our camp every evening, and these hobbled and guarded nightly. That not less than four men at a time should be on the watch after dark, to be relieved once every night, with a superintendent to each; and that as to our proceedings by day it was agreed that all hands should raise camp together, that no person should run ahead, either to hunt or to set traps, nor lag behind, that while travelling they should keep close together, that no traps should be put in the water before the party encamped and that no person should slip out of camp, the safety and success of the expedition depending upon a rigid observance of these rules, that any individual wilfully disregarding them should be punished.

We now proposed to advance through the mountains, without any plan as to our route; the appearance of the country for beaver and other local circumstances would henceforth regulate all our movements. Leaving therefore our mountain encampment we advanced in nearly an easterly direction, crossing in succession five small branches of the headwaters of the Missouri; on one of these it was that McDonald lost his man Anderson last year by the Piegans,[1] after proceeding some distance we followed down one of

---

[1] Anderson was killed during a parley between Finan McDonald's party and the group of Blackfeet warriors described on subsequent pages. The parley took place some days before the battle.

these creeks for upwards of twenty miles; but during all that distance we only met with one solitary tree on its banks! on this woodless creek we encamped the second day and took twenty beaver at the first lift; here however fresh Piegan tracks were frequently seen, which admonished us to take care of our horses, so that the new regulations were strictly enforced, both day and night.

At a little distance from our camp I found one of those hot springs so often mentioned in former expeditions; but this being the first I had ever seen myself I viewed it with some degree of curiosity; it was of a circular form ten feet in diameter and only about nine inches deep with a white sediment, the water reddish and tasted of iron, no grass grows about its margin; but although hot it did not boil.

On leaving Hot Spring Encampment the following day, and while crossing a large open plain, we were suddenly overtaken by a furious snow storm. In a moment the day was almost turned into night so that we got completely bewildered, the one running against the other, without knowing whither to go for shelter. In this perplexing situation I called out for each to shift for himself. In the meantime, myself and several others went off and after several hours wandering got to some woods a little before dusk, where we passed the night: but the storm continuing with unabated violence we could not start next day. The day following however, the weather clearing up we began to travel about in search of our lost companions, so that by night we had all got together once more excepting two of the Iroquois and their families, in all seven persons, and as their horses were found with their saddles and baggage on their backs, we expected that they had all perished in the storm. All hands went off in search of them; but we kept looking along the adjacent woods, never thinking they would have lodged in the low plains, until I and some others happened to cross the plains where the storm had overtaken us, and seeing a dog belonging to them howling in a low place, that at once confirmed suspicion that they had perished, we therefore approached the spot with anxious steps; after some time we by mere chance found them alive, buried however under two or three feet of snow! As soon as the storm broke out they dismounted, and rolling themselves up in a leathern lodge, lay quiet; they had tried to get up, and had made their way to the light of the sun but the snow having melted about them, their clothes had got all wet, and the weather so piercing cold that they durst not leave their hiding place, where they had been for three nights and two days without food or fire, and must have soon perished for want of both as they had nothing to strike a fire and were at least six miles from the woods. We however dug them out and wrapping them up in part of our clothing got them to our camp, when after some care they all recovered.

After leaving Stormy Encampment we kept wandering about through the intricate passes of the mountains, trapping and hunting with tolerable success for six days during which time we passed the middle branch of the Missouri,[2] and the track where Lewis and Clark crossed over from that river to the waters of the Columbia, on their journey to the Pacific in 1804.[3] While in the last defile we took ninety-five beavers one morning, and sixty more during the same day; but the next time we set we only took three! Before we got out of this part of our rugged road, we had in one place to ascend on the east side of a mountain for about two miles, and then descend the same on the west side; for the first miles the descent was so steep, that anything dropped from the top rolled down several hundred yards, without stopping, and for the next mile in length, the intricate tortuous windings were so short, so frequent, and so steep, sometimes up, sometimes down, sideways, crossways and perpendicular steps, that we had a thousand hairbreadth escapes with ourselves as well as our horses before we reached the bottom which however we providentially did without accident.

Being now relieved from the mountains on the east side we considered ourselves in the Snake country, a country comparatively more open than that which we had been wandering through for some time past. In advancing in a westerly direction,[4] we came to

2 The Beaverhead River.

3 1805, rather than 1804. They left the Beaverhead River near the site of Armstead, Montana, traveling west to Lemhi Pass and the Continental Divide.

4 That is, before crossing the Continental Divide.

that memorable spot,[5] where as already noticed, McDonald had lost seven of his men in a pitched battle with the Piegans the year before, and as we promised to notice in course of our narrative the particulars of that unfortunate rencontre we give it in the words of those who were eye-witnesses.

One day they had travelled till dark in search of water, when they found some at the bottom of a deep and rocky ravine down which they went and encamped: as they had seen no traces of enemies during the day, and being tired they all went to sleep without keeping watch. In the morning however just at the dawn of day, they were saluted from the top of the ravine, before they got up, with a volley of balls about their ears, without however killing or wounding any; but one of them had the stock of his gun pierced through with a ball, and another of them his powder horn shivered to pieces, and this was all the injury they sustained from the enemy's discharge. The alarm was instantly given, all hands in confusion sprang up and went out to see what was the matter, some with one shoe on and the other off, others naked with the gun in one hand and their clothes in the other, when they perceived the Indians on the top of the rocks, yelling and flourishing their arms; the whites gave a loud huzza, and all hands were collected together in an instant; but the Indians instead of taking advantage of their position wheeled about and marched off without firing another shot.

McDonald at the head of thirty men set out to pursue them; but finding the ravine so steep and rocky to ascend, they were apprehensive that the disappearance of the Indians all at once was a stratagem to entrap them when they might have been popped off by the enemy from behind stones and trees without having an opportunity of defending themselves; acting on this opinion they returned and taking a supply of powder and ball with them they mounted their horses to the number of forty-five and then pursued the enemy leaving twenty men behind to guard the camp, when our people got to the head of the ravine the Indians were about a mile off, and all on foot having no horses with the exception of five

5 Near Brenner, Montana.

for carrying their luggage, and before our people could get up with them they had to pass another ravine still deeper and broader than the one they were encamped in, and that before they had got down on one side of it the enemy had got up on the other side, and here again the Indians did not avail themselves of their advantage, but allowed our people to follow without firing a shot at them, as if encouraging them on, and so bold and confident were they that many of them bent themselves down in a posture of contempt by way of bidding them defiance.

As soon as our people had got over the second ravine they took a sweep, wheeled about, and met the Indians in the teeth, then dismounting, the battle began without a word being spoken on either side; as soon as the firing commenced the Indians began their frantic gestures, whooped, and yelled, with the view of intimidating and fought like demons, one fellow all the time waving a scalp on the end of a pole; nor did they yield an inch of ground till more than twenty of them lay dead! At last they threw down their guns and held up their hands as a signal of peace; by this time the people had lost three men, and not thinking they had yet taken ample vengeance for their death made a rush on the Indians, killed the fellow who held the pole and carried off the scalp and the five horses, the Indians then made a simultaneous dash to one side to get into a small coppice of woods, leaving their dead on the spot where they fell, our people supposed that they had just laid down their arms and next taken to the bush because they had got short of ammunition as many of the shots latterly were but mere puffs, and unfortunately for them, the scalp taken proved to be none other than poor Anderson's, and this double proof of their guilt so enraged our people that to the bush they followed them.

McDonald then sent to the camp for buckshot and they poured volleys into the bush among them from the distance of some twenty or thirty yards, till they had expended fifty-six pounds weight, the Indians all this time only fixing a single shot now and then when the folly and imprudence of our people led them too near, and on these conditions they seldom missed their mark. Here three more of the whites fell at this part of the conflict, two of our own people, an Iroquois and a Canadian, got into a high dispute as to who was the bravest man when the former challenged the latter to go with him into the bush and scalp a Piegan, the Canadian accepted the challenge when taking each other by the hand and a scalping knife in the other, savage-like, they entered the bush and advanced until they had got within four feet of a Piegan when the Iroquois said, "I will scalp this one, go you and scalp another," but just as he was in the act of stretching out his hand to lay hold of him the Piegan shot him through the head, and so bespattered the Canadian with his brains that he was almost blind; the Canadian however got back again to his comrades but deferred taking the scalp. McDonald and his men being fatigued with firing thought of another and perhaps more effectual plan of destroying the Piegans. It blew a strong gale of wind at the time and setting fire to the bush of dry and decayed wood it burnt with the rapidity of straw, and the devouring element laid the whole bush in ashes in a very short time; when fire was proposed a question arose who was brave enough to go and fire the bush, at the muzzle of the Piegan guns? "The oldest man in the camp," said McDonald, "and I'll guard him." The lot fell upon Bastony, a superannuated hunter on the wrong side of seventy, the poor and wrinkled old man took the flambeau of destruction in his hand and advanced trembling every step with the fear of instant death before him while McDonald and some others walked at his heels with their guns cocked. The fire was set, the party returned, and volleys of buckshot were again poured into the bush to aid the fire in the work of destruction, about one hundred yards from the burning bush was another much larger bush, and while the fire was consuming the one our people advanced and stationed themselves at the end of the other, to intercept any of the Piegans that might attempt the doubtful alternative of saving themselves by taking refuge in it and to ensure success the better, our people left the passage from one bush to the other open, while they themselves stood in two rows, one upon each side, with their guns cocked, when suddenly the half-roasted Piegans, after uttering a scream of despair, burst through the flames and made a last and expiring effort to gain the other bush; then our people poured in upon each

241

side of them a fatal volley of ball and buckshot which almost finished what the flames had spared, yet notwithstanding all these sanguinary precautions a remnant escaped by getting into the bush! the wounded Indians who fell under the last volley the Iroquois dealt with in their own way, with the knife!

After the tragedy was ended our people collected their dead, and returned to camp at sunset, not we should suppose to rejoice but rather to mourn, and we afterward learned that only seven out of the seventy-five which formed the party of the unfortunate Piegans returned home to relate the mournful tale! Although our people were drawn into this unfortunate affair with justice on their side yet they persevered in it with folly and ended with cruelty; no wonder then if they paid with their own blood.

Withdrawing ourselves from this spot we journeyed on to the westward for some time until we reached a strong and rapid stream about fifty yards broad[6] which empties itself into the great south branch,[7] called by our hunters, Salmon River:[8] I thought the more appropriate name would have been Lewis' Fork, as it was the first Columbia water the exploring party fell on after crossing the Rocky Mountains. This stream forces its way through a very bleak, sterile, and rocky part of the country, yet we crossed it and recrossed up the west side for upwards of ninety miles, till we got to a place called Canoe Point[9] where the different branches from the four cardinal points of the compass form a cross. It runs in the direction of north west.

But it did not prove rich in beaver, fifty-five at a lift being the most we took at any one time during our journey on it. Here however in many places the snow had begun to disappear and the young grass grew up fast; and here our horses for the first time since we left Flathead Fort fed without digging in the snow; the

6 The Lemhi River.

7 The Snake River.

8 Here Ross may have mistaken the Lemhi, which flows into the Salmon, for the Salmon River itself. The Salmon subsequently empties into the Snake River. In journeying westward the party had crossed the Continental Divide, moving from the Beaverhead to the Lemhi drainage.

9 Here the Lemhi joins the Salmon River.

further we advanced the scarcer were the beaver, often taking no more than twenty a day; but buffalo were abundant; immense herds of these animals were to be seen in every direction; they were not fat at this early season.

In one of the valleys through which we passed there could not have been less than 10,000 in one herd! out of which our hunters killed sixty and we passed on leaving them still feeding on the young grass; here game of every description were in the utmost abundance, the deer feeding in herds, wild fowls of every kind, covered the waters. Yet we seldom disturbed any of them except for amusement, for our camp teemed with provisions; nevertheless, so great was the temptation, and so natural for hunters and trappers to waste ammunition, that all the day whether travelling or in camp nothing was to be heard but shots in every direction.

With all this profusion about us we were not exempt from anxiety; Blackfeet and Piegan war roads were everywhere in our way, and fresh tracks of men and horses were not wanting; yet it was with the utmost difficulty I could convince our people of our dangerous situation and the necessity of watching their horses strictly at night.

One morning on getting up at break of day, for early rising is indispensible in these parts, I found twenty-four of the Iroquois horses out of the watch altogether, strolling at large among the hills; on calling the owners to account who had been on the watch that night, I found that they had turned them out to feed; I ordered the horses to be brought in and warned them against a repetition of such conduct; but the next morning I found six more out of the guard belonging to Martin, another of the Iroquois, who confessed that he had turned his out to feed, a practice neither allowed nor necessary as our horses had always time enough during the day to eat; I immediately took two men off for the horses, telling Martin that since he would not take care of them I should, that he owed the company a heavy debt, and that if the horses were stolen his hunt would be at an end, and without them he could never pay his debt, and moreover that himself and family would become a burden on the camp—that I should place the horses to his credit,[10] and that he and his family might henceforth provide for themselves without horses.

The next morning on raising camp, I ordered Martin's horses to be loaded and we set off, leaving him and his family sitting by the fire. The other Iroquois, not wishing to leave Martin behind, lent him some of their horses for the day, so that he journeyed along with us; on putting up at night, Old Pierre and two others came to intercede in Martin's behalf and after giving me every assurance that they would all take good care of their horses in the future and observe the regulations of the camp, I delivered Martin's horses up to him again; this was what I wanted, and the example had for a long time afterwards a good effect, not only among the Iroquois but among the others.

In consequence of the fresh tracks of Indians which had been discovered lately we selected a strong place for our camp, and after delivering a fresh supply of ammunition to all hands, I sent out two scouting parties to see that there were no enemies lurking about and at the same time to examine for beaver; but both returned unsuccessful, having seen neither enemy nor beaver, one of the parties however passed the defile where the veteran John Day, who died in 1819, was buried;[11] the other party fell on a branch of Reed's River; the day following I sent out two other observing parties; but after two days' search they returned, having met with very few beavers.

At last I applied to our Snake slave for information and he gave me to understand that he knew the country well, said that there were plenty of beaver in the western quarter, but that the roads were not passable with horses. I decided on sending him and some others to visit that quarter; at the end of three days they returned and reported that they had not seen much; but that the further we went the more beaver we should find; and what they had seen promised well to repay the trouble of going there to trap.

I was so pleased with this information that I gave Hakana, for that was the name we gave the Snake, a second-hand gun as a

---

[10] The value of the horses would be deducted from his debt to the Company.

[11] They were now traveling along the course of the Little Lost River.

present, which he was not a little proud of and the people among themselves gave him also several trifling articles; so that our Snake guide, for we honoured him with that title, was held to considerable favour and promised to be a useful member of our little community in future.

We had however reached a point where it became necessary for us to decide on the course we intended to pursue the rest of the season. I therefore called all the people together and described the country to them, and as it did not appear to me that one side was much preferable to the other I left it to them to make their choice; I then told them that the country to our left or southeast[12] would lead us along the foot of the Rocky Mountains to Henry's Fork, and crossing there Lewis River or the main south branch, we might proceed by the Blackfeet River[13] to the Buffalo Snakes, the Sherrydikas,[14] and Bear's Lake, where the country was already known; but on the other hand, if we took the west and southwest side, the country was in many places unknown to the whites, and we should have to run the risk of whether successful or not.

Old Pierre and some others observed, "We have already been through the country on our left, and have trapped in that quarter two years in succession; there is nothing very interesting there, we therefore prefer trying the west quarter"; this opinion they all agreed to and it was much strengthened by Hakana's late report, so we decided on trying the unknown and unfrequented part.

Having now settled our plan of operation we turned to the right, and entering a defile of the mountains, proceeded on the track our Snake guide had pointed out[15] as leading to a beaver country. We advanced in the direction our guide had been and found the rocky road most terrific. Yet in the hope of soon reaching beaver we continued till both man and horse were almost exhausted with climbing up and down, and then encamped on a place where our tired animals could neither feed nor ourselves get as much level ground as we could sleep on.

12 "South west" in the manuscript.
13 The Blackfoot River.
14 The Bear River.
15 Jesse Creek.

245

Next day we reached the point where our guide and his companions had turned back, and where it was said that the beaver there would well repay the trapper for his troubles: all we found was a small rocky creek with scarcely any traces of that animal; we encamped, and after putting one hundred and seventy traps in the water, we only got fifteen beaver! I then questioned our guide and we began to think that he knew nothing of the country, and that we had been duped. We left Creek Disappointment[16] and proceeded for three days further, but with no better success; here and there we found a brisk creek of running water among the rocks, but they seemed all to be formed from the melting snow; the place having not the least signs of beaver we encamped and resolved on turning back by the way we came.

The people had got into a bad humour with the Snake, and their disappointments in this quarter were such that they were ready to quarrel with their shadows, even the women got by the ears, for two of them fought like Amazons till they had scarcely a rag left on each other's back or a hair on each other's head! From Battle River,[17] for that was the name we gave this place, I sent off two or three parties on discovery in various directions, and taking three men with me we proceeded on the same business; but although we had travelled all day and slept out, such was the rugged nature of the country that we had not made the distance of ten miles till we were stopped by perpetual snows, no beaver were to be found.

Next morning I climbed up to the top of a high rock; but I could see nothing of the country around. This height I called Rock-Turn-Again; on the top of it I deposited six balls, two flints, and a bit of tobacco. We retraced our steps back to the camp. The other parties were likewise unsuccessful. In this perplexity some were for stripping our Snake imposter naked, others were for tying him to a tree and leaving him.

During the day on which we arrived at this place we had to make our way over a frightful country. In winding among the rocks on the top of one of the mountains one of our horses was killed, and a

16 Moore Creek.
17 Panther Creek.

246

child belonging to one of the persons was within a hairsbreadth of sharing the same fate; on this high ledge of rocks the horses and people leading them one after another formed a string of nearly two miles in length, nor was there in many places space enough for a person to turn around or look behind him, so narrow and dangerous was the pass. In this situation a child who had been tied to one of the saddles happened to slide saddle and all under the horse's belly, when the animal took fright and began to kick, he slipped over the brink of the precipice and fell down with the child along with it! but getting jammed between two pieces of the rock, the horse could not move; but long before it had reached the extremity of the line, the cause of the alarm was ended. We only heard the sound without knowing the cause in this difficulty, I and many others thinking we had been waylaid and attacked by the enemy tried to follow the sound and reach the spot whence it issued; but the whole party had got into confusion and some time elapsed before we reached the place. At last we succeeded, we then let down two men with ropes and extricated the child, but before we had got the men hauled up again the horse died from the injuries it had received.

On getting back to Canoe Point we resolved on leaving some of our beaver en câche, to lighten our horses. We therefore concealed in the face of a bank one thousand beaver, until our return. Our late trial to the west had however shaken our confidence as to that quarter; many therefore were for abandoning it altogether and proposed that we follow it up the east branch[18] before going again to the west.

We prepared to cross the river and after examining it for some distance we found a ford, and although not more than seventy-five yards broad, the current carried us so far down that the distance between where we entered it on our side to where we got out on the other was more than two hundred yards; being late before we got all over, we camped for the night on the south bank.

On moving camp we bent our course for Goddin's River,[19] in

18 The Lemhi River.
19 The Big Lost River.

the direction of which on our way thither, we met with several hot springs with which this country abounds. In some of these I was surprised to see a number of animalculae as large as flies swimming about, which seemed to their will in this hot element! I intended to try whether or not these little inhabitants of so warm a climate would not live in cold water; but there was not a drop to be found for miles around, and those I carried along with me died before we reached any cold water.

On passing the height of land between Salmon and Goddin Rivers we perceived five men on horseback coming towards us, but they wheeled about immediately on seeing us. Taking them for the advanced guard of a Piegan war party the alarm was given, and being our camping time we retreated for a short distance and after putting the camp in a secure place near some woods, thirty of us mounted our horses and set off at full speed in the direction we had seen the horsemen in order to try and satisfy ourselves who they might be. But having taken the mountain we lost all trace of them, so we hastened back to our camp and after putting it in a state of defence and a double guard on our horses, we passed the night in quietness and awaited the morning in suspense; long before day however we were all armed and ready for what might happen, but all appearing quiet we took a turn round before raising camp and seeing nothing we proceeded on our journey.

We saw but very few animals in these parts and began to get short of provisions, for notwithstanding the abundance we had met with on Salmon River we had laid in but a very scanty supply, it being the custom to let the morrow provide for itself.

On reaching Goddin's River, so named after one of my men who discovered it, I sent off eight men to trap it downwards but made them leave their horses with us, so that they might the better conceal themselves from the enemy, I promising at the same time to pick them up at the south end on a certain day, while the main party proceeded round a range of mountains in order to lay in a supply of buffalo meat, for we expected but few of these animals in the direction we were about to take, and moreover to prepare some

A CAMP IN THE ROCKY MOUNTAINS

A drawing by Henry James Warre

A BLACKFOOT INDIAN

A drawing by Charles Bodmer

of their hides for making canoes, in case we might afterward require them.

The second day we got to the buffalo and encamped in Day's Valley, the spot on which McKenzie and party visited in 1820. It was a most dreary looking place, the young grass scarcely got out of the soil so that our horses fared but poorly; nothing was to be seen but the tracks of buffalo and the traces of war parties.

While our party was employed in trapping and laying in provisions, I set off with ten men to examine the country to the southeast; we were absent for four days on our trip and at the extent of our journey we ascended high mountains, had a good view of the country, and saw the three Pilot Knobs quite plain, in the direction of east; we then passed for some distance along the waters of the main south branch and came to a spot among the rocks where some Snakes had left in a hurry as the fire was still alive, and in the little bulrush hut we found six beaver skins and several other articles which they had abandoned through fear at our approach. We searched about and tried to find them as I was anxious to fall in with some of the nation in order to obtain information about the country, but all was in vain; taking then the beaver with us and leaving instead articles of more value to them we returned to our camp, having seen but few beaver on our trip. But the buffalo were in thousands, a sure sign that there were no enemies about.

As soon as I reached the camp I dispatched two men to River Goddin in order to bring the eight men whom I had sent there to trap some time before to our camp, as we had changed our plan of proceeding and had resolved instead of going further to the east to turn immediately to the west and follow our first intention of hunting in that quarter for the season.

The two men set out early in the day and reached the place appointed a little before sunset; a little before their arrival they perceived a smoke and taking it for granted that it must be our people heedlessly advanced among the bushes with the view of coming upon them by surprise and frightening them, until they got within gunshot of the place, but on crossing the end of Goddin's River,

249

which was there but a mere creek, close to where the smoke rose they suddenly perceived that they had fallen not on their comrades as they expected, but on a Piegan war party! On discovering their mistake they threw themselves from their horses and ran in among the bushes and got into the creek, the Indians in the meantime uttering a hideous yell and seized their horses, while some others whooped and yelped about the bush in search of them; all this time, however, they were making their way, crawling among the mud and mire under the banks of the creek, the bushes being thick and night coming on they fortunately got off safe owing solely to the approach of night, their horses, their traps, and their blankets became a prize of the Indians.

While our men were advancing through the friendly dusk which so fortunately aided their escape they passed within ten yards of the men whom they had been in search of and who were at the time unconscious of their dangerous situation, sleeping within half a mile of the Piegan camp! The two men however continued their flight all night and all the next day, reached our camp in the middle of the second night in a sad plight, without shoes on their feet and their clothes torn to rags!

After hearing their story, no doubt remained in our minds as to the fate of the eight men! I immediately roused the camp, and all were ready for a start by the break of day. Leaving fifteen men to guard and conduct the camp after us, we to the number of thirty-five went in pursuit of the Piegans; on arriving at the place we found the nest, but the birds had flown. So we gave up the pursuit and proceeded up Goddin River in search of our eight men.

But we had not proceeded far before we had the good fortune to find our men safe, ignorant of our anxiety and their own narrow escape, for they had neither heard nor seen anything of the Piegans before we reached them. We returned to meet the main party and reached the camp long before dark; on this disagreeable trip, lost my spy glass. The following day I went to examine the Trois Tetons,[20] so named from their appearance, these three little hills standing in a group are very conspicuous in the middle of an open plain,

[20] The Twin Buttes and Big Southern Butte.

having hot springs at their base but no cold water nearer than the south end of Goddin's River.

On starting the next day we proposed following up Goddin's River all the way to its source, as it had never been either trapped or examined as far before. Following up this intention, we entered it at the extreme south point, where the two men fell on the Piegan war party; here that river enters the ground, and wholly disappears. The reader will be better able to judge of the body of water thus absorbed when we reach its source. Following up the river for about thirty miles to the head of the main stream, we found it thirty-five paces broad, the current strong and running on a rocky bottom. At this place, the river is formed by three branches emptying into it, one from the northwest and another from the southeast, and a third from the south, all of nearly equal size, which descend from the surrounding heights but none of them were stocked with beaver; from eighty traps one night we only got seven, and a few nights later in one of the traps we caught a deer, and I mention this circumstance because it was a novelty.

We ascended the south branch, which takes its rise in a ridge of mountains which divides River Goddin on the east from Salmon River on the west, and on the very top of which we encamped on the 16th June. From this height I dispatched two parties on discovery in different directions, one of which brought us accounts of having discovered a river with considerable appearances of beaver in it, on the south west.

The weather until this day during the present month has been extremely cold, I should suppose not less than 15 below zero on Fahrenheit's thermometer, weather for blankets, mittens, and leather coats! The ice is still thick on the water since the sixth instant; we have had almost a succession of storms and boistrous weather, and on the 14th there fell nearly a foot of snow! Here three of our horses died.

During our journey the Iroquois had been plotting to abandon the main party and hunt afoot by themselves; but more especially since my quarrel with John Grey in the Valley of Troubles and with Martin for disregarding the regulations of the camp and ne-

251

glecting his horses on Salmon River. At last old Pierre was drawn into the cabal, and came to me saying that if I would but consent to their going off that they would do much better apart. I listened with patience to the old man's story, but did not approve of it. I then refreshed his memory with Oskonanton's tale of 1819 and put him in mind of their conduct at the River Skam-naugh and their behaviour generally when left to themselves; he still persisted in saying that they would do well and pledged himself for their conduct. I weighed the matter in my own mind and at last consented, thinking it better to let them go and supply them with their wants cheerfully than to be dragging a disaffected party along with us, so I fitted them out and we parted friends, but to my surprise, Grey and Martin gave up the idea, saying they would still prefer remaining with the main party and run all chances. So we turned our backs on each other, Pierre and his party making for the south branch; while we steered our course southwest to the place where the discovering party had met with beaver. On Pierre's departure we had arranged matters to meet on the first of October, at the Trois Tetons, near Goddin's River.

On descending from this height of land we had to wind our steps over a prodigious height, the path leading along the edge of a precipice which overhung a foaming stream below. Our way was full of rocks, and the place dangerous. Here we had to make leather muffles for our horses' feet, for they were worn to the quick. On descending into the low bottom we found the climate changed for the better, the snow off the ground, the weather warm, and the new grass fully long.

Late in the evening we reached a stream running through a deep valley in the direction of the southwest, called Riviere aux Malades.[21] On its east bank we encamped at a late hour.

In the vicinity of our present encampment were the finest appearances of beaver we had yet seen. In one place we counted 148 poplar trees cut down by that animal in less than one hundred yards square, and our first lift was favourable. Fifty-two beaver in part of the traps. There were eight feet left and in others seven toes,

21 The Big Wood River.

besides fifteen that missed altogether by the sudden rising and falling of the water, which caused a total loss of thirty beaver in one night. It is always difficult and doubtful trapping where the water keeps ebbing and flowing, and the chances of success are small. Nevertheless the place was promising, the weather fine and grass good, so that our worn-out horses both fed and rested.

In the afternoon of the same day we had to turn our attention to something else than catching of beaver, for we perceived a Piegan war party descending the mountain when the cry "Enemies," "Enemies," sounded in our ears, and their appearance and numbers might have well justified our apprehensions, there being only three men in camp at the time.

Our first care on perceiving the enemy was directed to the. security of our horses, which were all scattered; for this purpose one man with some of the women set off to collect and bring them into camp, but the confusion and the fear operated so powerfully on them that they made but little progress, some driving them one way, some another, so that considerable time had elapsed before they were got into a narrow point behind the camp.

While the people were securing the horses the other men and myself lost no time in getting our gun pointed, the match lit, and the women and children out of the way; while all this was going on the uproar in the camp was great and presented an appearance of large numbers being placed along the woods, made the enemy still more doubtful of attacking us.

As soon as the Indians appeared on the heights and long before we saw them they were discovered by some of our hunters, who communicating their fears to each other scampered off in every direction to avoid the enemy and reach the camp, some throwing their beaver away, others their traps while some abandoned their horses, traps, beaver and all and took to their heels crossing the rock, which the Indians observing took them to be more numerous than they were. It was no doubt the chief cause why they did not at once make a rush on our horses and carry them off, which they might easily have done.

The Indians had no sooner got down into the valley when we

were busied running after our horses; then they assembled in a group together as if counselling for a moment, then extending themselves they made a demonstration of attack, and the only reason we could assign why they did not carry it into effect was the seeing of so many of our people here and there on horseback making for the camp or perhaps the want of ammunition, for they well knew that the whites were seldom short of that necessary article and would have given them a warm reception. A party of them intercepted two of our men, John Grey and another Iroquois, and had wrested a rifle from the hands of the latter but instantly restored it again on perceiving some of our people in an opposite direction.

At last the whole cavalcade advanced toward our camp in slow procession, our people having made for the woods and coming fast in by ones and by twos soon relieved my anxiety, so that by the time the Indians had got within a hundred yards of the camp, there were thirty men in it. At this time I went with a flag to meet them, motioned them by signs not to approach the camp but sit down and smoke where they were; they did so, and in the meantime, giving them some tobacco and having Kouttanais Jacques to smoke with them I returned to camp and we were soon ready to receive them.

When all our people arrived and I knew that the Indians were only ninety-two in number I invited them to our camp, where they passed the night in smoking, dancing, and singing; all our people were under arms; at the same time, as a further security, I ordered forty of their horses to be hobbled and put with ours and secured their guns. On the following morning I invited them together and questioned them as to their business in that quarter, and asked them if there were not land enough in their own country for burying ground without coming to the Snake country to trouble the whites and frighten the natives, when the chief replied: "We have been on an embassy of peace to the Shoshones. When we left our own country about three months ago our party consisted of three hundred men, but not finding the principal Snake chiefs, we went off to try and fall in with our friends the Flatheads; but the main party returned home." On questioning them about the party who had seized the two horses belonging to the two men at Goddin's River they denied all knowledge of that affair; but I said, "You tried to rob one of my men of his gun yesterday." For that the chief apologized, saying that they only wanted to look at it as it was a custom among Piegans to handle and look at every strange gun they might see, but their story carried an air of falsehood along with it, and I strongly suspected that they were the very same party which had taken the two horses, and moreover that they were not a party on an embassy of peace to the Snakes as the chief had stated but a scouting expedition on the lookout to take vengeance on the whites for the misfortunes that had happened to their people in the affray between them and McDonald's party last year, but the severe handling they had met with on that occasion made the present party hesitate to attack so formidable a party of whites as we were, and particularly since they had failed to surprise us.

Being harassed by the frequent appearance of such visitors and the party being completely in our power I intended giving them a fright in return, for they had given us many. I therefore seized on two of their horses and four of their guns, and told them I had done so as a remuneration for the loss of our two horses and traps at Goddin's River, as I suspected them of taking them, "and besides," I said, "you give us too much trouble and prevent us from hunting and trapping quietly in a country that you only frequent for mischief." This declaration humbled them. They made a thousand protestations of innocence, adding that they were always friends to the whites. Although I did not believe a word they said, yet as there was a possibility of their being innocent I returned the guns and horses, telling them to take care.

After smoking and talking I gave the chief five balls, powder, and a piece of tobacco, when according to Indian custom they exchanged some horses with our people, as a token of friendship.

It was however amusing to witness their maneuvering; in going off some went one way, some another, dispersing here and there in small parties until they had got to a considerable distance from our camp, then assembling in a crowd they stood for some minutes and marching off in a body, took to the mountains. For some time we could not account for their manner of departure till someone observed that none of them had gone off in the direction that the big gun was pointed.

As soon as they were out of sight, taking some men with me we mounted our horses and went a few miles to a neighboring height to watch their motions and there we saw them join the main party, the party the chief had told us had gone home! As soon as they had joined together they sat down as we suppose to recount their adventures, after which they all marched off taking the direction of the Missouri.

On the next morning the neighborhood being free of enemies, different parties were sent off in search of the traps and beaver that had been thrown away on the first appearance of the Piegans, all of which we had the good fortune to recover, and at the place where the Indians had made their demonstration of attack our people found six scalps stretched on circular bits of wood, and not yet dry! The day after this bustle we took sixty beaver; but taking only eight at the next trial, we moved our camp down the river and passed a bad night from thunder and lightning.

From this place we advanced by slow marches for five or six days farther down till we reached a branch of the river coming in from the west which we named West Fork,[22] and although the appearances of beaver were favourable yet our success came far short of expectation, owing chiefly to the unsettled state of the water; one morning between feet and toes we found no less than forty-two in our traps! And as the generality of our readers may not be acquainted with the process of trapping beaver, we shall here explain the causes of our failure. From the great heat during the day the snow melted so fast that the water rushed down the mountains causing a sudden rise in the river, but the cold nights as suddenly checking that rise its fall became as rapid, hence the cause of our traps missing so frequently. When a trap is set for the purpose of catching beaver it requires about six inches of water over it and still deeper water near it because the moment the animal is caught, which is invariably by the foot or toes, it plunges and drowns.

But should the water rise for several inches higher the animal can then swim over the trap without its feet touching it, and of course gets clear; on the contrary, should the water fall several inches lower, so that the animal on being caught could not, from the shoalness of the water, plunge and drown, it cuts its foot or toes off and makes its escape, so in either case a loss occurs. Our success had, however, during several nights past averaged fifty-five beaver at a lift.

There we found the black and red currant ripe, we saw the swallow, the black-bird, and wild pigeon for the first time this season; during the mornings and evenings the mosquitoes were very troublesome.

When we first fell on Riviere aux Malades I had intended trapping it from end to end before leaving it; but being anxious to reach Reed's River early and finding West Fork leading in that direction, I changed my first plan; leaving therefore the river to be taken on our way back in the autumn we resolved at once on proceeding up West Fork, and having finished trapping at its entrance we made preparations for advancing to Reed's River in the hope of reaching it as high up as possible, in order to trap it downwards.

For this purpose I directed the main party on raising camp one morning to proceed in that direction, while I and four men with me were to have remained until part of our people who had gone out in search of their traps arrived, and then we were to have brought up the rear and followed after. Turning therefore our backs on the Riviere aux Malades the main party continued their journey whilst myself and the men with me remained at the place appointed, which was the top of an high hill not three miles from the encampment we had just left. From this height, however, the weather being very sultry, we descended a winding pass to the creek below in order to have refreshed ourselves with a drink of cold water until the men arrived. During our stay the men we had been waiting for had passed us unnoticed; but had not got far before they met a courier from the main party ahead with news that the Piegans were at the camp; two of the men therefore wheeled round

22 Camas Creek.

and came back to look for us but had passed unseen and only dis-covered us on their return again; on seeing them coming as it were from the camp we had left that morning, we very naturally sup-posed them to be the men we were waiting for; but were a little uneasy at the gestures they were making to hurry our departure, and still more so on hearing them vociferously call out, "Enemies! Enemies at the camp!" and then start off like a shot in the direc-tion of the main party.

To extricate ourselves from our dangerous position and ascend the hill again was a work of some time; we however made all haste, and the more especially as we took it for granted that the enemy spoken of were at the camp behind us; ascending therefore to the top of the hill in order to pursue our journey and then seeing some of our people, we drove off at full speed, every now and then look-ing behind us, having the distance of ten miles to go before we could join our companions or get any support; three of our horses got completely knocked up and fell down with the excessive heat under their loads. We, almost as exhausted from fatigue, left them to their fate.

At last we got up with the party and found to our surprise that instead of running from the enemy we had been running to meet them! for they were before us. The Piegans all the time kept stand-ing in a body not far from our people as if determined to oppose our progress further, and perhaps rather hesitating whether to advance or retreat. Provoked by the loss of our horses and by this continual arrogance of the enemy, I immediately served out am-munition to our people and then told them we should go and put an end to this state of anxiety, so leaving only the big gun and five men to guard the camp, forty-five of us mounted our horses and set off with the full determination of having a brush with the Piegans. When we were within one hundred yards of the party, who were all on foot, two of them with a kind of flag advanced to meet us, but we made signs to them to keep off. They however kept advancing. We then presented our guns to them with orders not to fire, but they still unflinchingly advanced, so we resolved to wait their arrival and see what they had got to say.

The principal man on reaching us presented me with his flag, then clasping my horse's neck in his arms, began to crouch in a supplicating manner. I gave him however a push off with the butt of my gun, which I was immediately sorry for; he nevertheless still held fast hold of my horse by the neck. We then dismounted and entered into a parley with them. They proved to be Piegans and one hundred and ten strong but badly armed, having only twenty-three guns and scarcely a load of ammunition! but they had quivers well filled with arrows.

Seeing there was no appearance of coming to blows I invited the two Indians to our camp, intimating to them that the others should remain where they were. On reaching the camp I dispatched some men for the horses we had abandoned on the road, two of which, together with the property, were recovered; but the third had died.

I then questioned the Indians, as we had done the party before, as to their business in that quarter, for we had flattered ourselves that we should have been at all events clear of Piegans and Black-feet in that direction. On putting that question the chief smiling said, "We are not horse thieves. For if we had been so inclined, we might have easily taken yours, for we were among them two nights ago! Two of my people entered your camp at night, and as a proof of what I say, one of them took a piece of deer's meat which was roasting at a fire and stuck it on a pole at one end of your camp! rubbed two spots of red paint on a riding saddle at one of the tent doors. We were therefore not looking for horses, nor wishing to injure the whites but have come in search of sixteen of our rela-tions, who came to this quarter last year and have not been heard of since, and that is our business at present."

The circumstances mentioned by the chief respecting the roasted venison and riding saddle were both correct! We had noticed both but never thought that they had been the work of Indians, and it was certainly a broad hint for us to guard our camp better another time! We then questioned the chief as to the affairs at Goddin's River and gave him an account of the party we had seen at our first encampment on Riviere aux Malades; but he denied all knowl-edge of either.

For the fellow's candour and honesty I gave him ten balls and powder, a piece of tobacco, a knife, and shaking hands with them we parted good friends.

From Piegan Encampment, a name we bestowed on this place, we continued our journey onwards from the head of West Fork over a rugged surface in search of Reed's River, and although scarcely thirty miles it took us six long summer days to accomplish it; during one of these days we travelled ten hours before we made three miles! But never did man nor beast pass through a country more hazardous.

The rugged and rocky paths had worn our horses' hoofs to the quick, and we not unfrequently stood undecided and hopeless. After immense labour, toil, and hardship we got to the river, arriving on its rocky bank, and looking as if we were over a mighty precipice to the gulf below, we were struck with admiration at the roaring cataract forcing its way among the chasms and huge rocks over a bed it had been deepening for generations. But although we had reached the river we had still but little hopes of making our way along its precipitous bank. We journeyed sometimes in sight of it, and at other times miles from it until we had made the distance of one hundred and sixteen miles, which took us twelve days, and during that time we only caught fifty-one beaver.

But bad roads were not the only obstacle we had to overcome. We had starvation to contend with. For animals of the chace of every kind as well as beaver were scarce, and our hunters returned to camp more hungry and dissatisfied than they left it, so that at this stage of our journey the people began to murmur greatly against the roads and want of provisions, evils we could have neither foreseen nor prevented.

I now found that though I had got rid of most of the Iroquois I had not got rid of the troubles for there remained John Grey and Martin, and they were enough to poison the minds of the rest. I assembled all hands together and told them that we had met with nothing but what we might have expected, that as we had proceeded so far in that direction I was determined to proceed further and make the best of it and see the good as well as the bad side, that in the nature of things we must soon get to a better part of the country than that which we have been involved in for some time past. That a few days' perseverance might bring us relief, that we would soon get to the Snakes in the direction we were in, but if a week did not procure us the relief they desired I would be prepared to meet their views, so they all consented and order was again restored. Had they plenty of ammunition at the time they would have followed their own inclinations!

We had for some time past been anxiously looking for some of the Snakes, from whom we might get information respecting the roads and country we had to pass through, and had come to some places where they had been encamped. But they had always got the start of us, and having fled to the rocks eluded our search. But just as we were pondering over our difficulties two wretched beings were found among the rocks. They proved to be the sole remnant of a small band of the Bann-at-tee tribe consisting of eighteen persons whom according to their own account the Piegan party we had seen at West Fork had fallen on and had killed man, woman, and child! excepting the two men before us. These poor creatures were almost unintelligible through fear. We nevertheless understood their misfortunes. They were in mourning, had cut their hair, and were apparently destitute of food and raiment; we could scarcely get any information from them, but understood the roads were impassible. We gave them a few trifles and let them go back to their strongholds again.

Not an hour after the two Bann-at-tees had gone off a party which I had sent out on discovery arrived at the camp with two men and a woman whom they had surprised and brought by force, but they were so frightened that neither kindness nor presents could make them speak or look upon us as friends.

12. POISONED BEAVER

Notwithstanding, that we had seen some of the Snakes, as we so much desired, we still remained as ignorant of the country as ever. Following up the plan we were pursuing, we left the encampment and proceeded down Reed's River. At the end of three days' toil we got clear of the mountains and into a highly picturesque and open country well furnished with animals of the chace. Our first lift of beaver was 64, a number considered favourable in comparison with what we had been doing for some time past. Added to this charming prospect six elks and seventeen small deer coming into camp at once filled a starving and dissatisfied people with abundance. So that for the first time during the last twenty-five days I witnessed a smile of content throughout the camp.

The lower part of Reed's River furnishing us with plenty of beaver and other animals raised once more a hope of making good hunts, and for a moment my people were cheerful, industrious, and obedient. Here we had a visit from Pee-eye-em, one of the principal personages of the country, accompanied by a retinue of forty warriors, all armed with guns and mounted on horseback. They had a flag, the one given them by McKenzie, and arrived in state. This was the great sachem so frequently and favourably mentioned by our friends on former expeditions, and so remarkable for size; and he had not diminished since, but was dull and heavy in his manners, never smiled, spoke slowly, and in a low tone of voice. His answers were generally a nod of the head! leaving us often to guess whether he meant an affirmative or a negative. Both himself and his escort, according to their number, were as fine a set of athletic men as I had ever seen in the country.

Pee-eye-em appeared pleased to see the whites again on his lands, and often enquired with great eagerness about Mr. McKenzie. I offered the chief some tobacco but preferring his own, he declined taking ours. After remaining for some time with us he told me that his camp on the Sherry-dikas was far off, and that he had come a journey of two days to visit his friend Ama-ketsa, the principal War-are-ree-ka chief, whose camp, he said, was only a few miles distant; being the great Snake camp mentioned to us by the Piegan chief while at West Fork. Pee-eye-em then informed me that while he was at Ama-ketsa's camp a party of the Cayouse tribe from Fort Nez Perce had arrived there on a mission of peace, and that hearing of the whites being in the neighborhood he had come to invite me to their council in order to see the peace satisfied.

Putting my people in a secure place and taking ten men with me, I accompanied Pee-eye-em and his followers to the War-are-ree-ka, where we all arrived after a hard ride of ten miles after dusk. There I met my Cayouse friends, who were no less rejoiced to see me than I was to see them in a strange country. On the whole, nothing could possibly have happened better than that a person like myself, who had been at the beginning of the peace and instrumental in bringing it about, should have arrived so seasonably to witness its conclusion. The business was introduced at once. Each spoke in his turn and I among the rest. When done, Pee-eye-em mounted his horse with a singularly painted robe thrown round him, rode about for some time haranguing the people, when every now and then the cry "Ho! Ho! Ho!" was uttered by the surrounding multitude by way of confirmation. Then a number of the elderly men collecting in a group held a consultation, when they all uttered in a loud voice and a drawling tone the same cry, which appeared to convey the general consent and only wanted the ceremony of a council and smoking to conclude it.

The chief's lodge was then put in order with a fire in the center when the ceremony of ratifying the peace according to Indian form commenced. The two Cayouse plenipotentiaries were placed in the back of the tent by Pee-eye-em and I next to them, when eighteen Snake dignitaries next entered and squeezed themselves down on each side of us. Lastly Pee-eye-em sat opposite to us with

263

his back to the door, having Ama-ketsa on his right and another chief on his left, apparently with the intention of keeping out all intruders and preventing anyone from either going out or coming in during the solemn sitting. And this completed the diplomatic circle. After which, a silence endured for some time.

The great medicine bag was then opened and the decorated pipe of peace taken out of it and filled with the usual formality by Pee-eye-em himself, who immediately after took a handful or two of sand with which he covered a small hole by the fireside, then smoothing it over made two small holes with his finger in the sand large enough to hold a goose egg. This done, he then extracted from the medicine bag a small piece of wood like a sugar tongs, with which he took up a piece of burning horse dung and laid it in the hole of sand to his left, resting at the same time the bowl of his pipe in the hole to the right, holding the stem of the pipe all the time in his left hand. He then took up the same bit of wood or tongs and with it took the burning bit of horse dung out of the hole to the left and laid it upon his pipe, which was no sooner lighted than Pee-eye-em taking up the pipe with both hands drew three whiffs, allowing none of the smoke to escape; that is, he swallowed the whole of it, then taking the pipe from his mouth held it vertically in his hands, blowing each time he smoked the cloud out of his mouth on the stem, and this he did three successive times at each of which he uttered a short prayer, as if invoking a blessing.

Then holding the pipe horizontally and pointing to the east he drew three whiffs, blowing the smoke on the stem as before, then turning it to the west, next to the south, and lastly to the north he did the same, always observing to repeat the short prayer every time he turned the pipe, Lastly, pointing the pipe to the ground he drew three whiffs, blowing the smoke as before on the stem, signifying that the animosities of war might be forever after buried beneath the earth. But in all this ceremony, Pee-eye-em did not once, as is generally customary among Indians, hold the pipe to or blow the smoke to either the sun or firmament.

All this time Pee-eye-em was sitting on his hams, then rising up and turning the pipe stem he presented it to one of the Cayouses,

A BEAVER HUT

A drawing by Charles Bodmer

INDIANS HUNTING THE BUFFALO

A drawing by Charles Bodmer

letting him touch it with his mouth but not inhale any smoke; the Cayouse did so. Then withdrawing the pipe for a moment pointed it to him a second time with the same positive injunction, which the Cayouse observed. The caution was no doubt intended to impress him to reflect sincerely on the responsibility of what he was going to do, for smoking with them on such occasions is the same as an oath with us; then putting it to his mouth the third time he said, "You may smoke now," adding after he had drawn a few whiffs, "We are brothers."

The Cayouse after smoking handed me the pipe, but without any ceremony. The smoking thus went round and round the circle, with no other formality than that of Pee-eye-em always filling the pipe and lighting it himself, with the same tongs as before. The fire was always a bit of horse dung, till the ceremony on the part of Pee-eye-em was gone through.

The lodge during the time was like an oven, so that I got up to go out and get a little fresh air; but Pee-eye-em shook his head and made signs for me to sit down again. I then asked for a drink of water: but Pee-eye-em giving another shake of his head, I had to sit down and compose myself. So there we sat, half roasted, half smoked, thirsty and uncomfortable, until long after midnight, when Pee-eye-em getting up and opening the door went out we all followed, and the ceremony was ended.

I expected that the chief would have invited me and the Cayouses to supper and to pass the night in his tent, but supperless and houseless we had to pass the night in the open air, in a camp stinking with rotten fish and pestered with snarling dogs. The night being warm the smell was horrible. Next morning, seeing no signs of anything to eat, I purchased two fine fresh salmon which were cooked and on which we made a hearty breakfast. We then prepared to return to our camp, and I invited the Cayouse chiefs to accompany us; but just as we were mounting our horses Pee-eye-em with his flag in his hand and retinue of followers joined and accompanied us back to our camp. Comparing things, I thought that there was more honour than comfort in the Snake camp.

From the solemnity observed, it might have been expected that they were all in earnest, but so changeable and treacherous are savages that I was apprehensive the Cayóuse chiefs ran great risk of getting back safely. I therefore invited them to our camp, promising them an escort to convey them out of danger, and we learned afterwards that they got back to their own people in safety.

The peace having been occasionally progressing for the last seven years, I now for the first time began to entertain hopes that it might, after all, possibly succeed. The hostile feelings had of late changed, otherwise the Cayouses would never have ventured so far and in such small numbers into the heart of their enemy's country. The Snakes had also, as we have already noticed, been at the Nez Perce camp and returned with a favourable impression.

We have noticed that Pee-eye-em accompanied us to our camp, where having remained for the greater part of two days, he returned home; on which occasion I presented him with one hundred balls and powder and some other trifles for which he appeared very thankful and we parted with regret. The more I knew of him the better I like him. He was sincere, well disposed, and much attached to the whites. From this time forward, the Snakes became constant visitors at our camp but were not always so friendly as I could wish. We however occasionally bought a fine salmon from them, in order that they might become possessed of some useful and necessary articles; but especially to keep up a good understanding with them. A needle was given for a salmon, an awl for ten, and a knife for fifty! and they could have enriched themselves at that rate, had we been able to encourage the trade.

After our Snake visitors had left us we continued trapping down Reed's River with good success, taking from seventy to eighty every morning until we reached its mouth, being a distance where we fell on it of 170 miles. Remaining a few days on the main Snake River we steered our course northwest for sixty-four miles till we fell on River Payette or Middle River, up which stream we proceeded to its source, a distance of 110 miles, then crossing over in a course nearly north for some thirty miles fell on River Weiser, down which we hunted. At a distance of fifty miles we again reached the main river. We found large numbers of beaver, but for want of canoes could do nothing. We then proceeded in a southerly direction till we made the great Snake camp of Ama-ketsa, where we had concluded the peace treaty. During our survey of all these rivers including that of Riviere aux Malades we caught 1855 beaver.

Then let us take a retrospective view of a circumstance which occurred on leaving River Weiser. As we were about to proceed to where the Snakes were numerous I issued a certain quantity of ammunition to each hunter, cautioning them at the same time not to trade any of that essential article with the natives nor to waste it, as our safety depended on it and our stock was getting lower every day. The moment however the Iroquois and half-breeds found themselves in possession of a sufficient supply, the plotting was revived, so that the day we turned our backs on River Weiser they turned their backs on us; but I only discovered it on reaching our encampment at night. John Grey, Martin, and ten others had lagged behind with the intention of taking a different road to the one we had taken, and we were then too far apart to overtake them. So we continued in the hope that they might join us in a day or two.

On the fifth day, two of them with an Indian guide arrived at our camp with the news that the party had got into trouble with the Snakes, which did not surprise me. Our people had been exchanging horses, running races, and wrangling with the natives. Martin and a Snake having bet on their horses, the former lost the wager, when a bystander, seeing Martin dissatisfied, went up to him saying, "You do not know how to ride your horse to advantage, give him to me and I will beat the Snake and get back your ammunition again." Pleased at the proposal, Martin was simple enough to put his horse into the Indian's hands when off started both the Snakes. Martin waited in vain. No Snake nor horse ever returned. So in addition to his ammunition, he lost his horse.

After this trick our people and the Snakes quarreled, when the latter getting displeased drove off four of their horses in broad daylight. To revenge the act six of the whites, mounting their best horses, pursued in order to get ahead and intercept the thieves at a narrow place where they had to pass. They took a short cut, got there and dismounting, tied their horses in the edge of the woods. The men concealed themselves in the bush but the Indians not coming up at the time expected, the whites thought they might have taken another road, went further into the bush and set about cooking something for dinner before returning to camp, at the same time loosing their horses a little to feed; but while they were thus employed the Indians arrived and seeing the horses gave two or three yelps. The horses took fright and joining the other four, the Indians drove all before them, leaving the pursuers to return home on foot, with their saddles on their backs!

This was the story the two men brought us, and they very pressingly asked for assistance. Thus separated, one half of us involved in a quarrel with the natives and the other half in the vicinity of a formidable camp, requiring all our united strength, I was for a moment at a loss what to do, to have sent a party back to their assistance would have been exposing ourselves; to have left them without support would have been sacrificing them. As there was little time for hesitation I resolved at once on applying to our friend Pee-eye-em; but on rushing to the Indian camp[1] I was mortified to find that Pee-eye-em had gone off to join his own people at a distance.

I had then nothing left but to apply to Ama-ketsa, the next in power, but he raised many objections, said the guilty Indians were Bann-at-tees, over whom he had no control; the temptation of a new gun made the wily chief alter his tone, and he then undertook the mission and recovered eight of the ten stolen horses and arrived at our camp on the fourth day of his departure bringing the whole party along with him; but he had done well, having through cunning and under various pretenses got from them the remainder of their ammunition; but I had to overlook the sacrifice and was contented to see us all together once more.

When I reproached my people for their conduct the fault was shifted from one to another, and the Snakes blamed for all; be that as it may, we lost eight days' time, besides the risks we ran of more serious evils.

1 On Indian Creek.

Ama-ketsa's camp was ill constructed for defence and much exposed had an enemy assaulted it. But the division of labour was such that every person seemed to be well occupied. Horse racing, foot racing, gambling, fishing, camp making, wood gathering, water carrying, swimming, smoking, eating, sporting and playing went on in different parts of the Indian camp. The Snakes are not a lazy people. Their camp was however very dirty, as all fish camps are. All classes we saw, with the exception of a few persons, were meanly clad even for Indians. Very few of the men and scarcely a woman was painted, a practice so prevalent among other nations. But they were plump, oily and slick. They appeared sociable and friendly among themselves, but with countenances rather dull than expressive.

During our ramble we had several opportunities of seeing and examining their native tobacco in its manufactured state. I purchased a gallon of it for a scalping knife. I did not much like it. As a substitute for tobacco, it is better than nothing. The natives use it from habit. Ama-ketsa and several others smoked ours. We mixed with the people, stood and talked with them, amused ourselves in examining their manner of doing their work; but not one of them ever said to us, "Will you eat?" We likewise saw them make their cricket and grasshopper broth. It appeared to me however a most abominable and disgusting hodgepodge. We returned home in the evening very hungry, and with no very favourable opinion of their hospitality.

We saw but few beaver among them but at some distance from their camp appearances were promising, so that my people were more anxious than prudent the following day to set their traps although I had forbid them, in order to avoid difficulties with the natives; but the chief assuring us that there would not be the least danger of the Indians either stealing or touching them a few more were put in the water, and their success encouraged others to do the same. The first and second nights, not one of the traps were touched; but on a subsequent trial no fewer than twelve were stolen; this sudden check to our proceedings opened our eyes to the character of the natives and left us to judge how far their character was in accordance with the account the honest chief had given us. I spoke to Ama-ketsa on the subject, with the view of having our traps restored. The chief smiled and made light of the matter. The other Indians taunted and jibed our people for making inquiries after their traps.

Soon after this discovery I had to kick one of them for attempting to steal a piece of rope out of our camp. These little grievances we winked at for some time, trying to check them gently in order to keep on good terms with Ama-ketsa and his people. But this conciliatory plan only encouraged them to assume a still greater degree of boldness. And this went on until one evening a fellow picked up a bridle and refusing to deliver it up, it was taken from him by force, when he strung his bow and threatened the man who had taken it from him, but was wise enough not to shoot.

On observing the daring aspect and conduct of the Indians I assembled all my people together and stated to them that I had known the character of these Indians for many years past and that from their insolent behaviour of late it behooved us to keep a strict and vigilant eye on them, that it appeared evident to me that they were seeking to intimidate us, and if they once thought they could succeed they would rob us, and from that might attempt something else. But before they had gone too far we must let them know that they could not encroach on our property with impunity. That united we were strong, and might teach them to respect us; whereas on the contrary, if we allowed them to take the footing they were assuming we might regret having carried our forbearance too far. Twelve of our friends had already fallen victims to their barbarity, and what they had once done they might attempt again, and now they had stolen our traps and had shown a disposition to set us at defiance!

Therefore I said, we will go and seize just as many of their horses as they have taken of our traps, and keep them as pledges until they restore our property. It will show them that we are not afraid of them. But my people demurred to this proposition. Some said the Indians were too numerous, others that we should all get killed. The Iroquois objected because it would put an end to their traffic with the Indians, while those who had lost their traps were, like myself, anxious to get them back and show that we were not to be trifled with. Some however called out, "We will go and take their horses and after that fight them." I told them that we had not come on their lands to fight them but to treat them kindly, yet in doing so we would not allow the Indians to trample on us. "Follow my directions and there will be no fighting in the matter, make a bold stand in defence of our right." I then warned my people that if any person exceeded his orders he should be punished. At last, the whole party were convinced of the necessity of taking a decisive step to check the insolent tone of the Indians and to pave the way for our getting away without loss or disgrace.

Arming ourselves therefore to the number of thirty-five we sallied forth, seized bridles, and brought into our camp ten of their horses, then we put everything in the best order for defence, knowing the step would bring the matter to an issue. Two of the Indians being at our camp at the time we counted out one hundred gun balls before them and poured them into our big gun in their presence, so that they might have reported the circumstance when they got to the Indian camp. Then we sent them off with a message that as soon as the Indians delivered up our traps we should deliver up their horses. The two Indians returned with the message to their camp. I then instructed my people to have their arms in readiness, in such a position that each man could have his eye upon his gun, and could have hold of it at a moment's warning, but to appear as careless as if nothing was expected. That if the Indians did come as they certainly would to claim their horses and insisted on taking them, I would reason the matter with them, and when that failed I would give the most forward of them a blow with my pipe then, and that would be the signal for my people to act. The moment therefore the signal was given the men were to shout according to Indian custom, seize and make a flourish with their arms, but were not to fire until I had first set the example. During this time there was a great stir in the Indian camp; people were observed running to and fro, and we awaited the result with anxiety.

Not long after we saw a procession of some fifty or sixty persons, all on foot and unarmed, advancing in a very orderly manner towards our camp, in front of which was placed our big gun well loaded, pointed, and the match lit. My men were in the rear, whistling, singing, and apparently indifferent. On the Indians coming up to me and another man who stood in front of them near to where the horses were hid, I drew a line of privilege and made signs to them not to pass it. They, however, looked very angry and observed the line with reluctance, so that I had to beckon to them several times before I was obeyed, or could make them understand. At last they made a sort of irregular halt.

I then made signs to the Indians to sit down, but they shook their heads. I asked where was Ama-ketsa, but got no satisfactory reply. One of the fellows immediately introduced the subject of the horses in very fierce and insolent language. I however, to pacify him and make friends, spoke kindly to them and began to reason the matter and explain it to them as well as I could, but the fellow already noticed, being more forward and daring than the rest, sneered at my arguments and at once laid hold of one of the horses by the halter and wished to take it away without further ceremony. I laid hold of the halter in order to prevent him. The fellow every now and then giving a tug to get the halter out of my hand; the others kept urging him on; they were the more encouraged seeing my people did not interfere. They were however on the alert, waiting impatiently for the signal without the Indians in the least being aware of it. Beginning to get a little out of humour, I made signs to him that if he did not let go I would knock him down; but prompted no doubt by the strong party that backed him and seeing no one with me, he disregarded my threat by giving another tug at the halter. I then rapped him on the side of the head with my pipe stem and sent him reeling back among his companions, which was no sooner done than the men sprang to their arms and gave a loud shout! The sudden act, with the terror conveyed by cocking their guns, so surprised the Indians that they lost all presence of mind, threw their robes, garments, and all from them, and plunging into the river swam with the current until out of danger, every now and then popping up their heads and diving again, like so many wild fowl! In less than a minute's time there was not a soul of the embassy to be seen about our camp. Never was anything more decisive.

It may be a satisfaction to our readers to know what kind of pipe the people use in this country. The pipes generally used both by Indians and Indian traders are made of stone and are large and heavy, the stem resembling a walking stick more than anything else. They were generally made of ash, and from two and a half to three feet long.

We had intended raising camp the next day, but after what had happened I thought it better to pass the night where we were in order to give the Snakes as well as ourselves an opportunity of making up matters. Not a soul however came near us all that day afterwards, and we were at a loss to find out what was going on in the camp. I therefore got about twenty of my men mounted on horseback to take a turn round in order to observe the movements of the Indians, but they having brought me word that the women were all employed in their usual duties I felt satisfied.

On the following day ten persons were observed making for our camp who on arriving spread out a buffalo robe on which was laid all our stolen traps, some whole, some broken, with several pieces they had been flattening for knives, the whole rendered almost useless to us. Ama-ketsa, who had not been at the affair of the preceding day, accompanied this party and made a long and apparently earnest apology for the loss of our traps and the misunderstanding that ensued, but did not forget to exculpate his people from all blame, laying the odium of the whole affair on the Bann-at-tees. We know the contrary. The War-are-ree-kas were the guilty party and perhaps Ama-ketsa himself was not altogether innocent, at least some of his people said so. We however accepted the apology and the traps as they were, and delivering up all the horses treated the chief with full honours, satisfied that the business ended so well.

The chief had no sooner returned to camp with the horses than a brisk trade was opened, the Indians, men, women, and children, coming to see us with as much confidence as if nothing had happened. On the next morning while we were preparing to start, one of my men fell from his horse and broke his thigh. We however got

273

it so fixed as not to prevent our removal. Although everything wore the appearance of peace yet I thought it necessary to take precautions, in order to avoid any trouble with the natives in passing their camp. I therefore placed two men mounted on horseback to go before; the camp followed in order after, while myself and twenty men brought up the rear, and all was peace and good order.

From the great Snake camp our course lay south, I purposing to have taken a sweep around the Snake Falls,[2] with the view of trapping beaver and trying to get some account of our ten Iroquois. Fifty-seven beaver taken the first night rewarded the toil of a long day's journey. At the falls the concourse of natives resembled the Columbia narrows at Dalles des Morts this season of the year. But I was taught a little experience at Ama-ketsa's camp not to put up near them, so we passed on. While at the falls the Indians told me that they had seen the Iroquois about a month before and gave us to understand that they had got into difficulties with the Snakes, and were spending more time in hunting after women than beaver.

From the Falls we continued our course southeast for about seventy miles, till we had reached the south end of a long range of high land,[3] which we called Point-Turn-Again, and there encamped on the 24th of August, which was the extent of our journey south. From that point we turned our faces toward home. Up to this date we had travelled since leaving the Flatheads, including trapping excursions apart from our regular journeys, 1110 miles. Reconnoitering excursions for beaver and for practical passes and in search of new trapping ground 530 miles, together with our daily journeys, which amounted to 1320 miles. Making in the aggregate not less than 3450 miles!

From the River Weiser, where we turned from the west to the south, the distance to Fort Nez Perces is not more than one hundred and eighty miles due west, a distance which might be travelled with horses in a week, and yet we had been travelling by the Spokane and Flathead roads for upward of seven months! At this stage of our journey we had lost by casualties, chiefly from bad roads and

2 Just below the site of Twin Falls, Idaho.
3 The Goose Creek Mountains.

severe weather, eighteen of our horses and twenty-two of our steel traps and had taken, exclusive of the Iroquois, 3880 beaver. Anticipating therefore a successful hunt from the Iroquois party, our prospects were still fair. From Point Turn-Again we took a wide range and with tolerable success until we again fell on Riviere aux Malades, according to our original plan.

On our way thither[4] we passed over one of those natural bridges so frequently noticed on former trips. The span of which was about thirty feet, twelve feet high, and appeared to be one solid rock, and through which the water had found a passage. Under it passed a good stream which flowed over a gravelly bottom. Following down the current the water all of a sudden disappeared, making its way underground similar to the River Goddin. No water was then to be seen, we passing and repassing several times over the ground but saw nothing for a mile, when the water suddenly burst out again and flowed in a strong current, sufficiently deep to have carried a loaded boat upon it! After following it for some distance it disappeared and we, taking another direction, saw it no more. In the last opening we shot an otter and two muskrats! This subterraneous river flowed through one of the most delightful valleys I had ever seen, skirted on each side by a gentle rising range of high land, divided transversely between these ranges by descending riverlets whose limits were lines with rows of bushes, as if set off by the hand of man. As we journeyed along, we passed several cold and hot springs. This enchanting vale I named the Garden of the Snake Country. It surpassed both in beauty and utility the valley of the Wallamitte.

While journeying through this beautiful vale, which is some thirty miles in length, we were overtaken by a heavy deluge of rain accompanied by the most fearful thunder and lightning which drenched us to the skin before we could get encamped, after which, having made a large fire out of doors and while standing round it to dry ourselves, a flash of lightning passed as it were through the flame and almost blinded us, when the loud peal of thunder, instantaneously following, struck several of the party dumb for a

4 They were in the valley of the Raft River.

moment. Three of the men were thrown down upon the ground, others upon their knees, myself and another man were forced out of the position in which we stood for the distance of three or four feet. The whole group remained for some time speechless. Within a short distance the lightning struck a tree, setting it on fire. We had frequently this season been visited by heavy thunder and much lightening attracted to the mountainous quarter, but none of us had ever seen anything as terrifying as in this place. We therefore named it the Valley of Lightning!

We now turn our attention to Riviere aux Malades. On reaching that stream we found beaver in considerable numbers. The first lift, forty-nine. The prospect before us was encouraging. But here a misfortune clouded our hopes and made beaver but a secondary consideration. For after breakfast the second morning a number of the people were taken ill, and the sickness becoming general throughout the camp, it struck me that there must have been something poisonous in our food or water. Not being able to discover anything, I began to enquire more particularly what each person had eaten that morning and found that all those who had breakfasted on the fresh beaver taken out of the river were affected! Whilst those who had eaten other fare remained in good health.

Two hours had not elapsed before thirty-seven persons were seized with gripings and laid up. The sickness first showed itself in a pain about the kidneys, then the stomach, and afterwards the back of the neck and all the nerves, and by and by the whole system became affected. The sufferers were almost speechless and motionless, having scarcely the power to stir yet suffering great pain, which caused froth about the mouth. I was seriously alarmed. We had no medicine of any kind in our camp, nor scarcely time to have used it; so rapidly was the sickness increasing that every soul in the camp, in the space of a few hours, was either affected with the disease or panic struck with fear!

The first thing I applied was gun powder. Drawing therefore a handful or two of it into a dish of warm water and mixing it up I made them drink strong doses of it, but it had but little effect. I then tried a kettle of fat broth mixed up and boiled with a handful or two of pepper, which some of the people happened to have. I made them drink of that freely, but whether it was the fat or the pepper I know not, it soon gave relief. Some were only sick for part of the day, but others, owing perhaps to the quantity they had eaten, were several days before they got over it, and some of them felt the effect of it for a month afterwards.

We then examined the flesh of the beaver and found it much whiter and softer, and the people who had eaten of it said much sweeter to the taste than the flesh of beaver generally. As there was no wood about the banks of the river we supposed these animals must have lived on roots, and in their food have eaten some poisonous roots which although not strong enough to destroy them was sufficiently deletorious to injure us, and from this it was that I named this stream Riviere aux Malades.

Having trapped up the river to the place where we had left it,[5] we then crossed over in order to trap some creeks in the mountains. Here some of the horses had to swim, and several persons had a narrow escape of being drowned. On mustering on the opposite bank I perceived at a considerable distance a Snake among the bushes, as if in the act of hunting for ground squirrels; beckoning to some of my people who were already mounted and pointing to the individual we set off at full speed to cut between him and the rocks, that we might get hold of him in order to learn something of the country we had to pass through. So intent was he on his business that we were almost on him before he noticed our approach; but the moment he saw us he bent his bow, taking us for enemies. Regardless of his bow and himself, we rushed in and laid hold of him. On our dismounting from our horses the poor creature let his bow and arrows fall to the ground, stood speechless and almost frightened to death.

We however mounted him behind one of the men and carried him to our camp, where we treated him with every kindness, and at last, by means of our man Hakana, got him to speak a little. I ordered some beaver flesh to be set before him, putting some of the white or poisonous into one dish and some of the good into another

5 At the entrance of Camas Creek.

purposely to see if he knew the difference, but the two dishes were no sooner set before him than he gave us to understand that the Indians invariably roast but never boil the white kind! telling us by signs that it was bad unless roasted.

We then entered at some length with our captives on the subject of their living and how the Bann-at-tees generally pass the winter when he observed, "We never want for plenty to eat, at all seasons. We often suffer from cold, but never from hunger. Our winter houses are always built among the rocks and in the woods, and when the snows are deep we kill as many deer as we please with our knives and spears, without using our bows and arrows." To a question I put he answered, "The Snakes never build their winter houses under ground." To other questions he answered, "We can never venture in the open plains for fear of the Blackfeet and Pie-gans, and for that reason never keep horses. Six of our people were killed by them this summer. Were we to live in large bands, we should easily be discovered." In reference to our road he told us that the country ahead was very rocky and bad, and that we could never make our way through it with horses. This miserable being, although the very picture of wretchedness, was far more intelligent and communicative than those we had got hold of on Reed's River. After passing a night with us I gave him a knife, a small looking glass, a grain or two of vomition, and he went off highly delighted.

We continued our journey, winding through creeks and round rocks with great difficulty for eight days until we had reached the extreme height of land between the sources of River Malade on the west and Salmon River on the north. This ridge or height of land we passed on the 18th of September. The country was mountainous, but a little to our right was a towering peak at least 800 feet higher than where we stood.[6] Here remaining a day to rest and refresh our jaded horses. I took a man along with me in order to try and ascend this lofty peak. We set out at eight o'clock in the morning and only got back at sunset, so tired that we could scarcely drag ourselves along. But the view we had enjoyed repaid us well for our troubles. On the top of this height was six inches of newly

[6] Galena Peak (11,118), above Galena Summit (8,752).

fallen snow and a small circular pond of water, about twenty feet in diameter. This height I named after our governor Mount Simpson, and the basin of water on its top the Governor's Punch Bowl. No elevated height in this country can present a more interesting prospect than that viewed from the top of Mount Simpson, the west in particular. It is of a highly picturesque character. On looking to the north, "How," said I to myself, "are we to pass here?" The doubt remained until I turned to view the quarter we had come from, and seeing it nearly as rugged and wild as country could be it struck me that since we had passed through the one we might attempt the other.

We therefore left Mount Simpson and descending into the narrow and unknown strands of Salmon River shaped our course for Canoe Point, the place where we had left our beaver en câche. On getting down to the bottom of the valley, day was almost turned into night. So high were the mountains on each side of us that in many places the view was so confined that we could see nothing but the sky above and the rocks around us. Here the river, some three hundred and fifty miles long, was scarcely four feet wide, but many rills and creeks pouring into it from the adjacent rocks soon swelled it into a river.

It appeared to us probably that no human being had ever trod in that path before; but we were soon undeceived, for we had not been many hours there before my people, going about their horses, found a pheasant with a fresh arrow stuck in it and not yet dead! So at the moment we were indulging in such an idea, the Indians might have been within fifty yards of us. As we advanced the valley widened and the deer were seen feeding in numerous herds, and so tame that we shot many of them without alighting from our horses! or going off the road after them. But it was not until the third day that we put a trap into the water and seven beaver was all we got to reward us for so much labour.

At the distance of forty-seven miles from Mount Simpson we entered on the end of a fine stream nearly as large as the main reach, being from thirty to forty yards broad with deep water and a strong current. This place we called the Forks: the west branch of the river. On reaching the Forks we observed at some distance the appearance of a ploughed field, and riding up to see it found a large piece of ground more than four acres in extent dug up and turned over. On getting to the spot we observed no less than nine black and grizzly bears at work rooting away. We immediately gave them chace, and with the help of some twenty or thirty dogs got four of them surrounded in front of a lofty and crumbling precipice up which they endeavored to make their escape; but the place being steep and the stones and gravel loose they made but slow progress and the more so as the dogs kept attacking them behind. Our horses however were so frightened and got so restive that we could not manage them nor get them to approach, for no animal terrifies a horse more than a bear; at last dismounting we let them go and kept firing at the bears, which were still scrambling to get up the rocky precipice. We brought three of the four down, but they got so entangled and surrounded by the dogs that in killing the bears we killed seven of the dogs.

After our adventure, we set off on a trip of discovery up Bear River[7] for about thirty-four miles. The valley through which the river flowed was very pleasant, but became narrow as we advanced. Four inches of new snow were on the ground, and the ice an inch thick. The weather was cold and in those snowy regions indicated an early winter; yet we persevered in our search of beaver notwithstanding our course lay north, and we had yet before us some six or seven hundred miles before we reached our winter quarters. The wood on the bank of Bear River was only stunted willows, nor were there any of other description in the neighborhood fit for anything but fire, and but little were fit for that if we except, now and then, a solitary pine no bigger than a good broom.

On rounding one of the many rocky points we observed some distance ahead of us two animals frolicking in the water; on approaching the place we discovered two black bears and got so near as to shoot one of them in the water, but while dragging it ashore,

7 "Bear River" is actually the main branch of the Salmon River. About ten miles east of the town of Clayton, Idaho, it turns from east to north, and the northward-flowing branch that Ross had been following joins it at this point.

we noticed in the shoal water a beaver concealing itself, and this circumstance led us to examine why the bear had been standing so long in the water. We found by the number of tracks about the place that the bear had been in pursuit of the beaver, there being but one deep hole where it could have swum under water and made its escape. At that place was artfully stationed the bear we had shot, while the other kept pursuing its object in the pond of water where we found it, and would have succeeded in killing the beaver had not our arrival saved its life.

Leaving the men to trap, I and another man returned to camp the second day in order to examine the road where we had to pass down the main river, but found it so absolutely bad that nothing but necessity compelled us to undertake it. After trapping for three days up Bear River the six men returned to the camp, having killed one hundred and fifteen beaver. We then raised camp, left the Forks, and continued our route down the main branch of Salmon River.

About ten miles below the Forks we entered a narrow and gloomy defile, where mountains on each side closed in on the river, between which the river became confined like the water race of a mill and shot through the narrow channel in a white foaming cascade with the noise of thunder. Along the margin of the river in this dangerous place the rocks and precipices descended almost perpendicularly to the water's edge, affording only some fifty or sixty feet above the water, in the face of the precipice, a sort of zigging path. On this road we had advanced one day until we were abruptly stopped by a dangerous chasm where a piece of the hanging cliffs had slidden down, leaving a deep and yawning gap of some yards broad across the road over which we could not pass. Here the horses being unable to get forward or backward, not having room to turn around, we had to use ropes to extricate them from their perilous situation, all hands calling out, "Hold fast! Hold fast!" While we in front were engaged in this no less dangerous than difficult task the others, beginning at the rear got the animals turned back. We then retraced our steps about a mile, where we encamped. Here all our horses had to be tied; we spent a restless night. Under the apprehension that we would have to go back again to Mount Simpson and seek another pass to get clear of the mountains, which would have taken us, at that late season, some weeks and some hundred miles to accomplish.

After encamping, one of the men jocularly observed that we ought to call the place "Hold Fast!"[8] and the name remained. On the next day, however, we resolved on attempting to cross the river, examined it in several places, tried and tried again, but failed the first day. The next, with difficulty, we crossed to the opposite side, in which undertaking we drowned one of the horses and lost four of our steel traps and about twenty-five beaver. And with the utmost difficulty we saved ourselves. But although we had accomplished the laborious task, we were not yet sure of getting through. From the crossing place we wormed among rocks and other obstructions for nearly two days, without advancing for more than six or seven furlongs! At last however, getting down to the river we got the eighth day altogether clear of the defile,[9] from the end of which we reached Canoe Point after a few hours' ride and found the beaver we had left en câche, safe.

At Canoe Point we remained for two days to rest and refresh our horses, for nearly half of them were more or less lame, their hoofs being worn to the quick. Without being shod no animals can stand the journeys through such rugged country. After one Snake expedition many of them are rendered useless ever after. No less than seventy-seven of our horses had to be muffled about the feet with leather, which is at best a temporary makeshift.

The season having now arrived that I was to have sent to meet the Iroquois, who left us on the 16th of June, on leaving Canoe Point I dispatched six men to the Trois Tetons, south of Goddin's River, the appointed rendezvous, while we proceeded on our journey[10] in order to trap and make provisions for our voyage home, having appointed a place near the headwaters of the Missouri where we were all to meet again. On the third day after starting

8 Near the Petrified Forest.
9 The Upper Salmon Gorge.
10 Up the Lemhi River.

Jean Baptiste Bouché, one of the aged fur men, died in his sixtieth year. He had been ailing for some time, and for the last ten days had to be carried about in a litter. The deceased was a quiet, sober, and industrious man. We buried him in our camp and burned the grave over so that no enemy might disturb his remains, and near the spot stands a small friendly tree bearing the inscription of his name, age, with the date of his death. As we advanced we reached in a short time an immense herd of buffalo and commenced laying in a stock of provisions until the men I had sent for the Iroquois should return.

While on the subject of buffalo we may notice that there is perhaps not an animal that roams in this nor in the wilds of any other country more fierce and forbidding than a buffalo bull during the rutting season. Neither the polar bear nor the Bengal tiger surpass that animal in ferocity. When not mortally wounded they turn upon man or horse, but where mortally wounded they stand fiercely eyeing their enemy, all silent until life ebbs away.

As we were travelling one day among a herd we shot at a bull and wounded him severely, so much so that he could neither run after us nor from us. Propping his legs, therefore, he stood looking at us until we had fixed ten balls through his body, now and then merely giving a shake of his head, and although apparently unable to stir, yet we kept at a respectful distance from him, for such is their agility of body, their quickness of eye, and so hideous are the looks of the beast, that we dared not for some time approach him, till at last one man bolder than the rest went up and pushed him over, he was dead! If not brought to the ground by the first or second shot, let the hunter be on his guard! The old bulls, when badly wounded and unable to pursue their assailant, prop themselves as if in defiance of man and often stand in that position till dead. But the head of a wounded buffalo is invariably toward his pursuer and while in an upright position, if the hunter be in doubt, let him change his position to see if the bull changes his position, for the surest mark of his being mortally wounded and unable to stir is when he cannot turn his head round to his pursuer. In that case you may safely walk up and throw him down.

The cow calves generally at one period and that period later by a month than our tame cattle, when they all as if with one accord withdraw themselves from the mountains and rocks into large families and resort to the valleys, where there is open ground with small clumps of wood affording shelter and preservation, as there they can from afar see the approach of an enemy. The cows in the center. The bulls graze in the distance, all in sight of each other.

The calving season is May, when the heat of the sun is not pointedly strong for the preservation of their young in the open air, and on which occasion, as we have just noticed, the herd keeps feeding round and round the place, as if to defend the approach of an enemy or wolves from the young calves. The resident tribes seldom hunt or disturb the buffalo at this season, or before the first of July. The Indians often assured me that during the calving season the bulls keep guard! and have been frequently known to assemble together in order to keep at a distance any wolves, bears, or other enemies that might attempt to approach the cows.

The men whom I had sent some time ago from Canoe Point in search of the Iroquois had arrived, but had met with no Iroquois; they met with enemies and had a very narrow escape from a war party of the Blackfeet, who came upon them early one morning just as they were preparing to start, and so suddenly that our people had to leave one of their horses as a prey to them. Fortunately for our people the Indians were all on foot. I, however, lost no time in sending off on the second day after their arrival another party double in number to the first who fortunately got back safely on the 14th of October after an absence of ten days, bringing along with them not only the ten Iroquois but seven American trappers likewise.

But they arrived trapless and beaverless, naked and destitute of almost everything! And in debt to the American trappers for having conveyed them to the Trois Tetons!

For thus is their story. "We proceeded," said Old Pierre, "in a southerly direction, crossed over the main river, and struck into the interior to be out of the way of Indians and there we trapped with good success for nearly two months. At last some of the Snakes found us out. Cantayehari took one of their women for a wife, for whom he gave one of his horses. The Indians wished for another horse, but were refused. The wife deserted and we changed to another place to avoid the Indians. There a war party fell on us and robbed us of everything. We had 900 beaver, 54 steel traps, and 27 horses, all of which together with five of our guns and nearly all our clothing the Indians carried off! Naked and destitute as we then were we promised them forty dollars to escort us back to Goddin's River, where we arrived the morning before the men you sent to meet us. And the Americans came along with us here. They had a good many beaver, but put them all en câche till they returned back." And this is the tale Old Pierre told me. When it was ended I said, "Well, Pierre, what did I tell you at parting?" He held down his head and said nothing.

I then questioned the Americans, who appeared to be shrewd men. They confirmed part of the Iroquois story. Smith,[11] a very intelligent person and who seemed to be the leading man among them, acknowledged to me to have received one hundred and five beaver for escorting back the Iroquois to Goddin's River, although Pierre had not touched upon this circumstance at all. No two of them, however, told the story the same way. Nor did the Americans agree in their version of it. So that it appeared to me to be a piece of trickery from beginning to end. Sometime after they arrived, however, another story got into circulation, perhaps the true one. This story was not that they had been robbed as Old Pierre had stated, but that while on their hunting ground they fell in with the seven Americans noticed, who succeeded in seducing them to their side, under the pretext of giving them five dollars for every beaver skin they might deliver at the Yellowstone River, where the Americans had a trading post. That in the view to profit by their contemplated speculation, they had left their furs en câche with those of the American party when they had been hunting, and had come back not with the intention of remaining with us but rather, as the story ran, to get what they could from us and then to seduce their comrades to desert in a body with their furs to the Americans, as a

[11] Jedediah Smith.

party of them had already done in 1822, and this story I had no difficulty in believing.

I however thought it best not to say that I either heard or believed this last story; at the same time, I had to find out the truth of it. I knew there must be some cheating going on between the Americans and the Iroquois from the constant intercourse going on between them. I however took such steps as I expected would most effectually prevent the possibility of their being able to carry their intention into effect. And it aided my plans greatly that the enemy kept hovering about, and I of course exaggerated the danger and made that a factor for doubling the watch by night, and remaining on guard myself; but in truth it was to prevent either the Americans or the Iroquois from taking any undue advantage of us, and in the meantime kept forcing our march the nearer to home.

And the measures we adopted succeeded so well that the Americans at last gave up the idea, preferring the protection of our camp to the risk of turning back.[12]

[12] It should be noted that the conclusions drawn by Ross concerning Jedediah Smith are pure speculations. Smith, an American appearing here in "British" territory, embodied in person the threat that had been very much in the minds of the Company men for several years. See Dale Morgan, *Jedediah Smith and the Opening of the West* (Indianapolis, Bobbs-Merrill, 1953), *passim*.

13. JOURNEY'S END

W̲E HAD no sooner done with the adventures of our absent trappers than the people were thrown into confusion by the report that enemies were approaching the camp. And although such reports were not infrequent they never failed to create a momentary thrill, whenever a sudden alarm was given. This is unavoidable.

We prepared to receive them as friends or foes, but were soon agreeably relieved from our fears by finding that they were our friends the Nez Perces. These poor weatherbeaten wanderers, only ten in number, passed the night with us and amused us with recounting their wild adventures. We shall give the reader their own simple story.

"When we left our own country, about three months ago," said they, "our object was to fall in with the whites in the Snake country. We were then seventeen in number and on foot, the better to conceal ourselves from the enemy. We intended to have stolen horses for ourselves from the Blackfeet, had an opportunity offered, in revenge for those they had taken from us at Hell's Gates in the spring. One turned back, and in crossing a rocky defile at the headwaters of the Missouri we were discovered and waylaid by the Blackfeet. Six were killed in that unfortunate affray, and the rest of us had a very narrow escape and only got clear of the enemy by escaping in the dark. From that time we only travelled at night, but despairing of meeting the whites and seeing the buffalo moving to and fro, we knew there must be enemies lurking about and had to hide ourselves and suffer from hunger and thirst. So that we had almost given up hopes of ever getting back to our own country again when all at once we perceived the whites coming, which at first we took for a large war party." When they had related the story of their troubles they began mourning for their unfortunate relations who were killed in the defile, then they appeared over-joyed at getting under the protection of the whites and vowed vengeance against the Blackfeet.

The Nez Perces telling us that there were enemies lurking about and we having a suspicious defile to pass I thought it well to have the place examined before raising camp the next day. This being settled I took five of the Indians along with us when we set off to the number of six and thirty persons, taking care to have two of the Americans and the most troublesome of my own men among the party. Just as we had got the bad step examined and reached the other side we perceived at a long distance off a number of move-able objects making for the mountains, but whether men or deer we could not ascertain. Losing no time, however, we resolved on giving chace and therefore set off at full speed to get between the objects we saw and the woods they seemed to be making for. Be-fore we had advanced far we were satisfied that the objects were men and not deer, which made us quicken our steps.

The Indians on discovering us began to quicken their pace and make for a hiding place. We at the same time advanced at full speed. The match was hard contested, but the Indians won the race by a short distance and got to a bush before we could reach them. In their hurry, however, they had thrown away everything that maintained them, robes, shoes, and some of them even their bows and arrows! And yet after all, we had got near enough to have fixed upon the last of them before they had got under cover, had we been so disposed. Immediately on getting to the bush where the Indians had taken cover we dismounted and invited them to come out of the bush and smoke with us, assuring them that we were their friends but they answered, "Come in here and smoke with us, we are your friends." We then sat down on a little rising ground close to the Indians to rest our horses a little, for we had given them a good heating, keeping all the time in talk with the Indians. They gave us to understand that they were Crows, the name of a tribe on the Missouri, and although they spoke to us in that language the impression in our minds was that they were

Blackfeet, and we told them so; this they denied, on account no doubt of having killed the Nez Perces, some of whom they now saw with us.

Some of the people in the meantime went and gathered together what things the Indians in their hurry threw away, namely sixteen buffalo robes, six dressed skins, fifty-two pair of moccasins, and two bows and arrows! all of which was laid in a pile, telling the Indians we did not wish to injure them nor take away anything belonging to them. Then taking a piece of tobacco we stuck it on a forked stick at the edge of the bush, for them to smoke after our departure. To questions we put them they denied having seen the six men sent out to River Goddin, or the horse they had lost. Said there were several parties of Blackfeet and Piegans both, not far off. That they themselves had been looking for some of their absent friends but were now on their way back to their own country. We then prepared to return, but had some difficulty in preventing the Nez Perces from taking the spoil we had picked up and also from firing on the Indians in the bush, but I told them that since they were with the whites and put themselves under our protection they must do as we did, but that if they were bent on revenge they might stop where they were until we had gone away and then settle matters as they might think proper.

As we were in the act of mounting our horses to return, we perceived at a distance the appearance of a crowd of men and horses following the track the Indians had come, and making straight for us! From their appearance at a distance they seemed very numerous, and taking them for another war party, we considered ourselves between two fires! Not wishing, however, to run off we examined a small point of woods near to the Indians, where we were to retreat in case of being too hard pressed; there we secured our horses under a guard of ten men while the other twenty-six, with their guns ready, awaited the arrival of the suspicious party.

As soon as we had observed them we discovered the party to be but four men only, driving however a large band of horses before them, and when they got within a few hundred yards of us they made a halt, which they had no sooner done than I ordered twenty of my men to remain where they were as a guard on the Indians, while myself and the other fifteen set off to meet and see who the newcomers were, but on getting up to them what was our surprise on finding forty-three of our own horses and also the one taken from my men on their trip to the trappers, all of which they had stolen, and the four villains had stolen and were driving before them!

On our approach the thieves immediately fled; we pursued and got hold of three of them, the fourth making his escape among the rocks; they belonged to the party in the bush. Our first impression was to have punished the offenders on the spot. We kept them as hostages, to see how things might end. I therefore carried them back to our camp.

After the bustle was over we secured the thieves and collected all our horses; then returning to the place where I had left the twenty men to guard the Indians, we tried to open a communication with them again. They would not speak a word to us although they spoke to each other in our hearing, so we took all the property we had picked up belonging to them, also the tobacco I had left for them to smoke, together with our prisoners and returned to our camp, where we arrived late after a hard day's work.

On reaching the camp we were told that the stolen horses had not been missed till late in the afternoon, although they must have been driven off soon after we started in the morning. Two parties had been in pursuit, but none of them happened to fall on their trail and had they escaped us, we never should have seen one of them. The rest of our horses being safe we held a court martial on the three criminals when every voice in the camp, with the exception of myself and two others, were for having them shot and that was the sentence, but after giving them a good fright, I managed to procure their escape the next day. Raising camp thereafter, we commenced our journey through the defile we had examined the day before, the condemned criminals being still prisoners. With a view of preventing sentence from being put into execution I selected some men on whom I could depend and delivered them into their hands with strict orders to let them off while passing through the defile. The Nez Perces, Iroquois, and I for obvious reasons went on ahead and all ended as I wished.

I was very happy that the miserable wretches got off with their lives. For depriving them of life would have done us no good, neither would it have checked horse stealing in those barbarous places.

Having once more got out of our troubles with the natives, we pursued our homeward journey[1] with great eagerness as the cold winter was closely pursuing us in the rear; we, however, continued trapping and hunting in order to make up in some degree for the loss we had sustained by the misconduct of the Iroquois.

It not infrequently happened, however, that natural causes operated against us, for we had to break the ice in order to relieve our traps almost every morning nor was this all; the immense flocks of wild fowl which kept hovering the numberless rivulets and pools at the headwaters of the Missouri and other minor rivers in their passage to a warmer climate tempted even the most industrious of us to forego the more prosperous pursuit of trapping for the gratification of shooting geese and ducks. Much time was therefore lost and much ammunition spent to little purpose.

But this superabundance of wild fowl was not the only attraction to divert our attention. We were at the same time surrounded on all sides by herds of buffalo, deer, moose, and elk, as well as grouse, pheasant, and rabbit. From morning to night therefore, scarcely anything else was to be heard about our camp but the sound of arms and the cries of wild fowl and other animals.

As we journeyed among the rocks and defiles, the Nez Perces took us a little out of our way and showed us the spot where their six companions had fallen a sacrifice to the fury of their enemies, and also the place where the Blackfeet, who had killed them, lay in ambush. That one of them escaped with their lives was a matter of wonder to us. These victims had, according to Indian custom, been all scalped, cut to pieces, their limbs strewed about the place.

1 They crossed the Continental Divide by way of Lemhi Pass.

On arriving at the fatal spot the poor fellows wrought themselves into a frantic state of mourning, tearing their hair, cutting their flesh, and howling like wild beasts for some time; then gathering up the remains of the dead, they buried them at a distance.

After a few days' hard travelling with more or less success in the way of hunting, we encamped at the foot of the celebrated mountain where we had spent so much anxious labour in the spring, cutting our road of eighteen miles long through a mass of snow from eight to ten feet deep; but the scene was changed. The mountain, then so terrific, was now the reverse. All the old snows had been swept away by the summer heat. A sprinkling of new fallen snow not six inches deep was all that concealed the features of the surface from the eye and the next day in six hours' time we crossed it without alighting from our horses and encamped in the Valley of Troubles, equally celebrated as being the vicinity of perpetual snows and our hopeless exile for thirty-five days. But its appearance at this season, although still wrapped up in the white mantle of snow, was more cheering than it was in the spring. At this time we could smile with contentment, inasmuch as every step put our difficulties farther behind us. Then we set our traps, but only obtaining two otters and no beaver, our trapping ceased.

Soon after we encamped fresh tracks supposed to be those of enemies were discovered, which made me remark that there was no passing that place without troubles. We therefore doubled the guard on our camp and horses; but next morning all were safe. Raising camp therefore, we bade farewell to the Valley of Troubles, continued our march, and visited the Ram's Head. Our road was embarrassed with ice and snow over which we had to make our way with difficulty till we reached Hell's Gates. At that place our troubles were not diminished, for the river which we had to cross was partially frozen over with ice, both solid and drift. With our utmost care one of our horses was drowned, and two of our men were nearly sharing its fate.

Hell's Gates being now behind us as well as our dreaded enemies, we looked upon the dangers and troubles of the journey as ended. We quickened our pace; every step now became more and more

292

cheering till the termination of our journey at Flathead House, which place we reached at the end of November. As the reader may wish to know the extent of our success in the object of our pursuit after all our toils, we may say that all things considered our returns were the most profitable ever brought from the Snake country in one year, amounting to 5000 beaver, exclusive of other peltries, and I had the satisfaction of receiving from Governor Simpson a letter of thanks on the success of the expedition. Which brings our Snake adventure to a close.

INDEX